GENRE IN POPULAR MUSIC

GENRE IN POPULAR MUSIC

FABIAN HOLT

THE UNIVERSITY OF CHICAGO PRESS

CHICAGO AND LONDON

FABIAN HOLT is associate professor of music and performance at the University of Roskilde.

The University of Chicago Press, Chicago 60637
The University of Chicago Press, Ltd., London
© 2007 by The University of Chicago
All rights reserved. Published 2007
Printed in the United States of America

16 15 14 13 12 11 10 09 08 07   1 2 3 4 5

ISBN-13: 978-0-226-35037-0 (cloth)
ISBN-13: 978-0-226-35039-4 (paper)
ISBN-10: 0-226-35037-1 (cloth)
ISBN-10: 0-226-35039-8 (paper)

Library of Congress Cataloging-in-Publication Data

Holt, Fabian.
    Genre in popular music / Fabian Holt.
        p. cm.
    Includes bibliographical references (p.   ) and index.
    ISBN-13: 978-0-226-35037-0 (cloth : alk. paper)
    ISBN-10: 0-226-35037-1 (cloth : alk. paper)
    ISBN-13: 978-0-226-35039-4 (pbk. : alk. paper)
    ISBN-10: 0-226-35039-8 (pbk. : alk. paper)   1. Popular music–United States–
History and criticism.   2. Genre (Popular music)   I. Title.
    ML3477.H65 2007
    781.64—dc22

                                                              2007005046

♾ The paper used in this publication meets the minimum requirements of the
American National Standard for Information Sciences—Permanence of Paper
for Printed Library Materials, ANSI Z39.48-1992.

FOR

Anja, Dante, and Victor

We're all under construction, trying to rebuild, you know, ourselves. Hip-hop that gained respect from, you know, not even respect from, but just like rock and roll... and it took us a lot of hard work to get here. So all that hatin' and animosity between folks, you need to kill it, with a skillet! You don't see Bill Gates and Donald Trump arguing with each other 'cuz both of them got paper, and they got better shit to do. Git more paper! So all I'm sayin' is let's take hip-hop back to the rope. Follow me.

—Missy Elliott, *Under Construction* (2002)

CONTENTS

ILLUSTRATIONS

ACKNOWLEDGMENTS

This book would not have been written without the support and encouragement of Professor Philip V. Bohlman, my editor Douglas Mitchell, my wife Anja Spangsvig, and my parents Paul Holt and Ninon Schloss. Bohlman has been my second mentor, if I may say so, following Erik Wiedemann in Denmark, who died in 2001 at the age of seventy. They have taught me more than I can say, and I am deeply grateful for their faith in my work. One of the most important things I have learned from them is that reason and human love should go together, regardless of the object or method of study. At one of our first meetings, in Chicago in 2003, Bohlman encouraged me to develop my ideas about genre into a book, and he has broadened my perspective considerably in many discussions since then.

I am grateful for the two major fellowships I received from the Danish Research Council for the Humanities and the Humanities Division at the University of Chicago. The Danish fellowship funded a two-year position as research assistant professor at the Department of Musicology at the University of Copenhagen. There, Peter W. Christoffersen encouraged me to move beyond jazz, and Jette B. Hansen, Nila Parly, and Søren M. Sørensen deserve mention for being supportive at times when this was needed. I wish to thank my students over the years for their inspiration and support, especially Simon L. Andersen, Mads Brammer, Jens Hartmann, Thorkil Jolin, Anders Juhl, and Ole Pedersen. My former colleague Jesper J. Jensen kindly did the final computer design of the musical examples. Many thanks also to Jeremy Llewellyn and Nils H. Petersen at the Center for the Study of the Cultural Heritage of Medieval Rituals. Parveen Akhtar worked hard as a cleaner in the music department, but also found a few minutes every day to tell a story of another world.

The music department at the University of Chicago hosted me twice, first as a visiting scholar and then as a postdoctoral fellow in ethnomusicology. Chicago was an exceptionally stimulating and supportive environment, and it changed my worldview. I should like to give special thanks to the students and faculty that gave direction to this project and helped me by establishing contacts, exchanging ideas, or reading chapter drafts at various stages in the preparation of the manuscript. They include particularly Martin Stokes, who had a decisive influence on the entire project, as well as Jayson Beaster-Jones, Thomas Christensen, Byron Dueck, Jeffers Engelhardt, Travis Jackson, Donald James, Jaime Jones, Joshua Pilzer, Erin Stapleton, Suzanne Wint, and Lawrence Zbikowski. I should also like to thank the University of Chicago for bringing me into contact with Harris Berger, Jane Florine, and other fine scholars. Ronald Radano of the University of Wisconsin–Madison, deserves special mention for his brilliant ideas and criticisms, which helped me much in clarifying the objective of this book. Radano has long been a role model for my thinking about music and what musicology should be.

Over the course of writing this book I have had the privilege of presenting material for various audiences and colleagues. In this regard, I wish to express gratitude to the ethnomusicology workshop EthNoise! at the University of Chicago; Franz Krieger at the University of Music and Dramatic Arts in Graz, Austria; Wolfram Knauer at the Jazz Institute of Darmstadt, Germany; Henry Stobart at Royal Holloway in London; Ian Biddle, Richard Middleton, and Goffredo Plastino at the University of Newcastle upon Tyne; Leslie Gay at the University of Tennessee, Knoxville; and, finally, Gregory Barz and Helena Simonett at Vanderbilt University in "Music City" (I'm teasing you!).

It almost goes without saying that the reports from the anonymous readers for the University of Chicago Press were of extremely high quality. The press gave me the best possible editorial staff to work with. They were Peter Cavagnaro, Alice Lee, Timothy McGovern, Douglas Mitchell, Mara Naselli, and Barbara Norton.

Much of my field research has been conducted as case studies for individual chapters. This would not have been possible without the collaboration of many people. For chapter 2, I did multi-sited field research on the circulation of the soundtrack to *O Brother, Where Art Thou?* The first site was the folk and roots music scene in San Francisco where bassist and banjoist James Schneider was of great help. In New York City, Julia Van Nutt took plenty of time to discuss her design of the "Roots/Americana" room at the Tower Records store at 692 Broadway. Frank Youngwerth at the Tower store on

Wabash in downtown Chicago provided a contrasting perspective and further insight into the world of music commerce. On a field trip to southern Illinois and western Kentucky, during which I was fortunate to collaborate with Byron Dueck, I learned a lot from talking to country music veteran Billy Grammer, to Jason McKendree of the McKendree bluegrass family band, to Ryan Patrick at Z100 FM New Country, and Vince Hoffard at the *Southern Illinoisan*. Thanks also to Becky McKendree; Larry Kelley at WGKY; everyone at Trail's End Ranch in Lovelaceville, Kentucky; Fred's Dance Barn in Carterville, Illinois; and Glen Campbell at the Kentucky Opry in Draffenville, Kentucky. The wise country fan John Holmes in Metropolis, Illinois (Superman's hometown), was also very helpful in more than a few follow-up correspondences.

Many of those voices also speak directly or indirectly through chapter 3, for which I did research in Nashville. Two of my students, Kelsey Cowger and Greg Weinstein, kindly invited me to join them on a cross-Tennessee trip in March 2004, which served as a background for my stay in Nashville in November that same year. I am grateful to the country music experts who agreed to be interviewed and offered rich insight into the chapter theme: Harold Bradley, Paul Kingsbury, Robert Oermann, Ronnie Pugh at Nashville Public Library, and John Rumble at the Country Music Hall of Fame and Museum. At the museum, Denny Adcock, Dawn Oberg, and Lee Rowe provided excellent assistance with archival materials and photographic illustrations. Jim Slone in Tucson, Arizona, was a remarkable source on the history of commercial country music radio.

Chapter 4 is largely based on the study of commercial recordings and printed materials, many of which I have found in the archives of the New York Public Library, the San Francisco Public Library, and the Institute of Jazz Studies at Rutgers University in Newark, New Jersey. This research was informed by interviews and correspondences with the former *Down Beat* editors and writers Lawrence Kart, John Litweiler, Dan Morgenstern, and Neil Tesser. Pauline Rivelli responded via mail to questions about her time as editor of *Jazz and Pop*.

Chapters 5 and 6 are based on ethnographic fieldwork in Chicago in 2003 and 2004. Above of all, I wish to thank Jeff Parker, who not only made this study possible but greatly amplified its ethnographic richness in the process. Others who sat down with me for one or more interviews or discussions include Josh Abrams, Scott Amendola (San Francisco), Fred Anderson, Aaron Cohen, Dave Jemilo, Bob Koester, Jason Koransky, George Lewis, Howard Reich, Bettina Richards, Mike Siniscalchi, Ted Sirota, Charles Walton, and

Frank Youngwerth. Some of them commented on draft versions of the chapters, as did various people at the University of Chicago, including Nathan Bakkum, Marina Peterson, Aram Shumavon, and several others mentioned above. Thanks also to Saverio Truglia, to Deborah Gillaspie at the Chicago Jazz Archive, and to everyone at Delmark and Thrill Jockey.

Chapter 7 grew out of the "Music In-Between" course that I taught with Bohlman in the winter quarter of 2004. I shared the first, embryonic version with Celia Cain (University of Toronto), Suzanne Wint, and Helena Simonett. Their superlative feedback helped me focus and develop my ideas. All three also offered useful reactions to the final draft version. A number of practical questions were clarified with the help of Todd Harvey at the American Folklife Center, Chris Strachwitz at Arhoolie Records, and Roberto Gutierrez at Del Bravo Records in San Antonio, Texas.

In the final stage of preparing this book, I was very grateful for the encouragement and support from my new colleagues at the University of Roskilde.

CHAPTER ONE

Introduction

This is a book about the work of genre categories in American popular music. I explore the diversity of musics subsumed under the category of popular music and deal with its boundary areas with folk music, art jazz, and world music. Popular music is a powerful cultural and economical force in modern capitalist societies. Individual genres and artists have been strong symbols of social groups, places, and time periods. In recent decades, rock/pop has become a cultural mainstream and increasingly functions as a discourse for articulating public memory of peoples and nations at major official events such as the fall of the Berlin Wall, Princess Diana's funeral, the Soccer World Cups, and the media spectacle ahead of the G8 summit in 2005.[1] The growing acceptance of popular music in the twentieth century and its power as a marker of a new era in music history generate tremendous optimism (think of the jazz boom in the 1930s or the rock boom in the 1960s), but there are also reasons for ambivalence. Some forms of popular music accompany racism, sexism, and political disengagement, while others have had unparalleled power in struggles against these social problems and succeeded in overthrowing cultural hierarchies. Popular culture is really one of the major domains of social life for which academia has a responsibility to act as a humane and critical voice (as opposed to merely embracing or ignoring popular taste). This was a central concern when the International Association for the Study of Popular Music (IASPM) was founded in 1981, and it is still pertinent today even though the field has become more established institutionally.[2]

The field is not very organized, however. It has developed from such diverse traditions as British cultural studies, German musicology, East Asian media studies, and American folklore studies, and that partially explains the absence of a common methodological ground. Although this ensures some diversity, stronger integration of the field could above all reduce some of the discursive and institutional gaps between music-centered and culture-centered approaches. The concept of genre is taking on a new centrality, as we shall see, and it has precisely this potential to strengthen our common ground without sacrificing diversity. Popular music studies may indeed turn to genre for ontological reasons, to lay claim to a musical and cultural raison d'être.

The very term genre emerged in the mid nineteenth century when the processes of modernity were accelerating and new forms of popular culture were beginning to emerge, including what became known as genre fiction and genre painting ("Genre" 2006; Neale 1995, 176). Bourgeois aesthetics valued the notion of the unique and organic art work with a life of its own (Solie 1980), and that mind-set informed images of popular culture as trivial mass culture derived from mechanical formulae. Genre has since become part and parcel of the vocabularies for many musics, and it should be clear that generic categories underpin all forms of culture.[3] Human agency is never formless, and even the simplest cognitive functions depend on categories and typologies. At a basic level, genre is a type of category that refers to a particular kind of music within a distinctive cultural web of production, circulation, and signification. That is to say, genre is not only "in the music," but also in the minds and bodies of particular groups of people who share certain conventions. These conventions are created in relation to particular musical texts and artists and the contexts in which they are performed and experienced.

Genre is a fundamental structuring force in musical life. It has implications for how, where, and with whom people make and experience music. Without paying attention to genre, we would be poorly prepared to discuss a number of important questions: How is rhythmic and melodic variation regulated? What do we listen for in music? How do musicians communicate? What are the functions of rituals in a musical tradition? What do various people understand music to be and how do they use it? How can we think comparatively about music?

Genre is also fundamental in the sense that the concept of music is bound up with categorical difference. There is no such thing as "general music," only particular musics. Music comes into being when individuals make it happen, and their concepts of music are deeply social. Humans are enculturated into particular musics and ways of thinking about musical difference. For me, and probably many others, this began in childhood, when I was introduced to the musics of my family and encountered a distinction between music for children and music for adults. My immediate surroundings taught me that age and gender are determinants of musical preferences, and these are also articulated on the level of genre. As teenagers, my peers and I got spending money and became consumers, conscious of the role of musical taste in defining identities. The music I heard then now evokes memories of particular people and places. Genre thus continues to create cultural and historical horizons over the course of life. It is also a tool with which culture industries and national governments regulate the circulation of vast fields of music. It is a major force in canons of educational institutions, cultural hierarchies, and decisions about censorship and funding. The apparatus of the corporate music industry is thoroughly organized in generic and market categories. From the moment an artist starts negotiating with a major label, he or she is communicating with a division specializing in a particular kind of music, and the production then follows procedures of that division before finally the music is marketed and sold as a product with a label and registered with a generic code in the database of retail stores. These various agents can use the same term and be interested in the same music for different reasons. Sociability and musical passion may be important factors in private life, whereas professional music makers also have to think about the business side, and governments are concerned with institutions and politics.

Genre not only appears in many areas of musical life; it also has the capacity to connect them. A piece of music is created and heard in the context of others, but the contextual dimension is much broader than that. Genre is always collective, musically and socially (a person can have his or her own style, but not genre). Conventions and expectations are established through acts of repetition performed by a group of people, and the process of genre formation is in turn often accompanied by the formation of new social collectivities. A typical example is how music scenes are organized around particular musics.

Discourse plays a major role in genre making. A genre category can only be established if the music has a name. Naming a music is a way of recognizing its existence and distinguishing it from other musics. The name becomes a point of reference and enables certain forms of communication, control, and specialization into markets, canons, and discourses. This process also involves exclusionary mechanisms, and it is often met with resistance. Alternatives to dominant names and definitions are proposed, and some people are skeptical of categories and refuse to deal with them. "There are only two kinds of music, good and bad," goes an old saying that evokes a general skepticism toward categorization. Some cultures of categorization are excessive and narrow-minded, and many people feel that genre boundaries create artificial divisions between things they love. But it is problematic to replace genre with taste and suggest that there are universal standards. Nor does it help to counter one rigid distinction with another or to discard all labels and leave an undifferentiated mass. Struggles about names and definitions are often an integral part of the histories of individual musics and their cultural dynamics. Why do people have different names for the same music? What happened when "hillbilly music" became "country music," when jazz was defined as art music, and when zydeco was presented as world music? Did such changes in nomenclature create or reflect musical changes? Why have people debated whether salsa is a distinct genre or nothing more than Cuban music in new clothes? Who fought the battles, where, and what were the stakes?

Framing the Project

If genre is fundamental to understanding musical culture, one might ask why there is relatively little scholarly writing about it and why it has been relatively marginal despite the growth of interest in issues of identity and culture in music studies over the past couple of decades. Hamm has also noted that genre has been ignored (2000, 298). Several explanations can be offered for this.

One reason genre has been ignored is that although genre is important, it is more difficult to establish useful genre theories for music than for other art forms. Genre theory is most firmly established in film studies, and a comparison with music studies can begin with differences in production and signification. When film studies arrived at the conclusion in the late 1960s that genre is a necessary conceptual tool, it was argued that popular American cinema required a different approach than the traditional arts because it is more standardized, in part as a result of the enormous investments in real estate, personnel, technology, and marketing (Ryall 1998, 328 and 337). The forms of production in music are more diverse. In popular music, major labels do enforce a high degree of standardization, but there are also many specialized independent labels, and many different live music venues, not to mention amateur music making. "Nowhere," says Walser, "are genre boundaries more fluid than in popular music. . . . musicians are ceaselessly creating new fusions and extensions of popular genres" (1993, 27). In much popular music, a great deal of creativity and genre negotiation occur on the level of the individual performing artist. Many artists perform "their own music" in the sense that songs and arrangements are frequently made specifically for them or by themselves. Performers can, moreover, make the material their own by performing it in their own style and negotiate or even challenge generic boundaries in the course of a performance. Individuality is also valued in many genre discourses. Fans praise their favorite artists for having a unique style, and artists applaud their colleagues for this and encourage young aspiring artists to "find their own voice."

One could also argue that music genres are more difficult to theorize because of the nature of musical signification. Music is not referential like literature or film, for instance. From a Peircean perspective, musical sound is a symbolic form of representation. Music does not have the precision of iconic or indexical representation even when it accompanies words. Born has argued that because music's representational meanings lack denotative "back-up" they need to be established through other sociocultural dynamics (2000, 32 and 46). As a result, the connotations attached to music are potentially more labile and unfixed. This means that musical meaning is highly contingent, and that the ontologies of the semantic codes that form the musical basis of generic categories are fragile. The argument is supported by the fact that a mimetic relation to reality is less central to music genres than to film genres. In a process unique to the photographic arts, the film image is in a sense produced by means of reality itself, and that affects how the film "text" is evaluated. Incidentally, the specificity of musical signification is one of the reasons for the strikingly limited success of semiotics in musicology compared with film and literary studies.

A more direct explanation for the limited interest in genre in contemporary cultural theory of music is that the strong interest in hybridity has drawn attention away from categories.[4] The erosion of cultural hierarchies and the massive increase in the circulation of cultural products have created new forms of categorical complexity and given rise to critical reactions against the large philosophical systems of Western modernity. The paradigms that emerged in the Age of Discovery and evolved in the greater Enlightenment movement were characterized by detailed universal systems of classification and by imperialism. The narratives of modernity dominated the first hundred years of the social and human sciences (ca. 1850–1950), as evidenced by the paradigms of evolutionism, positivism, and structuralism that also had a great impact on music studies.[5] Influential postmodern thinkers have criticized these paradigms and claimed that the world has arrived at a new condition. Much writing about "late modernity" and "postmodernism" has been preoccupied with diagnosing a general social condition and has in effect created new forms of reductionism. Moreover, the antifoundational stance of postmodernism and the fetishization of hybridity do not get us very far. In popular music studies, Hesmondhalgh has recently stated: "We need to know how boundaries are constituted, not simply that they are fuzzier than various writers have assumed" (2005, 24).

Popular music categories have gained some attention among scholars, and interest in genre has grown since the mid 1990s. In 1982 Fabbri proposed a general scheme for popular music genres, but it was never really followed up, and the concept of scene stole the show in the late 1980s and early 1990s. In the mid 1990s, Fornäs (1995) presented a general discussion of genre formation in rock, applying perspectives of contemporary cultural studies and focusing on discursive mechanisms. Frith included a chapter on genre in his book *Performing Rites* (1996), a work that represents a move away from the somewhat distanced theoretical gaze of early popular music studies toward a more textured insidership. Informed by Fabbri, he discusses how collectivities are organized around individual genres and adopts the term genre world to indicate that a popular music genre constitutes a distinct sphere with a "complex interplay of musicians, listeners, and mediating ideologues" (1996, 88). That genres are rooted in their own distinct social spheres is perhaps not particular to popular music, but it is an important feature and one that is less prominent in, say, Western art music. For one thing, popular musics have a more direct relation with everyday life and emerge from a wide array of contemporary lifestyles and social formations. One might get the sense from reading Frith that genre worlds are somewhat self-contained entities and freestanding ontologies. The boundaries between genres and the broader field of popular musics, however, are fluid, and there is much interaction between them. It should also be mentioned that popular music cannot be portrayed merely as a series of genre-specific cultures. Other specialized cultures, occasionally crossing genre boundaries, are organized according to musics of a particular culture area (such as heritage music) or an instrument (such as choirs and fiddle societies, and even deejay competitions). A highly visible form of specialized collectivity is celebrity fan culture. Louis Armstrong, Dolly Parton, and Flaco Jiménez are examples of artists who crossed over from genre-specific cultures to a broader mainstream characterized by less generic and cultural specialization.

Negus, in *Music Genres and Corporate Cultures* (1999)—so far the only advanced-level book on genre in popular music—draws on Neale and Frith in his development of the term genre culture. It includes not only the aesthetic debates on which Frith concentrates, but also the organizational structures of the music industry, and Negus's focus is on the latter. His book is an excellent account of how categories of major musical formations and markets structure corporate agency. *Popular Music Genres* (Borthwick and Moy

2004), another British book, provides rudimentary introductions to eleven popular categories, some of them genres, others sub-genres. The book has little theory and can be viewed as a somewhat conventional genre history of popular music since the mid-1960s. A few briefer studies of more recent date also deserve mention: Toynbee has suggested in *Making Popular Music* (2000) that genre is central to popular music studies, and the chapter he devotes to the concept indicates that the agenda in the emerging discussion centers on the relation between music and collectivity.[6] Brackett (2002) has examined the relation between various types of categories in mass-media contexts, and Hesmondhalgh (2005) has discussed musical collectivities, rejecting the concepts of tribe, scene, and subculture, claiming that genre is a more useful concept. Finally, genre has been assigned a significant place in the canon of critical concepts, as defined by a monumental handbook from Routledge (Frith 2004).

The present book broadens the field of inquiry and refigures the critical toolbox in a number of ways. Above all, I wish to bring genre scholarship closer to musical practice and experience. Several of the above-mentioned scholars have noted that the relation between music and the social is important, but they have focused heavily on the social. This is understandable: they all have a background in the social sciences or in media studies (except Brackett, who is a musicologist but has published little on the subject). Writing about the musical dimension of music requires a serious engagement with particular musical performances, but it is possible to communicate nuanced listening in a meaningful way without using very technical language. Furthermore, although I present analytical observations on performances or recordings thereof in every chapter, readers are not expected to have extensive knowledge of music theory.

Secondly, this book aims at understanding music genres in the totality of social space, and the field of inquiry thus encompasses a wider area than just the corporate world. Other spheres of production are taken into account, including independent record labels and avenues for live music in rural and urban areas. As the field of inquiry is broadened, the need for more differentiated analytical perspectives increases. Genre draws attention to the collective and the general, and a great deal of genre research forgets that culture cannot be adequately understood without paying attention to the individual and the particular. This critique can also be raised against studies of genre worlds and cultures because thinking about the general and systemic dimensions has dominated. We need to examine the dynamics of genre formation at many different levels and sites. The best way to do this is not to develop an all-encompassing master theory. I employ multiple critical models, explore plural narratives, and develop "small theories" in relation to particular musical and social realities in a series of individually designed case studies. This allows for a more direct confrontation of theory and the empirical.

My methodological approach is deeply influenced by the unique community of ethnomusicologists that has grown up around Philip Bohlman since the late 1980s at the University of Chicago. Bohlman's sophisticated thinking about boundaries has been a remarkable source of inspiration for this project. Like his colleague Martin Stokes, he has developed rich approaches to understanding music as a complex phenomenon with many dimensions—aesthetic, ethical, historical, performative, social, and so on—approaches that are important in genre studies, too. The discussions I had with Bohlman and Stokes during my stays at Chicago have influenced the entire project, and the only reason they are not cited more often in this book is that their publications concentrate on other topics and musics. A special case is the final chapter, which is a direct response to some of the arguments Bohlman made in a course I co-taught with him in 2004. My ethnographic informants, moreover, have also had a much broader impact than the number of pages on which they are explicitly represented might suggest. From elder country music people to young urban hipsters, archivists, business executives, and musicians, I have been fortunate to draw on rich vernacular knowledges of music outside academia.

One of the basic principles of ethnography is to ground theory in fieldwork, and this has not really been done yet in the study of popular music genres. All except Negus and Brackett have theorized genre without grounding it in empirical research in any substantial way, and the general schemes outlined by Fabbri, Frith, and Toynbee suffer from typical problems of armchair research. Negus's empirical research is strong, but, again, he focuses on the corporate world and says little about individuals and local microcosms. The field research I conducted in the United States in 2003 and 2004 informs my entire project. Not all the case studies are based on ethnographic research in a rigorous sense, but they all look comparatively at how music and musical difference are socially situated by particular individuals in particular places. My base of operation was Chicago, and other field sites included Nashville, New York, and San Francisco, as well as rural areas of southern Illinois and western Kentucky.

It should be clear by now that this book is about *understanding* rather than *defining* genres. Definitions and categories serve practical purposes and tell us something about how people understand music. But we should be suspicious because they create boundaries, because they have a static nature, and because they have political ramifications and draw attention away from more important matters. Traditional genre theory has tended to shift scholars' focus from practice and experience to structure and object.[7] Moreover, short definitions of hundreds of popular music categories are already available in handbooks and on Web sites, which also feature systematic lists of styles and substyles.[8] What journalism does not provide is detailed accounts of how music categories operate in cultural processes and how people make sense of them. If you picked up this book to learn the difference between hard rock and heavy metal or how many subgenres there are in rock music, you may find other sources more useful. I hope, however, that you will find tools to deal with these questions and pick up on other issues.

Organization of the Book

To add more detail to the picture, in this introductory chapter I continue with a discussion of terminological issues and outline a general framework for understanding genre formation in popular music. The framework is an account of important mechanisms in a number of existing popular music genres in the United States. It is an open-ended model, not an all-encompassing theory. By starting from my own ideas about the histories of individual genres, I have developed a framework that differs in some respects from existing genre theory, but I also synthesize elements of existing theory. The framework is necessarily raw because genres are too diverse and fluid to be captured in a detailed, exhaustive theory. The nature of the framework is such that it can form a background for studies of particular genres, but it is not suited as a model that can be applied in its entirety. Individual components and terms must be adjusted to the particulars of each genre.

The introductory chapter is followed by a series of case studies that examine musical and cultural issues of genre making at various sites and moments. Together, the case studies explore a range of popular musics and share a commitment to understanding musical genre differences in relation to cultural difference and cultural diversity. The overall site of inquiry is restricted to one country because the case studies can then build a context for understanding genres and how they are embedded in the histories and cultures of a society. The United States has a complex history of nation building, from early encounters between European empires and Native Americans to multinational migration. I am Danish, and my experiences of living in the United States made me more aware of the social and political dimensions of musical boundaries. My attention to social inequality and racial segregation in the United States was amplified by the outbreak of the Second Gulf War, which began right around the time I started working on this book. It was further amplified when Denmark joined the coalition and became one of the "masters of war." Living in the United States, however, also made me attentive to the one-sidedness of much European anti-Americanism.

Chapter 2, "Roots and Refigurations," examines the role of genre in a contemporary revival culture. The chapter evolves from a case study of the film *O Brother, Where Art Thou?* (2000) and its representation of the American South in the 1930s. The film appeals to the fantasy of authentic history, and yet that history is redefined and adjusted to the needs of the present. I look at the soundtrack of the film and its connections with the culture of American roots music. Based on ethnographic encounters with various people in rural and urban areas around the country, I conclude that the different responses to the film reflect tensions between established genre discourses and new revivalist discourses.

It is known that the rock and roll revolution caused major changes in American musical life, but it is surprising that no one has studied these changes in terms of genre. By comparing how various genres reacted to rock, we can locate broad connections and open up new perspectives. I have designed the double session "Reactions to Rock" to examine this problematic. The "prelude" gives a broad introduction to reactions to rock and roll and outlines a theoretical model. This is followed by case studies of transformations in two different genres, jazz and country music. Chapter 3, "Country Music and the Nashville Sound," argues that country music lost its market share and that the Nashville industry's efforts at moving country closer to mainstream pop led to the hegemony of the Nashville Sound. In the early 1960s, country was more popular than ever before, but fans of traditional country felt that the genre had lost its soul, and alternatives to the Nashville scene emerged in other parts of the United States. Rock and roll and the corporate industry's growing engagement in country music played a significant role in the genre's move away from its folk basis in southern working-class consciousness and toward urban middle-class pop.

Chapter 4, "Jazz and Jazz-Rock Fusion," begins by locating different dimensions of the jazz network in the mid 1950s. Jazz had splintered into different fractions, with art-oriented modernism as the dominant genre discourse. There was less centralization and standardization than in country music because jazz had become marginal to the general public and hence to corporate media. Jazz was not affected very much by rock until the mid 1960s. The British invasion contributed to a genre transformation that has structural similarities with that in country music a decade earlier. Rock music became a big issue in jazz after the Monterey Pop Festival in 1967, but rock was only one of the components of the new musical territory of jazz-rock fusion. In contrast to country music, jazz moved toward rock and black popular music, not mainstream pop, and jazz-rock fusion did not achieve hegemony like the Nashville Sound did in country. Miles Davis gave direction to this style, and his role as a genre subject is critical to understanding the transformation of jazz.

The relation between art jazz and popular musics is also a theme in the double session "Urban Boundaries," whose primary aim is to analyze genre boundaries within the space of a city. To this end, I present an ethnography of connections between the jazz scene and other music scenes in contemporary Chicago, focusing on a community of younger musicians who are based in jazz but engage in particular forms of genre mixing and play different genres of music. This indie jazz community, as I call it, emerged in the mid 1990s as part of a vibrant neighborhood scene that forms an interstitial space between larger, more genre-specific scenes. I begin chapter 5, "Jeff Parker and the Chicago Jazz Scene," by exploring tensions and contradictions in local discourses on jazz in Chicago. Narratives cluster around distinctions between mainstream and non-mainstream music and comparisons with New York, both of which issues create divisions within and alliances between various genre scenes. I chose the guitarist Jeff Parker as my main subject because his activities cross many boundaries and because he is an excellent focal point for understanding the structure of the jazz scene. He is part of the indie jazz community which is concentrated in city zones shaped by the processes of gentrification and economic globalization. Chapter 6, "A Closer Look at Jeff Parker and His Music," continues the discussion by examining Parker's subjectivity and musical practice in greater detail. Parker is ambivalent about defining himself in terms of genre but primarily thinks of himself as a jazz musician, even though his main job for extended periods of time has been playing in the rock band Tortoise. The chapter concludes with four case studies of his different areas of activity from the perspective of the role of musical grooves. The groove concept has important genre functions in popular music, and it provides a useful perspective for comparative thinking about genre and the collaborative ethos in some of the indie music communities in Chicago.

The final chapter, "Music at American Borders," takes a somewhat oblique approach to the concept of genre and shows how it can be used as a tool in the study of cultural history. The basic question is why some of America's native popular musics are considered American while others are considered to some extent foreign. I begin by looking at the work of genre in canons of "American music" and their discursive contexts. Discourses on American

musical identity have privileged particular genres and created fixed notions
of genre, place, race, and ethnicity. In popular music, the engagement with
nationalism became pivotal after 1970 in attempts to situate this music at
the center of national history. Also noted is how the continuing hegemony of
Anglo-American identity governs the boundaries of American popular music and obscures our understanding of cultural diversity and cross-cultural
genre formations. To counter these problems, I propose a poetics of music
in between genres. My poetics is built around a decentered concept of genre
and draws on metaphors of transgression and heterogeneity. It employs plural narratives and embraces polymorphous semantic textures. I illustrate
how this poetics may be applied by conducting three case studies of musics
that have taken root in a core region in American mythology, the South,
and at the same time complicate conventional boundaries of "American
music" and southern musical geography. The first case study involves a
Ricky Martin song and its performances at major public events that illustrate some of the complexity of the national and transnational boundaries
of Latin pop. The second is a 1934 ethnographic recording of *juré* music in
southern Louisiana, seen in relation to the recent popularization of zydeco
as world music, with an excursus on Paul Simon's *Graceland*. The third
case study is a 1976 Flaco Jiménez recording of music that is rooted in the
conjunto tradition but also embedded in processes of hybridization in the
Mexican American border region.

The case studies in this book are intended to do more than explore an
array of examples. I try to chart a path that at once recognizes and defamil-
iarizes the role of genre in canon formation by reconsidering major and minor figures as well as introducing some new and unknown. I make efforts to
identify a new set of milestones along the peripheries of popular music and propose new ideas for how it might be understood. The case studies also serve
to illustrate the general point that popular music is an unstable and contingent category. These perspectives are strategically emphasized in the final
chapter, in which I foreground the idea of case studies as juxtapositions of
difference and argue that categorical transgression is a fundamental condition of musical life.

Terminology in a Wild World

In everyday discourse, terms such as genre, style, and idiom are often used
interchangeably, as if they represented an undifferentiated generic category.
In common usage, they usually have the unspecific meaning "type of": "The
festival presents many styles of music from all over the world"; "There are

various musical idioms in this culture"; "What's your favorite genre of music?" Sometimes the choice of words is accidental, but these words can also
have different meanings. A group of young rock fans with antiauthoritarian
attitudes might be more inclined to say "idiom," whereas their high school
teacher is likely to use "genre" for the same category because this term is
common in the professional language of the institution. Many people make
systematic distinctions between genre and other generic categories, and although there is no universal agreement on how this is done, there can be no
doubt that there are situations when it is useful. It allows us to create more
nuanced representations of musical culture.

The origins of "genre" and "generic" in the Greek word *genós*, Latin
genus (kind and lineage), point to the role of biological metaphors in genre
discourse. One of the most influential paradigms of thinking about categories in modern Western societies was Darwinian evolutionism, which
developed after the publication of *The Origin of Species* in 1859. Darwin
showed that the evolution of animals and plants could be tracked with the
tools of biology and mapped in diagrams of family relations. He also argued that changes could be explained by the principle of natural selection,
and his theory implied that the laws of nature are not dictated by God but
follow their own logic. This set of ideas about the lives of organisms was
not detached from ideology, and its ideological dimensions were amplified
in social and cultural theory. Darwin's refiguration of race as a typological
and essentialist concept sustained scientific racism across the board and
consolidated the notion that race is a biological determinant of culture. In
addition, discursive modes of thinking about classification and genealogy
were adopted and used to legitimize distinctions between "primitive" and
"modern" societies. The principle of natural selection was used to legitimize ideology as nature, although Darwin had actually been inspired in
this by Malthus, who in 1798 had claimed that poverty was an unavoid-
able product of population dynamics, implicitly arguing against the poverty
reforms in contemporary Britain (Malthus 1798/1989; cf. Emmeche 1995,
305). Malthus's theory was rooted in Christian moral philosophy and had
become a classic in the literature on political economy by the time Darwin
read it.

Cultural evolutionism was refuted a long time ago, but it serves as a
lesson in the political ramifications of categorization and the fallacies of using nature as a model for understanding culture. It may be that the laws of
nature are universal and that many organisms can be distinguished geneti-
cally as relatively fixed types that evolve with a high degree of predictability.
But culture is constituted and evaluated differently. Certainly, there are no

standards that allow us to create universal distinctions and or taxonomies of expressive culture. Genealogies of cultural traditions are difficult to document and map, and multisensory experiences are difficult to categorize. They are embedded in particulars, and discursive mediation has many limitations.

Metaphor extends the range of language and works productively across many phenomenological domains through select comparisons. Cognitive semantics has pointed out that much of our language and understanding is grounded in everyday bodily activities such as eating, seeing, and moving in and out of buildings (see, e.g., Johnson 1987). Musical terminologies contain rich examples of how mental spaces for physical and spatial conditions are mapped onto culture. Expressions such as "a *heavy* beat" and "a *dry* sound" and the terms "*cool* jazz" and "*heavy* metal" refer to the physical, whereas the spatial is present in "a *high* note," "*outside*-playing," "a hybrid *between* salsa and rap," "*crossover*," and "*beyond* blues." Discourse on the temporal dimension of categories is saturated with organicist metaphors, as in discussions of how genres are *born*, how they *grow*, *mature*, *branch off*, *explode*, and *die*. These metaphors have great explanatory power, but they often create a false sense of unity and support general claims about the state of a genre. As a rule, general claims about a genre are reductive, and this is especially true when someone sounds the death knell. In short, nature can be a useful source of inspiration on a figurative level, but not as a model for constructing large generic systems, as has happened in foundational moments of various fields of study.[9]

Using such a model would also be difficult because music categories are context specific and have different kinds of markers. Dancing is a defining aspect of disco and salsa, but not of symphonic rock or country gospel, and one artist may be categorized differently at a festival, at an "'80s night" among friends, or on MTV. Dancing creates interesting forms of genre mixing in a variety of contexts, from multilayered grooves to eclectic practices of deejays in dance clubs (Lawrence 2003; see also chapter 6). Genre boundaries are contingent upon the social spaces in which they emerge and upon cultural practice, not just musical practice.

Categories of popular musics are particularly messy because they are rooted in vernacular discourse, in diverse social groups, because they depend greatly on oral transmission, and because they are destabilized by shifting fashions and the logic of modern capitalism. The music industry daily invents and redesigns labels to market musical products as new and/or authentic. Most of today's consumers of R & B are also too young to have experienced how the term was used in the 1950s. Yet another factor is that some of the main sites of popular culture are still "the street" and other so-cial spaces where many value their relative independence from or even resistance to social authorities, educational institutions, and the music business. These oppositions play a role in defining creativity, freedom, and pleasure for many fans. Moreover, no single group of agents or institutions has the power to sanction its typology as the standard for everyone. Typologies of European American art music have enjoyed a higher degree of stability and monopoly because of the music's position in education and because of stable support from social elites. Notions of stability have also become standard in popular narratives of classical music as a body of timeless masterpieces.

All is not chaos, though. Many terms for Western popular musics are in global circulation, and there are more specific conventions in local and national traditions. Although some of these conventions are not systematic, we cannot afford to ignore them. Theoretical distinctions such as the taxonomic levels suggested by Middleton can help scholars work more systematically (Middleton 1990, chapter 6; Brackett 1995, 9f.). But problems arise if scholarly definitions become the rule and not the tool, because that creates barriers for understanding how categories work in culture. It also forces scholars into a corner where agency is eliminated and categories are perceived to be a property of the music itself.

I have arrived at my concept of genre by studying common perceptions of genre and how it is used in comparison with other types of categories. Because I have not had the means to conduct extensive interviews with large numbers of people and do not find questionnaire surveys meaningful in these matters, I follow broad conventions among the informants in my case studies and in popular and academic writing about American popular music.[10] For practical reasons, I have narrowed the perspective to categories that many perceive to be genre categories and that belong to a group of genres common within American popular music with some certainty. The resulting list of nine genres is intended to give a rough idea of my general concept of genre and of the body of material for my theorizations in this chapter. The categories do not fit into a system, but I have used, with some flexibility, chronology as an organizing principle. This also applies to the examples of subcategories listed in parentheses.

Blues (country blues, urban blues, Chicago West Side blues)
Jazz (traditional, swing, bebop, cool jazz)
Country music (old-time/traditional, bluegrass, honky-tonk,
    Nashville Sound)
Rock (rock and roll, classic rock, glam rock, punk)

Soul/R & B (R & B, Memphis soul, Motown, soul-funk, contemporary
   R & B)
Salsa (salsa dura, salsa romántica, soul salsa, dance club salsa)
Heavy metal (black metal, death metal, doom metal, speed metal,
   trash metal)
Dance (disco, techno, house, trance, ambient)
Hip-hop (old school, East Coast, West Coast, gangsta rap)

Such a list can only be tentative. It serves a rudimentary purpose and should
not limit the agenda for our thinking about genre. Nor is it a representative
overview of the musics featured in this book. Any discussion of such lists
must deal with their nature and not only their individual choices. My list
represents a retrospective overview of musical formations that have evolved
over time. They are what Todorov (1976) called historical genres, as opposed
to theoretical or abstract genres, which could include ensemble genres such
as piano music and acoustic music or social genres such as wedding music,
religious music, and background music. In the early 1950s, for instance,
there were only about three major genres in American popular music (jazz,
blues/R & B, and country). A music such as mambo might have momen-
tarily attracted a great deal of attention, but it was imported from another
country and did not become as established as the others. The positions of
subcategories have also changed, and more recent ones may evolve into new
genres, as when hard rock evolved into heavy metal in the 1970s. Another
historical problem is that although older, canonical genre categories are
more stable than newer ones, some of them are not important to everyone
everywhere and do not show up in typologies based on sales figures (see,
e.g., Recording Industry Association of America [RIAA] 2003). Obviously,
few people operate with such a long and organized list, but groupings of
fewer genres are common. This is reflected in magazines and festivals that
feature a broad range of music, but not all musics, and in statements such
as "I am really into blues and jazz" or "I grew up on rock and soul." Genres
are often grouped according to ethnic and racial boundaries (see chapter 7 in
particular).

   Numerous questions could be raised about how these nine categories
relate to the larger world of popular music. What about formations structured primarily by celebrity fandom, instrument appreciation, or cultural
taste? These forms of appreciation are not primarily structured by the principles of music genre, but they do not eliminate genre; rather, they provide
complementary perspectives. Genre should also be studied in the context
of marketing categories, as illustrated by Brackett (2002), and in relation to

other types of music categories more generally. In later chapters, I go into detail about relations between genre and categories such as roots music, mainstream, indie rock, Latin pop, and "American music."

What about less specialized domains such as mainstream popular music and Muzak?[11] The relation between mainstream and genre is complex and must be understood in particular contexts. It often involves a relation between a smaller culture with a distinct identity and a larger market or a dominant culture. The term mainstream is associated with hits, stars, and corporate production. It is a keyword in discourses of high art and underground authenticity, in which it denotes conformity, predictability, and superficiality. Within the broad spectrum of mainstream popular music there is "pop music," a category that I am reluctant to define as a genre in a strict sense. George Michael, Madonna, Céline Dion, Sugababes, Backstreet Boys, Justin Timberlake, Britney Spears, and other contemporary pop stars specialize in similar forms of production, with professional teams of producers and managers, and their music shares certain conventions and forms a component of certain kinds of collectivity. But the culture has a different social structure, with its heavy focus on mass-media texts and the individual celebrity. It also stands out from genre cultures, if sometimes only in an imagined sense, by reason of its high-volume sales and massive public exposure, which is a source of tension in genre cultures and underground scenes (see chapter 5). Many artists are attracted to mainstream success, but also to smaller music spheres and categories that embody a different kind of authenticity and prestige. Artists move back and forth and create fusions, so the boundaries with mainstream pop are fluid in many genres, and especially in contemporary popular genres such as country music (see chapter 3), dance, soul/R & B, and rock. We should also remember that for minority populations, the notion of "crossing over" to mainstream pop is sometimes less a musical than a social issue (see chapter 7). Segregated labels such as soul, urban, and R & B are routinely imposed on African American artists, even when their music is based on much the same conventions as that of white colleagues whose music is sold as pop or rock (see also Garofalo 1993).

Muzak confirms the rule that genre ascribes meaning and value to music— that genre formation is also canon formation. There are no strong discourses asserting the musical values of, say, elevator music and music in pornographic films. Musics identified as "hybrid" usually reside at the other end of the spectrum because of their perceived power to transcend genre. They are attached to genre cultures as more sophisticated formations. The flip side of this logic is when hybridity is viewed as a dilution, a loss. I confront these problems of genre centricity most directly in chapter 7.

A few remarks on some of the many musics that might have been included: I have suggested that contemporary pop music can be understood as a category with a special position as a mainstream formation, but it also has genre functions and could be defined as a genre or style in a loose sense. The same could have been said about Tin Pan Alley up until its decline in the 1950s, and there is a sense in which new forms of pop music have taken its place. Genres such as reggae and flamenco are not included because they do not have the same type of cultural network in the United States as the examples on my list. Many reggae and flamenco recordings are imported, and much of the genre making happens abroad. Mexican American musics such as *conjunto*, *banda*, and *orquesta* are American, too, but whether any of them is a genre or whether they are a series of coexisting styles in Mexican American culture remains an open question.[12] In some cases it is hard to decide whether genre or style is the most appropriate term, not so much because the musical formations are complex, but because they are rather similar. Much of my genre theory also applies to major styles such as conjunto, disco, and techno, which some readers may consider small genres.

Following the principles outlined above, we can identify a few criteria of the concept of popular music genres around which I develop a framework for the inquiries in this book, a framework that is reflexive rather than normative because it is designed to have explanatory power for multiple, even contradictory, concepts of genre. The genres on my list are defined in relation to generic boundaries of musical texts and practices within musical traditions. Each category has a social basis in music scenes and magazines devoted to this particular kind of music. The social basis lies in the power that the categories have in cultural practice and their embodiment in objects, places, and people, and it is constituted through communication in what I call networks. The network of a genre can be understood from the perspective that the genre is a constellation of styles connected by a sense of tradition. These aspects distinguish genre from marketing categories and labels because it has a more stable existence in cultures of musical specialization among musicians, listeners, critics, pedagogues, and others. Categories such as "race records," "Top 40," and "chill-out music" are primarily used to present and market recorded music to unspecialized consumers and do not coincide with some of the categorizations preferred by musicians and fans (cf. chapter 2). Like Muzak, lounge, and easy listening, chill-out music is a category that is frequently used to repackage music of different genres for consumption as background music, typically as discreet accompaniment and stimuli in shopping, transportation, and leisure activities. Yet such categories are sometimes located in genre contexts. For instance, in May 2006 the lower level of the Virgin Megastore in downtown Chicago was partitioned into two main sections, hip-hop and dance music. Within the dance section was a row of bins respectively labeled chill-out, lounge, house, trance, and trip hop. Many of the CDs in those bins were anthologies produced by the same record companies, with similar styles of visual design and much overlap in the musical content. The chill-out bin was particularly eclectic. It mainly contained smooth contemporary rock and dance music with meditative grooves, but also nineteenth-century German art music, Zimbabwean mbira music, and Indonesian gamelan. This practice of categorization reflects how consumer cultures and culture industries are finding new ways of using recorded music as a consumer-directed product in everyday consumption, from the CD anthologies for specific private occasions to Apple's iTunes software for the private library and the Muzak made specifically for the Ann Taylor, Armani Exchange, or Starbucks customer.[13]

Following Frith and Negus, I adopt the term *genre culture* as a concept for the overall identity of the cultural formations in which a genre is constituted. It makes sense to view popular music genres as small cultures because they are defined in relation to many of the same aspects as general culture. Genres are identified not only with music, but also with certain cultural values, rituals, practices, territories, traditions, and groups of people. The music is embedded in all these things, and the culture concept can help us grasp the complex whole because of its capacity to represent a large entity of connections and sharing among many people. Culture also stresses the social and historical dimensions that are ignored when categories are defined only in relation to the music itself. Although genre cultures are embedded in general culture, they are concentrated in a smaller domain of social space and do not have a fixed position in the social order. In chapter 3, I develop a model of genre transformation inspired by large-scale processes of cultural modernization, but the similarities between the different concepts of culture are limited, and comparisons should not be carried too far.

Frith and Negus do not say much about the dimensions of their concept of genre world or genre culture. Studying the local formations of genre cultures known as *scenes* allows a bit more specificity. All genres on my list have crystallized in local scenes in a few cities in the United States, and some have taken shape in other countries as well. Genre scenes are translocal because they share ideas and representations of the same genre with scenes in other cities and often position themselves in relation to each other, with competing localized conceptions or branches of the genre. Genre cultures have a transnational network, but like culture in general they are structured on various territorial levels. Among the fundamental structuring principles are core–boundary structures and the interconnected processes of musical and social specialization. Bottom-up perspectives and other ontologies are also important, so I do not use the concept of genre culture as a master frame but as a tool for analyzing and contextualizing various notions of genre among different groups of people. Genre is in a sense always cultural, but the relation between the two varies greatly.

A General Framework of Genre

To understand the complex work of genre we need more than a systematic account of individual dimensions. We need explanations of fundamental connections and moments in the trajectory of a genre. The nine genres on my list above have evolved differently, but they have all gone through two basic processes: They have been *founded* (and *codified*) in what I call "center collectivities," and they have changed through *further negotiations*. It is reasonable to distinguish between formative and subsequent stages in a genre's history.

Emergence and Basic Operations

It is difficult to say exactly when individual genres were created, because they have emerged out of various existing musical formations. The formative process has been characterized by intense work on defining an emerging canon or tradition in relation to a number of core artists and "texts." Early negotiations have resulted in a set of shared ideas about the music and its values and origins, and in the hegemony of a single term. Dominant genre discourse thus conceals genre's immanent complexity, especially the musical and social heterogeneity of the genre. It is useful to explore this heterogeneity and differentiate between various aspects of the genre category. To this end, we can distinguish between "networks" and "conventions."

NETWORKS (SOCIAL AND DISCURSIVE) I adopt a broad and inclusive concept of *network* for the communicative relations between the many different agents that create and sustain a genre's identity. The network of an individual genre remains broad and fluid, interwoven in complex cultural textures. Its connections have been established in social and historical moments through the articulation of both strong and week affiliations between different groups of people across vast territories. Not all parts of the network are in direct communication with one another, and some parts are remote and may not feel as though they are part of a larger whole. But if they identify with the genre, they share some ideas about this particular kind of music and are familiar with some of the same recordings and artists. Each network is different in size, structure, and power. The role of discourse is also different from one genre to another. Criticism has had a limited role in country music, for instance, in comparison with jazz and rock, where groups of core writers have formed discursive networks with specialized fan readerships.

The interconnected processes of musical and social specialization have crystallized in various kinds of group affiliations for which we have the general concept of *collectivities*. The term comprises everything from the intimate relation between a couple of fans or a band to communities and scenes. Some collectivities have positioned themselves as core subjects and insiders of the genre. These *center collectivities*, as I call them, are clusters of specialized subjects that have given direction to the larger network. Recognized as authorities and experts, they have distinguished themselves from outsiders and the general public. They include influential fan communities, critics, record producers, and above all artists whose iconic status marks them as "leading" figures. The largest groups of influential insiders live in cities, where resources are concentrated. Center collectivities deserve attention because of their influence, but it is also important to look beyond them and not blindly accept their hegemonic discourses. Nor are they completely self-contained entities. Mass mediation plays an enormous role in genre formation, and corporate companies form a major part of the institutional network.

To illustrate briefly, let us take the cases of jazz and salsa: In the 1920s, jazz was more or less synonymous with popular music for many people, but dedicated fans and musicians who identified themselves as insiders were more discriminating. They began creating a canon of recordings by Jelly Roll Morton, Louis Armstrong, and others. Although jazz grew out of many musical formations, including ragtime, blues, and the white dance band tradition, critics primarily framed it in opposition to Tin Pan Alley. The term jazz was destabilized by the swing boom and the bebop movement, and it was not until the 1950s that jazz was consolidated as a genre with a narrative that connected various styles of the past and present in a canon. The center collectivities were first located in New Orleans and Chicago and then expanded to Harlem. New York City has remained the symbolic capital in the global network of jazz.

Similarly, salsa drew on many musics, but the formative moment occurred in fairly specific settings. Salsa was founded in the late 1960s and early 1970s in center collectivities of the Cuban and Puerto Rican diasporas to New York City, with the roster of artists on Fania Records forming the core. Unlike jazz, salsa was rooted more directly in recent foreign musical developments, especially the modern Cuban *son*. The salsa network became more complex and less centered on scenes and communities as the corporate industry moved in on the market in the 1980s.

CONVENTIONS (CODES, VALUES, AND PRACTICES) The processes of communication and signification in the network require several conceptual approaches. Music can be performance, practice, recorded sound, and text at the same time or in different situations, and we should explore how these ontologies operate in relation to genre. Adding to the complexity is the role of surrounding visual and verbal representations. It is impossible to distill this totality into a single theory and model of analysis, so I shall instead point to three central concepts for understanding the conventions of a genre, for a genre is not only defined by its boundaries—by what it is not—but also by its interior.

The aim of this outline is not to create catalogs of conventions in various genres, because such catalogs would be banal and highly reductive. Elaborate definitions may work in specific contexts and for some subcategories, but even there a catalog has limited explanatory power. Exclusive definitions are problematic because it is hard to find something in one genre that does not appear in other genres.

In structural linguistics, the concept of *code* implies a relatively strong and fixed convention that can be identified in concrete correlations between discrete entities in the communication process. A cultural code exists in the socially sanctioned correlation between a linguistic, visual, or aural sign, for instance, and a concept thereof. In many societies traffic law presumes a fixed correlation between a red stop sign and a concept and word for understanding and representing it ("stop," "arrêt," "alto," "светофор," "dur," "ق.ف," etc.). Musical signification is far more complex than this, of course. Many aspects of music are hard to describe even in native language, and music terminologies are very language and culture specific. Music involves polymorphous semantic textures and multisensory experiences that highlight limitations of language in general and concepts such as structure and sign in particular. Another problem is the unspecific and nonreferential character of musical signification (see p. 5).

Structuralist and semiotic approaches can be useful in exploring conventions on the level of discrete musical elements. For instance, certain twelve-bar chord schemes are strongly identified with the blues, certain vocal techniques with soul, certain distorted guitar sounds with rock, and steel

their fight for survival—their fight against "pop" versions and "sellouts" and their defense of "the real thing" or insistence on "keeping it country."

The relation with mainstream pop is also pertinent for understanding how genres negotiate the steady stream of new sound technologies, shifting clothing fashions, and musical innovations. This is illustrated by the process of *modernization*, in which divisions in a genre culture are exacerbated by the pressures of new fashions. Usually, elders have felt challenged and younger people energized by the new. The swing boom in the 1930s, rock in the late 1960s, and later disco, techno, and hip-hop were powerful signifiers of contemporary youth pop culture. The power of those musics to draw large numbers of youth has increased the intensity of reactions against and borrowings from them in other areas of musical life.

In addition to such general mechanisms, the trajectory of a genre has been determined by the social status of the people with which it is primarily identified. Unspecialized mainstream tastes have had a strong position in popular culture, and the elites have preferred high art. The center collectivities of genre cultures have rarely represented dominant social groups. Musical specialization, racial segregation, and social marginalization have been interlocking processes in American society. Musics of minority populations have suffered from the general conditions of these social groups. African American genres, for instance, have gone through more or less the same process of appropriation and exploitation. The classic story is that they were initially ridiculed and subjected to suppression, and as resistance gradually eroded they became absorbed and redefined in ways that reduced their association with blackness (Hall 1997, 32). Similar processes have occurred in white youth subcultures, although they were not doomed a priori by racism. One example is heavy metal, which emerged in small subcultures of primarily young, white working-class males in the early 1970s, received virtually no airplay, and entered the mainstream in the 1980s when it became popular among a more gender-balanced, middle-class audience (Walser 1993, 3).

GENRE AND THE CORPORATE MUSIC INDUSTRY I have noted that in the corporate industry musics are organized according to generic and market categories on more than one level and that corporate interests do not always coincide with those outside the organization. The corporate industry has been a major force in standardizing and popularizing genres. A classic strategy of popularization has been to adjust genres to the mainstream and create crossovers, so that artists sell in a broad market. This is one reason why celebrity promotion often lifts artists out of genre contexts. Although the corporate industry has sustained rising genres, it has also compromised them. Rather than being exclusively committed to genre cultures, the industry has oriented itself toward major market segments and adopted categories that are not genre categories in a strict sense. "Race records" and "world music" are but two examples of categories that have been used for targeting various musics to specific markets. When Negus (1999) identifies genre as an organizing principle in corporate practice, he is using the term in a general sense, because the industry uses whatever categories do the job, not just genre, although genre and style are central ones.

In some cases, the corporate industry has changed the dominant course of genres and styles. The shared interests of a trade organization, commercial radio, and major labels pushed country music toward mainstream pop in the late 1950s to a point where traditional country was marginalized, leading to a sense of great loss among core insiders (see chapter 3). Similar situations have occurred in rock in the early 1970s and hip-hop in the mid 1990s. Indie labels and underground magazines have offered alternatives to the corporate world, but many of them have had limited access to the main media channels, though a growing number of indies collaborate with major labels. Major labels have also challenged the continuity of genres by cutting down on production when sales decrease. Market changes are registered through portfolio management according to music categories, and production can be regulated directly because it is organized in discrete departments for particular musics (Negus 1999).

Executives, artists, and other agents in the corporate industry work within rather than outside of a larger musical culture. The Frankfurt School and early cultural studies approached the culture industry as a somewhat bounded world in which owners exercised control over workers and produced capitalist culture. Negus and du Gay have critiqued this "production of culture" approach and moved toward a more textured and situated understanding of corporate practices. According to Negus, "Production does not take place simply 'within' a corporate environment structured according to the requirements of capitalist production and organizational formulae" (1999, 19). Yet agents on all levels are required to maximize profits, and institutional capitalism creates an environment that is different from that of other domains of musical life. Music Row in Nashville is a good example of a distinct corporate industry sphere. It is an area of several square blocks inhabited by recording studios, labels, publishers, business agencies, and so on, and many country music artists have felt alienated there and complained about its power to regulate the genre.

Genre cultures are divided in relation to corporate production. Some artists and fans are happy with it, while others repudiate it or have a peripheral position because their music does not sell enough to be of corporate interest. It is important to represent both sides and to counter prejudice, but it is also important to recognize the ideological dimension of cultural production. The industry does not merely serve the needs of society as a whole, although this is often suggested by the claim that the industry is only giving people what they want. Massive sales of a product do not necessarily mean that the industry produces music of high cultural value and advances social health. Obviously, the space for musical diversity is limited when more than 80 percent of the global trade of recorded popular music is in the hands of about four major record labels.[15]

MEDIA AND CULTURAL PRACTICE Mass mediation brings music into wider circulation and complicates the spatial boundaries of social collectivities. The mass media have been necessary for establishing broad genre networks. Sustained production of particular musics has depended on the circulation of music, words, and images across great distances, and translocal histories have evolved in the process. The commercial phonogram, a core object in popular music since the 1920s, has essential features for genre formation: it is regulated, fixed, repeatable, and sold by category. Recordings have constituted the musical "texts" of translocal canons. In addition, the musical production of genre has occurred in close relation with the professional production of recordings. The formative moments in jazz, blues, and country music were all shaped by the recordings that major labels produced to capitalize on the so-called ethnic markets. Cities have been recording centers for individual genres—Nashville for country music, Memphis and Detroit for soul, New York and later Miami for salsa, and Detroit for techno—although major labels have tended to centralize their production in New York and Los Angeles. As more of the creative process moved into the studio in rock and other genres in the 1960s, individual record producers became more important to shaping generic boundaries. A few examples include Chet Atkins in country music, Phil Spector and Brian Eno in rock, Teo Macero in jazz, and DJ Premier and Dr. Dre in hip-hop. Artists who have presented, mixed, and sampled recordings have also shaped boundaries. Deejay pioneers include David Mancuso in disco, Grandmaster Flash in hip-hop, and Kevin Saunderson in techno (Brewster and Broughton 2000; Lawrence 2003).

The circulation of recordings is regulated by genre specific business structures, but the recording is a disembodied object, separate from its context of production, and it can gain meaning only when it is actively brought into being in a signifying context in various other locales. This translocal work of contextualization involves fans and cultural brokers such as writers who have looked to the genre canon and its mythologies in center collectivities. Country fans and artists from all over the world make pilgrimages to Nashville or Texas and have clear ideas about the clothing styles and attitudes associated with this genre. There are heavy metal fans in Finland who display tastes in fashion and standards of behavior very similar to those of their counterparts in Japan, and they have most likely read some of the same magazines and invested in the same American rock canon.

We can understand the ways in which genre categories are connected to recorded sound by looking at rituals of consumption and forms of mediation. Conventional music stores are designed for types of consumers and present music in product categories in discrete physical spaces. Mainstream music and genres with big sales are placed in the foreground, so store interiors reflect the market shares of different musics. Stores are designed so that individuals can find a particular item or browse spaces of interest with minimal help from store personnel. To this day, the standard organizing principles for popular music are first music categories and then artist names. One may meet other fans there, but most shoppers go into the store just to buy the recording and then share it with family and friends elsewhere. Personal and portable technologies of reproduction multiply the possibilities for individualized consumption. Affluent people have all sorts of opportunities for customizing their music consumption according to their individual tastes and lifestyles, somewhat independently of music collectivities.

Much the same can be said about the Internet. Online music stores such as Amazon.com, CDNow, and the Internet arms of Tower and Virgin are pushing into the market of traditional music stores because they serve the same basic functions, in some respects more effectively, with database utilities and accompanying reviews by critics and consumers. Online stores are modeled on traditional stores and allow for further separation of the music from spheres of specialized music making because more focus is on mass audiences and individualized consumption, which eventually weakens the community basis of genre. At online stores, music is a database object without physical presence, a hypermobile commodity. The downloading of digital music via online stores such as iTunes and Music Now or illegal file sharing represents a further step in this direction: the purchased product itself is no longer a physical object. In 2005, digital music sales only constituted about 6 percent of the total market, but the market was growing fast.[16] The growth continued in 2006, especially in the market of digital subscription services offered by media conglomerates such as AOL Time

Warner (via Music Now), Virgin (Virgin Digital), Napster Inc. (Napster), RealNetworks (Rhapsody), and Trans World Entertainment (FYE). MTV Networks launched Urge, which was integrated with MTV and embedded in Microsoft's Windows Media Player 11 (Garrity 2006).

Online reviews and music writing in general have so far displayed fairly conventional forms of musical discourse, including genre discourse. Nor has the Internet eliminated traditional forms of social interaction in genre collectivities. Even in cyber-oriented techno music, insiders have congregated in live music venues and adopted the traditional ritual form in which artists perform on a stage before an audience. Music categories and artist's names play a key role when fans communicate on Listservs and engage in downloading. Listservs and message boards enable fans of a genre from all over the world to connect: in 2006, MySpace.com had over 200,000 music groups and Yahoo! over 100,000 genre-specific music groups.[17] Online discourse can be viewed as an extension of offline discourse, and it is often complementary to the professional mass media. However, electronic communication is not only empowered but also limited by its relative independence from face-to-face interaction. For one thing, one cannot see and feel how categories are used in various social contexts. For another, e-forums of people living in many different places lack the forms of knowledge and sociability that exist among insiders of the same scene. Verbal as well as musical genre discourse can become disoriented if its social basis is reduced. In the early years of Napster and Kazaa, for instance, when everyone could upload song files to the same database, the database would sometimes list the same song in five different genre categories. The explanation for this confusing situation is that different cultures of categorization operated in the same database but somewhat displaced and removed from their social basis. In sum, categories have little value in themselves. What matters is how they are used and embodied in communicative relations to become structuring forces in musical life.

The framework outlined above presents general ideas for further exploration, and I do not consider it final in an absolute sense. In concluding this chapter, I wish to stress that small theories and frameworks serve the need for ongoing revision and integration of methodical approaches in close relation with the empirical. To understand the changing horizons of popular music, we need to engage critically in musical life and conduct case studies from which new theories can emerge, and this is what the following chapters are about.

Figure 1 Still from *O Brother, Where Art Thou?* Photo courtesy of Photofest, 2000.

CHAPTER TWO

Roots and Refigurations

The idea of folk music, going back to Johann Gottfried Herder in early modernity, has had a pivotal role in shaping the aesthetics and boundaries of popular music.[1] The relation between folk and popular musics, however, has frequently been one of opposition. A classic example is the dichotomy between the notions of commercial popular music produced *for* "the people" and authentic folk music created *by* "the people" (cf. Middleton 2004). The two were also framed in exclusive terms when popular music studies started defining its field of inquiry in the late 1970s and scholars came up with general distinctions between folk, popular, and art music.[2] By that time musical and discursive components of folk and art musics had long circulated widely within popular music cultures and stimulated the formation of styles such as folk rock and art rock. Today, it no longer makes sense to view art, folk, and pop music as separate cultural spheres or as a trichotomy into which all musics can be organized. But the categories are still relevant for distinguishing between different forms of musical culture in more particular terms. Also important is their existence as myths and ideologies. Folkloric images of life in a rural past, for instance, have been a major source of fascination in popular music, even in urban settings, where people had little or no experience of what they endorsed. Like other forms of expressive culture, music has the capacity to stimulate the human imagination and mediate between myth and reality.

In the mid nineteenth century, the opposition between notions of a simple life in the preindustrial rural South and a complex modernity in northern cities was a basic scheme in American popular culture, including literary fiction, blackface minstrelsy, and various forms of popular song. The refrain of Stephen Foster's classic "Hard Times Come Again No More" (1854) is a remarkable example: "Many days you have lingered around my cabin door," it goes, but neither Foster nor his predominantly urban audience had ever lived in a cabin.[3] The song was presumably inspired by the skepticism about industrialization in Charles Dickens's novel *Hard Times*, published the same year. This cabin myth reappears in country music all the way from the Carter Family through Hank Williams to Dolly Parton's songs about her childhood in "a shingle covered cottage" in the Tennessee Mountains.[4] There is a mythical notion of the cabin as an ideal site of old-fashioned, simple, and nonmaterialistic values. The film *Cabin in the Sky* (1940), with its all-black cast, demonstrates the interracial legacy of the cabin myth, and it goes without saying that it does not have the same implications across racial lines. African Americans have been imprisoned by racial stereotypes and had less mobility in all domains of society.

O Brother, Where Art Thou?

A recent example of folklore in popular culture is the film *O Brother, Where Art Thou?* (2000). The screenplay transposes elements of Homer's *Odyssey* into a story of a man who travels not in ancient Greece, but in the American middle South of the 1930s. Part of the story is situated in Mississippi, and the press speculated that the action took place in 1937, but the locale and time are generic rather than particular, as Malone has pointed out (2003). The journey of the protagonist, Everett (George Clooney), primarily leads through remote rural areas. The few people he and his two companions, Delmar (Tim Blake Nelson) and Pete (John Turturro), meet along their way are rather odd, including a white criminal who shoots haphazardly at grazing cows.

The first person they encounter is a blind black man riding a hand trolley on what appears to be an endless road to nowhere. With a voice like an oracle in a fairy tale, he declares that the three men are going to travel a long, difficult road and find a fortune. There is an ironic tinge to the film's approach to such mythical and existential themes and to its own subjects. Everett is not an honorable king who is about to return to his royal castle like Odysseus. Rather, in order to escape prison he tells two fellow prisoners to believe that he has buried a large sum of money and will give them a share if they follow him. He just wants to get back to his wife Penny (i.e., Penelope [Holly Hunter]). Everett is nonchalant and charming, but there is nothing elevated or sacred about him. His distanced attitude to his surroundings bears the mark of a contemporary urban subject, and he can be viewed as a mediating figure between past and present.[5]

Almost every scene is accompanied by music, and a lot of it is diegetic. Musical performances are central in some of the momentous scenes but also function as entertainment in scenes of minor importance to the general narrative. The music is a major attraction in itself and not merely an accompaniment to the visual. As in most Hollywood films, the soundtrack (produced by T-Bone Burnett) is targeted toward a broader audience rather than a specialized genre culture. This is reflected in the distanced and stereotypical approach to the musical cultures represented. Emphasis is on early country music and bluegrass, and there are a few performances of African American work songs and the blues. Music is named in only a very few instances. In one, a radio deejay claims to play "old-timey music." In another, a blind record label owner says he does not record "nigger songs," only "old-time material," and believes he is recording a white band when in fact the three protagonists have brought a black singer and guitarist with them. Generic categories are indexed by displaying typical genre elements in the music as well as in its social context and iconography. Classic images of blues, for instance, are articulated in the scene where the protagonists meet this black guitarist and singer, named Tommy Johnson (played by Chris Thomas King), at a crossroads. Johnson's character is fashioned after the now famous Robert Johnson (1911–1938) rather than his lesser-known contemporary who actually bore the name Tommy Johnson (c. 1896–1956).[6] His trickster image is reinforced when he says that he has sold his soul to the devil.

One of the scenes in which music is essential to the story is where the three protagonists perform with Johnson in a community hall. They are doing what is supposed to be a traditional, rural music show. Because they are escaped prisoners, they perform their comedy routine in disguise, but the actors also create a meta-irony in relation to their characters in the film. They first do Jimmie Rodgers's "In the Jailhouse Now," in which Delmar exhibits his yodeling skills. Singing and playing music seem to be as natural and easy as breathing, and yet music has tremendous power. When the group starts to perform "I Am a Man of Constant Sorrow" (traditional, arranged by Carter Stanley), it is clear that their recording of the song has become a hit. The crowd cheers enthusiastically, but the performance is soon interrupted by a candidate for the gubernatorial election in Mississippi, Homer Stokes (i.e., the Cyclops [Wayne Duvall]), who proudly declares that he is with the Ku Klux Klan and condemns Johnson's presence on the stage. The crowd boos, and the sitting governor, Pappy O'Daniel, does not hesitate to turn this to his advantage by embracing the band and accusing Stokes of bad taste. The response from the crowd indicates that this event has consequences for the outcome of the election and that the music was able to exert pressure in the negotiation of social issues such as politics and racism.

In several ways, then, music is ascribed magical power. This is characteristic of other scenes, too, for instance in the redemption scene, where a
gospel choir draws our three fellows into a mass baptism in the river. Another example is the Sirens, who seduce the men with their sexual body language (they are wet through, one lifts up her skirt, and another touches her
breast) and with their gentle, bluesy singing, in a slow tempo appropriate to
their catlike movements.

Making History Attractive

O Brother is a larger-than-life Hollywood adventure that glorifies the past
in accordance with dominant sensibilities of the present. The whole visual
dimension is the result of extensive manipulation using some of the most
advanced studio technology. The production short "Painting with Pixels"
included on the DVD edition tells us that Joel and Ethan Coen, two brothers
who wrote and directed the screenplay, made suggestions for the look of the
film. To meet their expectations, a collaboration was initiated with Cinesite, a Kodak subsidiary. The narrator of "Painting with Pixels" tells us that
this is "the first time the look of an entire live-action feature was digitally
manipulated." A handful of people involved in the production are interviewed, and they all seem to be fascinated with the idea that the technology
helped create a more authentic representation of the past. The director of
photography, Roger Deakins, mentions the Dust Bowl era and says that they
wanted the film "to look very dry and dusty and have a sort of feel of an old
picture book."[7] Great importance is attached to the enrichment provided by
color, not least by the vice president of business development at Cinesite,
Randy Starr:

> I believe the color in the movie became a character. I believe it washes
> over the audience as you view it, as a character. It lets you feel the period
> of time. It lets you feel the heat in the air. It lets you feel the sweat on
> their body [sic], and that is something that the filmmaker could not cap-
> ture in camera and could only use digital technology to let them capture
> that.

Capture what? On the one hand, this statement represents the realist
view that there is a truth to be captured and that history is finite. On the
other hand, technology is praised for its ability to transform and connect.
Starr imagines a kind of metamorphosis of technical material into living nature and implies a correspondence between emotional power and historical

authenticity. He is essentially talking about creating a more realistic image of reality by using more advanced technology, and that turns most thinking about authenticity on its head. This fascination with technology is not revealed in the film, which presents a fantasy of the unmediated.

In addition to the technical beautification, the image of the past also modifies the reality of serious issues such as racism. Tommy Johnson's identity has elements of the fairly traditional stereotype of the African American male as a sympathetic subordinate subject with great musical talent. He is kept at a safe distance from white subjects, but he is not confined to the rigid stereotypes of classic Hollywood. The atmosphere in the scenes with Johnson and the three protagonists is relaxed, and the interracial music making in both the recording studio and the community hall is slightly romanticized. It is unlikely that an interracial performance could have happened publicly in the South in 1937, and the filmmakers' attempt to harmonizing racial history with a more moral present is obvious in their representation of the Ku Klux Klan as a bunch of stupid and evil men.

Fantasies of authentic and unmediated history govern the representation of music, too. One could easily overlook this aspect because these fantasies are performed so professionally. But music never happens by itself. The musical dimension of the film is the outcome of a process that has involved performing artists, a sound designer, a music editor, music producers, a musicologist, and many others. Each song is selected, performed, recorded, edited, and inserted into the film and the CD soundtrack.

Most of the songs are more than fifty years old, some of them classics by the likes of the Carter Family and Jimmie Rodgers, and it is striking that almost all of them were performed specifically for this film by contemporary artists. The only exceptions are two Alan Lomax field recordings and two recordings by Harry McClintock and the Stanley Brothers.[8] It may be that the decision to request new performances primarily derives from financial concerns, because Universal could hope to maximize sales of artists in its roster, but the decision also has cultural implications. Most of the music is performed by popular and professional artists born long after 1937, notably Emmylou Harris (b. 1949), Gillian Welch (b. 1968), and Alison Kraus (b. 1971). These performers automatically attract an audience, and they deliver a professional product.

Older artists such as Ralph Stanley (b. 1927) and the Fairfield Four represent the authority of tradition, while the many younger artists signal a move from older genre traditions toward contemporary mainstream popular music. In their performances, these artists transform old song material for contemporary sensibilities. Kraus sings the traditional "Down to the

River to Pray" in her pop-inflected style, which contrasts with the less trained voices one might have heard from the characters portrayed in the film. There are also disjunctures between the acoustics of the locales shown in film and the acoustics of the music that accompanies those images: In this scene, the locale is a riverside in a flat field, but the clearly audible reverb effect situates Kraus's voice in a concert hall. As with photographic technology, sound technology is used to enhance the sensuous quality of the material of representation and thus seduce the spectator.

Film Music Outside Cinema

O Brother has contributed to the growth of the emerging culture of American roots music. This is a revival culture invested in the notion that a number of vernacular musical traditions form a common authentic national heritage. The notion of American roots music is embedded in a unitary narrative that connects musics that in some cases have been rather separate. The central objects of this revival are iconic artists and the recordings they made decades ago, so the refiguration of generic and historical boundaries primarily happens in the representation, marketing, and consumption of the music. In its dominant form, roots music is largely a reception phenomenon. It is typified not by specialization into blues, country, folk, or gospel, but by the eclectic juxtaposition of all these musics into one section of the record store and private record collection. However, we shall see that roots sensibilities can be found in contemporary musical practice.

Through encounters with people in various parts of the country in 2003 and 2004 I learned that the film and especially the music in the film were celebrated as something that was exciting and authentic. The input I got from fans and clerks in a few video and DVD rental stores indicated that the audience was diverse, but that a large segment was white middle-class people aged fifteen to forty. Fans and performers who had specialized in some of the musics represented in the film were mostly happy with the growing young audience but did not take the film very seriously. The bluegrass and country music people I talked to on a field trip to southern Illinois and western Kentucky in May 2004, for instance, liked the film, and none of them felt uncomfortable with it. An experienced deejay at a commercial country radio station argued that the film helped bluegrass:

RYAN PATRICK: It helped to get bluegrass back on mainstream radio for a brief
    time. [...] A song like "I Am a Man of Constant Sorrow" got a lot of radio
    airplay.

AUTHOR: Did you play it on your station [Z100 FM "New Country," in Carterville, Illinois]?

PATRICK: We played it on our station, yeah. And a few of the larger artists did
some bluegrass songs based on the success of that, but it slowly started phas-
ing out. Now, what I think that movie did, though, it brought a lot of bluegrass to a lot of new fans. There are probably more bluegrass fans now than
there ever have been because of that movie, seriously, and so I think a lot
more people were introduced to it and then saw it more as being OK to listen
to that music. You know, bluegrass used to be, "Hmm...I don't listen to
that!" but it's okay to listen to it now, it's acceptable. (Conversation with
author, Carterville, Illinois, 6 May 2004).

The soundtrack was identified with bluegrass, but people with a strong
background in bluegrass and country music made a point of telling me that
only one or two of the songs are actually bluegrass songs. There are also
old-time country, gospel, and blues songs in the film. Several artists also
felt a bit strange about the new mainstream image of bluegrass, parallel-
ing the early 1960s, when bluegrass was introduced in the urban folk revival
(Rosenberg 1985, chapter 6). A serious young banjo player in a bluegrass family band in Kentucky said that his colleagues did not call their music roots
or folk music, but that I could probably find it under that label at Wal-Mart;
thus, he associated those categories with mass-culture consumerism (Jason
McKendree, conversation with author, Draffenville, Kentucky, 7 May 2004).

During a stay in San Francisco in the spring of 2003 I encountered a community of musicians who identified with the concept of roots music. They
had been attracted to bluegrass and other kinds of music from a folk-oriented
perspective and felt compromised by the film. Said the bassist James Schneider: "While many of my musician friends welcome the new group of listeners, many also see their work with roots music as an oppositional stance to
not only popular genres of music but also modern forms of capitalism such
as the very commodification and mass marketing of musical genres that the
film and soundtrack promote." This reaction also has a parallel in the folk
revival of the 1950s and 1960s. Purists of what was known as the esoteric
camp would stop singing a song if it was recorded and became a hit, because
they felt that it had been lost to the world of commerce and did not need
their preservationist effort anymore. The singer and folklorist Joe Hickerson
told me in 2003 about an episode at Oberlin where one day a fellow student,
having heard the song on the radio for the first time, came running into the
classroom and burst into tears: "They have taken 'Rock Island Line' from
us!"[9]

O Brother did indeed boost the popularity of musics that were largely unknown to younger generations. The soundtrack went platinum and was on both the country and pop charts for years. In 2002 alone, it sold 2,736,000 copies, making it the no. 10 album in sales in the United States that year, and by the spring of 2003 it had passed 7,000,000.[10] Fan Web sites, newsgroups, commercial vendors, record labels, magazines, and newspapers devoted a lot of attention to the film and the soundtrack. A publicity Web site for the soundtrack was set up by the label at www.obrothermusic.com, and that was of course accompanied by other forms of publicity produced by the corporate apparatus of Universal. The soundtrack was released on Mercury in Nashville and moved in 2001 to the new label Lost Highway Records, which is based in Nashville and also owned by Universal (Christman 2003; Farley 2001).

This was not the first time a film had jump-started a revival of musics of the white southern working class. *Bonnie and Clyde* (1967), for instance, also gave bluegrass a new image and brought it into the pop market. However, *O Brother* sold more and was accompanied by a larger wave of albums produced to capitalize on its success.[11] The pop-oriented and slightly exoticized image of country music in the film *Urban Cowboy* (1980) started a country fad in mainstream popular culture that had been developing since Dolly Parton's crossover success in the late 1970s. In other words, a brief turn to bluegrass or country music had occurred a couple of times, but it had been a while since it had last happened, and so *O Brother* might have been perceived as a novelty. Indeed, the popularity of the film was conditioned by the fact that the majority of the audience was too young to have experienced its predecessors, among which we can also count *Deliverance* (1972) and the television series *The Beverly Hillbillies* (1962–71). Like most revivals, the roots revival is fueled by a strong sense of excitement about discovering a hitherto unknown past. The young urban audience is not deeply traditional and does not faithfully explore the history of the genre traditions with which they connect.

Roots Music Discourse

Beginning in the late 1990s a discourse on American roots music developed in music magazines, CD anthologies, encyclopedias, and a four-part PBS documentary series entitled *American Roots Music* (2001).[12] The PBS series, largely the work of journalists and independent scholars, was done in collaboration with the Smithsonian Institution and the Rock and Roll and Country Music Halls of Fame. Additional grants were received from the National

Endowment for the Arts (NEA), AT&T, and others. Bill Ivey, an ethnomusicologist and the chairperson of the NEA, met with the producers in 1998, and the bulk of the work was completed between March 2000 and August 2001. The series was broadcast in prime time in October 2001, about fifteen months after the premiere of O Brother and ten months after the release of the soundtrack.[13] Adding to the media hype of roots music was a video/DVD edition of the series as well as an accompanying CD and a coffee-table book, all of which have the same cover image, which is modeled on an old photo album.

In the vein of Ken Burns's documentaries, the PBS roots series offers a light and rosy history that caters to a nonspecialist, white, middle-class audience who wants to enjoy the music together with positive images of their past (cf. Dornfeld 2002). There is also an element of tourism in the series's search for authentic sounds as exotic treasures, on one hand, and its concealment of its own identity as a mass-distributed commercial product, on the other. The discursive network of the series extends to fans and magazines that identify with the roots category, but the discourse does not have a strong social basis in music scenes or genre cultures. Sponsors of the PBS series are national rather than regional, and a closer study reveals that the PBS products and the O Brother soundtrack to a great extent have been created by and for the general rock/pop domain of mainstream popular culture.

The PBS products illustrate that the word roots is being used as an essentialist metaphor for timeless authenticity in the context of a common cultural history. It is not difficult to see that this mythical and transcendental notion of roots fits with the poetics of magic realism and revivalism described above. Roots music becomes a more or less freestanding category detached from the recontextualization that is going on at present.

The term American roots music is rarely defined, but it is applied to a more specific body of music than the sweeping narratives suggest. A rough distinction can be made between contemporary roots music and roots music of the pre-rock era, beginning in the 1920s, when commercial recordings became available. Roots music of the pre-rock era focuses on legends of country music, blues, and the folk revival, which boomed in the early days of rock. Contemporary American roots music is more loosely defined, because it is less canonized, but it has included folk-oriented rock (e.g., Bob Dylan and Neil Young), bluegrass and country (e.g., Alison Kraus and Emmylou Harris), and, in a wider sense, also roots-oriented jazz (e.g., Bill Frisell, Cassandra Wilson, and Norah Jones). At the center of this particular concept of roots music are country music, the blues, and the folk revival. The PBS series also includes music of Cajuns and Native Americans, for instance, but this is more the exception than the rule. Tin Pan Alley, jazz, and genres that arose after 1960 are generally not included in the roots category.

If roots music culture draws so much on folk music discourse, why not call it folk music? The main reasons for using the label roots music instead are its novelty effect and its ability to reach across a wide range of genres and styles, but the term could also signal that the distinction between folk and popular have collapsed. Working against the term folk music are its associations with moaning about dying traditions and with socialism, which is not very popular these days. Under pressure from the booming markets of popular music, the folk music world was marked by a sense of crisis in the 1970s, and the crises led to attempts to replace the term folk music with traditional music (Bohlman 1988, xiii–xx). "Traditional music" is less stigmatized but also less sexy and not the most obvious tag for a new fashion in popular culture. The term roots music has been used as a marketing label in the world music field since the 1980s, with the same focus on essentialist notions of authenticity (Holt, in press). It has been embraced by underground discourses but also exists in the mainstream sphere of the *Rough Guide* music and travel products, for instance. Notions of roots world music, moreover, are shaped by anxieties about modernity and globalization (Feld 1994b, 269), just like the American roots music trend can be seen as a nationalist response to the same processes. Interest in American roots music greatly increased in the immediate aftermath of the 9/11, but it would be reductive to see its popularity as a mere reflection of rising patriotism and postmodern nostalgia.[14]

Benjamin Filene is so far the only scholar that has used the term American roots music as the central concept in a monograph (Filene 2000). It is interesting that in the process of turning his 1995 dissertation into this book, he changed the title by replacing the term vernacular music with roots music. This decision was hardly unaffected by the growing popularity of the term. Filene also served as an advisor for the PBS series. Like several of the other members of the advisory board, Filene has a background in American studies, and he works in the museum sector.[15]

Filene uses the concept of roots music as an umbrella term for several musics that until recently were named differently. He says that the terminological change shifts attention from the music itself to perceptions of the music (2000, 4), but he does not say whose perceptions and does not reflect on the differences between past and present terminology. It is surprising that the book provides no etymology of the term except for a passing mention that it comes from rock criticism. I return to rock criticism later (p. 157); here I should like to add that the general meanings of the roots metaphor include origins, heritage, lineage, and solidarity, as in Alex Haley's novel *Roots* (1976) and in the concept of grassroots. Nor does Filene discuss the formation of American roots music discourse in the 1990s. He motivates his choice of the term roots music by arguing that the term folk music is too restrictive and conflict ridden. That this is also a negation becomes clearer when he states that he will "substitute" other terms for the term folk music. Filene adopts the concept of vernacular music to include folk, popular, and roots music. Things get more complicated when he goes on to define roots music: "I use "roots"... to identify musical genres that... have been glorified as the 'pure' sources out of which the twentieth century's commercial popular music was created" (2000, 4). This definition raises more questions than it answers, but he clearly adopts a linear narrative of a general transformation from folk to popular music.

A Live Performance in San Francisco

During the above-mentioned stay in San Francisco in 2003 I observed that the myths of the 1950s' beat generation and the 1960s' counterculture still attracted many tourists to the North Beach and Haight-Ashbury neighborhoods. The Fillmore Auditorium, the Bottom of the Hill, and other venues for popular music chiefly presented national acts, and the local popular music scene did not have a strong local identity. An important medium for exploring categories used to navigate the city's popular music scene was the *SF Weekly*, the primary guide to the city's nightlife. Several fans and musicians complained to me that the paper provided little more than listings and scattered ads. One consequence of the sparse information was that communication depended more on the seven standard categories used to organize the listings.[16] Roots music was not one of those categories, but the term was used in individual entries, and a great deal of the music in the category "folk/country/Irish" had connections with the roots trend.

One live performance illustrated important aspects of the local roots music scene. The show was at the Make-Out Room on Twenty-second Street between Valencia and Mission Streets in the Mission District, a multicultural neighborhood with a large Latino community and street soundscapes dominated by international dance pop. This music could also be heard a couple of nights a week at the Make-Out Room. In a word, it was not a place where one could expect a celebration of traditional Southern music, but that was nonetheless what happened at this event, where three bands played before an audience of sixty to eighty people. Most people were between the ages of twenty-five and forty and dressed casually, in neither mainstream nor alternative fashions, and while there was a gender balance, almost everyone appeared to be white.

The audience consisted of people with different tastes and levels of genre specialization. Part of the audience seemed somewhat insecure and quiet, like curious newcomers, whereas others were enthusiastically engaging in improvised square dancing, clapping hands, and being in general very spirited. A small crowd routinely shouted "Yeee-haaw!", as if delighting in an unaccustomed form of revelry. These people exoticized music from their own country. Yet James Schneider, who performed at this event and who comes from a white southern middle-class background assured me that the southerners he knows would not have been offended. They would have been doing "the same thing," he said: "I say that this is unfortunate because I would almost rather see folks offended and willing to engage the classicist stereotypes that such behaviors display" (Schneider, e-mail to author, 27 September 2003).

The three bands only played acoustic instruments, several of which were old or vintage, and their music was based in genres formed in the pre-rock era. The Creole Belles announced that they were going to play "Cajun music from southern Louisiana," and the female lead singer wore a traditional Cajun dress. She also told the audience that band members had made field trips to study Cajun culture. Incidentally, the band had recently performed in a record store as part of a concert series titled "The American Roots Music Show" that had been running every Sunday since April 2002.[17]

The lead singer of an old-time/bluegrass band named the Crooked Jades wore a country-style vest and presented two songs by saying that he had learned them in North Carolina and Alabama, as if he, too, wanted to authenticate his own performance. He introduced a young dancer who performed with the band by saying, "Now we're going to have some barn dancing." Barn dancing in the Mission District! I later found out that the band proudly represented itself as a "traditional" band on its Web site, which also revealed that several reviewers had associated the band with "the *O Brother* phenomenon."[18] Some of the band members were on the board of the San Francisco Bluegrass and Old-Time Festival, the first of which took place in 2000. In 2001 the festival organized a series of live shows with local bands at evening screenings of the *O Brother* concert movie *Down from the Mountain* (2000) in the Red Vic Movie House on Haight Street.[19]

The third band was named Hot Club Sandwich and came from Seattle (the other bands were local). It played a mix of swing music and classic Latin American genres in the revivalist spirit of the evening. No one in the Make-Out Room this evening could fail to recognize how the whole event was marked by a sense of difference in relation to other parts of the city's live scene. The music, the people, and the atmosphere were strikingly different from the electronic dance music that proliferated in so many venues with a slightly younger audience. The audience at the Make-Out Room had little interest in electronic dance music and instead invested in what they perceived to be the more authentic and natural values of traditional music. A revival culture had emerged, but its social network was relatively small and not very organized.

Tower Records in New York and Chicago

About a week later I walked into a Tower Records store on 962 Broadway in New York City and found a remarkable offshoot of the roots trend. Having looked in vain for a particular bluegrass CD in the country music bin on the second floor, I asked the nearest clerk for help. The young woman did not know of bluegrass or where I could find the CD, though it turned up on her computer screen after some effort. She assumed it was sold out. Then I spotted a large wooden sign at the far end of the room saying "Roots Music/Americana." It hung over a door to a room that was richly decorated in mythic iconography, including portraits of legendary musicians, three musician automatons named the Splinter Bottom Boys, a window treatment based on an Amish quilt, and an object representing the Oracle Chicken. There were large "Americana/Roots" signs all over the room, throwing into relief the various symbolic objects.

To find out more about the room and how the music industry handled roots music, I contacted the store upon my return to Denmark a few weeks later. It turned out that the room was the creation of a marketing representative named Julia Van Nutt and her husband, Robert, an artist. The couple had come from the South, gone to graduate school in North Carolina, and worked in the Broadway theater business for some years. Julia started as an everyday clerk and had been at Tower for only about a year before she organized the room in the summer of 2002. Says Julia: "I got the idea for the room very much based on the vastly increased interest that the public had in this bluegrass genre, thanks to the success of *O Brother, Where Art Thou!*" (Van Nutt, e-mail to author, 5 May 2003). In other words, this initiative did not come from Tower's headquarters.

Experts in the headquarters had organized a central catalog in which every CD was registered under a label with a numerical code. For example, bluegrass and folk shared number 324, and blues was 325. Neither roots music nor Americana figured in this catalog, so those categories were organized by Julia. "After choosing my core roots musicians I gleaned the store for CDs to bring into the room," she explained. Her core artists included the Carter Family, Jimmie Rodgers, and Hank Williams in country music; Robert Johnson and Blind Willie Johnson in blues; and Woody Guthrie and Leadbelly in folk; but also Buddy Holly in rock. Julia's selection of roots music was informed by existing canons, but she occasionally made changes based on input from customers, magazines, and books. Her selection of Americana largely consisted of contemporary music and changed all the time according to weekly radio playlists and sales figures, some of which were provided by a trade organization for Americana (Van Nutt, e-mail to author, 3 May 2003).[20] The fact that so much was managed locally by Julia alone and not by corporate headquarters shows that the roots music market had not been developed on a larger scale. A hierarchy in this store was evident in the foregrounding of rock and pop music on the first floor and the more remote location of jazz, classical, country, and folk music on the second floor. This is standard in major chain record stores.

A meeting with the product manager at Tower Records in downtown Chicago about a year later taught me more about the relationship between genre and consumption in chain stores. While Julia was obviously trying to connect consumers of the *O Brother* soundtrack with country and blues, her colleague Frank Youngwerth in Chicago looked at the soundtrack as a singular novelty with a much more peripheral relation to genre cultures. Youngwerth recognized that the soundtrack boosted sales of bluegrass, but many of his customers bought only this one album, he said. He had worked in the store since 1987 and argued that the majority of consumers were not specialized listeners:

> From the start of me working at the record store I was amazed because I always considered, like, you track things down and you read. You know, if you're interested in something, you read everything can about it, find out what's available, try different things out. And that's not the way most people buy records. Most people don't have the time to do any of that. They sort of, you know, catch something on the newspaper or something that's a big phenomenon, and then they sort of come in and they want that, you know the big thing everybody's talking . . . the thing that, when they went to a party, their friends had that record. That's the way people buy records. They don't buy records by trying to find anything out about, you know, reading a book or even reading an article. Well, of course a lot of people read magazines, but I think music consumers in general—although I like to think that we got an exception to that in

what comes to our store—but in general the people that made *O Brother, Where Art Thou?* such a success were people who are very superficial in their approach to buying music. But they're like in denial about it, and so that makes them feel very good that they're picking up something so authentic. Now, if they go and they check out some real... rural... if they go on and buy a Jimmie Rodgers album it's like, OK, great for you, you learned the lesson. But they're just sort of waiting for the next thing that's worthy enough to come along.... I have a kind of a cynical point of view because it was marketed. They bought it because it was marketed, and there was a certain appeal that it had for the content, but basically they only found out about it because it was so well marketed. You know, marketing is one of those mysterious things. Nobody knows how to make it happen, but... it's fascinating.

Youngwerth helps us understand why chain stores such as Tower have not integrated the category of roots music in their system of classification. The industry renames and repackages music products, but it continues to operate with established genre categories such as classical, rock, and jazz. Moreover, Youngwerth said that he was surprised how few copies were sold of the soundtracks that tried to use the same combinations of factors that supposedly made *O Brother* a hit. His examples included T-Bone Burnett's soundtracks for *Divine Secrets of the Ya-Ya Sisterhood* (2002) and *The Lady Killers* (2004). He also mentioned Martin Scorsese's PBS series on blues (2003), which followed the model of the Ken Burns jazz series and the PBS roots music series. The blues series, he said, failed to generate a significant increase in sales, and the compilations accompanying the series "were just sort of trying to follow the formula, but it just wasn't very effective." One of the reasons formulas cannot be transposed across genres is that genres have a degree of cultural specificity, and this is one reason it is relevant to study them culturally.

Americana

In Julia's roots/Americana room I found the bluegrass CD I had been looking for. I was struck by the existence there of several Americana anthologies. Americana had existed for little more than ten years. But why was it juxtaposed with roots music? Like roots music, Americana has an acoustic sound and plays with national mythologies and the opposition to mainstream pop. However, Americana is situated in a contemporary world of hip young musicians—"citybillies"—who essentially play rock music or rock-influenced country music. The opposition to pop is defined not only in the image of a pure past, but also in self-consciously subcultural identities in the present. Americana has roots in punk and in the outlaw country music of the 1970s. It was first defined as a distinct movement when bands such as Uncle Tupelo and Souled American emerged on the scene in the early 1990s. Later, the category became broader, and artists previously identified with another category were recategorized as Americana artists. Among them were Lucinda Williams in country-folk music and Johnny Cash, Kinky Friedman, and Emmylou Harris in country music. Americana is still a vague term used interchangeably with "alt.country" and the "no depression movement." The categories of American roots music and Americana overlap, and the two are often coupled in the market, as in the case of the Tower room and the catalog of Lost Highway Records, which has a distinctive Americana profile but also includes the *O Brother* soundtrack. Americana has not been supported by museums, scholars, and journalists as roots music has, perhaps because it has not attained status as national heritage music.

One of the Americana CD anthologies in Julia's room was *Another Country: Songs of Dignity and Redemption from the Other Side of the Tracks* ([1996–2002], Agenda, 2003). I suspect that avoiding the term country music in the title is advantageous from a marketing perspective because many potential Americana listeners have negative stereotypes of country music. The CD's cover photo is a landscape, and the notion of country is invoked in the general sense of land rather than the genre of country music. The photo shows an old railroad sign and the wide open spaces of a prairie with mountains in the distance. There are no people or houses, only a few shacks in the distance. This image of a remote area is represented in black and white with subtle shades of grey that create a sensuous, evocative atmosphere of silence and loneliness. The railroad sign points to the past, but the photographic technique and the use of modern sans serif typefaces create a trendy early-twenty-first-century look. It resembles the art design of the German record label ECM, which is known for its fetishization of deserted nature as a signifier of pristine, timeless, and universal culture.

The music on the CD is eclectic. One of the unifying elements is the atmosphere, which is generally relaxed, melancholic, and slightly dissonant. The tracks by Sam Prekop and Peggy Honeywell, for instance, have little to do with country music. Prekop sings a song in a slow tempo with a stoned feeling as if he had endless time, a feeling generated by his lazy, whispering voice and the bossa nova–inflected accompaniment. Honeywell sings with an assertive, sexually suggestive, and nonchalant attitude to a rock and roll accompaniment with a dry sound reminiscent of the early Elvis Costello.

A song with stronger connections to country music is "The Littlest Birds" by the female trio the Be Good Tanyas. They begin a cappella in a style reminiscent of the Carter Family, with a rustic phrasing of the words "I feel like an old hobo, all sad and lonesome and blue." This fantasy of a life far from reality echoes Stephen Foster's "Hard Times" and the barn dancing in San Francisco. In a long interview in the Americana/alt.country magazine *No Depression* (founded in 1995), one of the band members, Samantha Parton, said that she became so fascinated with Woody Guthrie's "Hobo's Lullaby" some years ago that she "wanted to become a hobo." She pursued this dream in the early 1990s by working in the summer season together with other young "bohemians" from Vancouver in the Kootenay Mountains at the eastern edge of British Columbia (Himes 2003, 71–73). Evenings were spent sitting around a campfire singing songs by Guthrie, Hank Williams, and Muddy Waters. "It made me want to find the real roots of American music," said the young Canadian (ibid., 73).

The song acquires a more contemporary sound after the opening gesture, but it retains a simple and traditional feel: The rhythmic accompaniment simply consists of brushes marking the beat, the melody consists of a few tuneful phrases, the harmony is a basic three-chord vamp, and the form is a simple verse-chorus. There is something about the soft and sincere emotional idealism in the music and self-representation of the Be Good Tanyas that reminds me of the young Joan Baez and the young Joni Mitchell. The trio's clothing style is casual, but in a conscious way, and their neotraditional aesthetic is influenced by the particular style of Americana hipness among people in their generation (they were between twenty-three and twenty-seven years old when the trio was founded in 1999). This influence is evident in their vocal style. All three women have experience in rock culture, and in the *No Depression* interview Trish Klein, another band member, suggests that her early interest in punk was triggered by its outsider and folk ideologies: "The radio bands played in these big arenas where you couldn't get close" (Himes 2003, 70–71). She therefore got into "folk coffeehouses," in which "punks and hippies hung out together, because we were all the rejects." Since hippies did not allow anger and punks did not allow tenderness, she continues, "the second alternative community was folk" (ibid.).

Parton and Klein thus adopt a pragmatic approach to genre. Deciding what kind of music to play is apparently a matter of finding the community that best satisfies one's needs, and that involves a close relation between music category and group identity. The case of the Be Good Tanyas also shows that it is important to explore the idiosyncratic life stories and experiences of individuals. If we only looked at the systemic dimensions of genre, we would not be able to understand the dynamics of genre categories in social life.

Conclusion

The culture of American roots music that crystallized in the late 1990s is not a genre culture in a strict sense but a revival culture that draws on existing genre traditions and draws them into a national canon. From this perspective, the roots revival is illustrative of historical dynamics in contemporary cultures of categorizing popular music. It shows how history can be simplified and remain largely unknown even to the enthusiastic revivalist. Mainstream popular culture tends to center on the present and on youth, and it remains a challenge and responsibility for educators to explain to students and others that history is not always what we think it is. Confronting disjunctures between past and present strengthens our ability to deal critically with our culture and shape our future. In the study of music categories, historical disjunctures may serve as crossroads at which one can begin to understand the different histories and realities of a music. At these disjunctures it becomes clear that the engagement with roots ultimately leads to their refiguration and thus brings their nature into question.

In the case of American roots music, various musics have been lifted out of the cultural and historical contexts in which they were created and appropriated into new contexts through discursive and technological mediations. The move away from the specialized genre audience to a broader mainstream audience has involved a redistribution of power over the representation of the music. Contemporary American roots music is mainly constituted around mass-mediated representations, and media professionals such as record producers and journalists have targeted voyeuristic consumers rather than experienced insiders. To be sure, the *O Brother* soundtrack was not designed for the traditional bluegrass fan. Moreover, media professionals seized the moment and collectively began using the name American roots music. Fueled by its power as a metaphor in narratives of American cultural identity, this name has been a strong discursive vehicle in the recontextualization and remarketing that sustained the broader processes of mainstreaming and revival.

In several ways, then, this chapter extends the arguments of the introductory chapter about genre, mainstream, and media (p. 24–29 and passim). Music created in a small genre culture can circulate far beyond that culture, but its core collectivities typically continue to inform and respond to the music's wider circulation. The music may evolve in new branches of the genre culture or in mainstream culture in which individual types of music have a less distinct social basis. Above all, this chapter has extended the historical perspective of chapter 1. Whereas the framework in chapter 1 mainly focused on the formation and transformation of genre cultures, this chapter has explored the reimagination of music and music categories more than forty years after their emergence. Much of the "roots" value of blues, gospel, and bluegrass derives from their mythical status as old and stable components of *the* national canon.

I should finally like to suggest that the roots revival can serve as a source of inspiration for reexamining the folk and roots impulses across rock, country, and jazz. The Band, Neil Young, Ry Cooder, J. J. Cale, Bonnie Raitt, Joni Mitchell, and others have remained somewhat peripheral in academic histories of popular music, not only because of taste biases but also because they have not been identified as key figures of a major collective movement or style (nor have they been superstars).[21] It is also worth confronting the jazz canon with the roots-influenced music of artists such as Bill Frisell and Cassandra Wilson. They have been underrepresented in jazz history writing because of the dominance of the modernist narrative of a linear development from folk and pop to art.[22] The contemporary American roots music revival creates a new context for understanding some of these roots impulses. Like other revivals, it opens up new opportunities for comparative thinking about past events, and it helps us see connections between them.

Reactions to Rock

Figure 2 Elvis Presley, 1956. Courtesy of the Library of Congress, Prints and Photographs Division, *New York World-Telegram* and the *Sun* Newspaper Photograph Collection, LC-USZ62-115589.

D uring a stay in Nashville in November 2004 I interviewed witnesses on the subject of how the advent of rock and roll affected country music. They did not say much about what had happened locally. In the experience of these fans, musicians, and writers, the rock and roll revolution was primarily located in the national mass media and was associated with stars, among whom Elvis Presley was by far the most influential figure. Again and again, my informants turned to Elvis, from the fan who had been too young to understand the sexual meaning of "Hound Dog" to the radio deejay who remembered that it sounded strange when he first put on "That's All Right, Mama." Listeners called in asking, "Who is that? Would you play that again?" (John Rumble, conversation with author, Nashville, 8 November 2004; Jim Sloan, conversation with author, Tucson, 4 November 2004). For a musician who had worked with virtually everyone in Nashville since the mid 1940s, the introduction I gave him to my project simply translated into a short question: "So basically you want to talk about what happened to country music when Elvis came along?" (Harold Bradley, conversation with author, Nashville, 12 November 2004).

The event that stood out in everyone's memory was Elvis's first appearance on *The Ed Sullivan Show* on 9 September 1956. His performance of "Hound Dog" was revered for its distinctive rock and roll energy and sex appeal. It was faster than Big Mama Thornton's recording of 1953 and less tied to traditional blues. The producers of the show wanted to improve their ratings, so they hired Elvis and paid him $50,000. However, they censored his body: the producers requested that he should not be filmed below his waist. This is significant because Elvis's performance was a culminating point in the rock and roll boom. A native Tennessean and expert on country music said to me:

> There were parents, especially in the South, who thought, "What is this? Kids are jumping around to all this black music?!" The controversy surrounding rock and roll was intense because massive numbers of white youth started dancing and listening, and some parents were worried: "Oh gosh, not only are you engaging in all of this wild dancing..."—with all the young girls screaming and fainting, you know, with Elvis. It was very sexual. It was black.[1]

The Ed Sullivan Show was watched in the domestic sphere by a broad audience, by families, by people of all ages. A variety show, it presented various forms of popular entertainment, and the radio business tried to regain market shares by developing a genre-specific alternative. The emerging concept of format radio meant that radio shows and entire radio stations dedicated themselves exclusively to one kind of music, and that reinforced genre divisions and led to more segmented consumer cultures. From early on, rock and roll was associated more with some people than with others, with youths and dances rather than with the family and Ed Sullivan, and there were insiders who were deeply familiar with the music. However, even insiders felt unsure about what rock and roll was and where it was going. In *Feel like Going Home*, Peter Guralnick recalled:

> Like nearly everyone I knew I was unsure how to react to rock 'n' roll. I was twelve when Elvis scored his first success, and he wasn't much older. The excitement, the exhilaration, the *novelty* of that moment is something it would be impossible to recapture.... We measured ourselves against the judgment of our elders and believed what they told us even when it rang false to our own experience. There were at that time certain immutable standards, and if they said that rock 'n' roll was a passing fad, like swing and Frank Sinatra, it seemed unimaginable that it was not. That's why our first reaction was necessarily so ambiguous. There was, at least among my acquaintances, not the faintest suspicion of any Woodstock nation. (Guralnick 1971/1999, 15)

Although the book is a historical project, it is striking that Guralnick emphasizes the pastness of his experience of early rock and roll. The book was first published in 1971, so the time distance was only about fifteen years. Guralnick's statement points to the big musical and social changes in rock during this period. Definitions of rock had not been firmly established, and rock did not evolve into the kind of larger and more differentiated cultural formation we call genre until the late 1960s and early 1970s, when the social basis became more specialized and self-sufficient, with its own festivals and magazines. Around the same time, writers began to build a canon that started with Elvis.[2] Said Nik Cohn: "Elvis is where pop begins and ends" (1969, 12).

Rockin' Other Genres

Rock and roll affected musical cultures in the West and beyond. Other musical discourses have tended to focus on their own relationship with rock because it was so powerful and because genre discourse by nature renders other kinds of music exterior. This sort of thinking tends to isolate each genre's encounter with rock and thus create reductive binaries. In fact, though, a number of genres that are usually considered separately registered some of the same reactions to rock.

If genre is this broad category that comprises different styles and circulates in diverse ethnoscapes, we should not expect a genre culture to react uniformly to a new musical formation just because is it perceived to be external. Internal struggles over rock have proliferated in many genres, and yet little has been done to theorize connections. My tenet is that different genres have reacted differently to rock but that some of the mechanisms and themes have been the same.

It is common knowledge that cultural boundaries evolve around differences in style, identity, capital, and other interconnected symbolic elements, but boundaries are sometimes defined in a larger process of change characterized by tensions between different cultures or cultural "systems." I have argued that genres are not systems but that they have system functions (p. 23). The constitutive aspect in this context is that collectivities within a genre culture have a sense of being a cultural sphere that is distinct from others. Insider-outsider distinctions do exist, even though in many cases they are ambiguous and fluid. Cultural boundaries are increasingly complicated by globalization and the forms of mediation enabled by modern technologies.

As sources of inspiration for understanding some basic mechanisms, I should like to evoke the concepts of modernization and westernization to think about how one musical culture can change under the influence of another. In the acculturation theory of mid-twentieth-century anthropology, modernization and westernization referred to large-scale processes of change as a result of contact between major world cultures.[3] Modernization was described as a situation in between the extremes of survival without change and complete westernization in a traditional non-Western society (Nettl 1983, 347). In a related and more common sense, modernization refers to the process of modernity and its transformations of traditional life in rural areas or developing countries. Acculturation theory fell out of fashion in the 1970s, and theories of cross-cultural formations have gone in other directions and established key concepts such as hybridization and globalization (Holt 2006, 15–17). But the older theories are worth studying at least for historical reasons. Their models are plagued by mechanic structuralism and bounded notions of cultures and nation-states, but their focus on long-term change is valuable, and some of the basic mechanisms still exist. Consequently, I am only using certain components of the older models as a source of inspiration and not without reframing them.

A few analogies about tradition can be drawn between mechanisms of modernization and genre-specific reactions to rock. One is the typical split between younger people, who are attracted to new and outside influences, and older people, who are witnesses to the loss of tradition. Such situations have produced images of the young as mobile, pleasure-seeking consumers or as rebels, and of older people as protective or conservative authorities. From Hollywood films such as *The Jazz Singer* (1927) to Bollywood films such as *Bombay* (1995), contemporary popular music has sustained the narrative of youths breaking away from their parents' traditions. In the former, jazz is central to the protagonist's move away from his Jewish immigrant background to a modern American identity. In the latter, a Michael Jackson–style performance accompanies the wedding of a young Muslim and Hindu that have fled to Bombay from the boundaries of traditional life in their rural hometown.

Another analogy is the power-regulated direction of cultural flows. Powerful national and urban centers are like magnetic fields in which financial and cultural resources concentrate, and the flow of influence and cultural products goes more from center to periphery than vice versa. Similarly, genre cultures with a smaller market than rock have felt that rock dominated the flow of influence and drained their resources. Indeed, insiders in country music, blues, jazz, and the folk revival have all expressed anxieties about rock's hegemonic status.

Rock and Roll and Popular Music Landscapes in the 1950s

Chapters 3–4 examine the problematic outlined above through a comparative study of reactions to rock and roll in country music and jazz in the mid 1950s. For reasons that will be obvious later, the case study of jazz will also look at reactions to the boom in the mid 1960s when the dominant term for the emerging genre became rock music. When rock and roll emerged, country and jazz had just become established as genres with a canon, and that constitutes some common historical and structural ground for comparisons between two genres associated with different places and social groups.

In both case studies, the focal point will be the first style that emerged in response to rock music (including 1950s rock and roll) and was motivated by crossover interests. I have chosen this strategy because reactions to rock were strongest and most visible at the time when it was perceived to cause a new wave of influence from outside and change the general situation in the genre. This strategy also allows us to deal directly with musical and not only social and discursive reactions.

The mid 1950s was a time of decline for the culture of live swing music and dancing. Many of those who had been involved in it during the 1930s and 1940s were now making television the primary medium of family entertainment. A teenage market emerged with films like *Rock Around the Clock* (1956) and the Top 40 radio format. Top 40 operated with playlists that were basically dictated by the *Billboard* charts, and they included only music that was expected to have a broad appeal to the newly record-buying teenagers. This was particularly hard on genres with a small market because they did not attract advertisers. Commercial radio was and is an advertising business in that stations basically sell consumers to advertisers, so the music is a way of reaching consumers of other products (Jim Sloan, conversation with author, Tucson, Arizona, 4 November 2004).[4]

To make a long story short, the changes in media culture and markets and the advent of new social and musical styles were important components of a new era in popular music dominated by rock.[5] For decades, Tin Pan Alley had dominated the market, the industry, and the main media channels such as film and network radio. Genre cultures had been forced to deal with the Tin Pan Alley mainstream and partly existed on its premises because it defined some of the basic rules of the industry. Rock and roll quickly gained a large audience and hit the media spheres of mainstream popular music, and it complicated the infrastructure of the field of popular music. The popularity and novelty of rock and roll made it a strong point of reference for other musics. Genre cultures have always defined themselves in relation to dominant genres and genres in their cultural proximity, and the corporate industry continuously adjusts to cultural changes. Today, this industry has little interest in folk music, blues, and jazz, for instance, and instead concentrates on producing stars in rock, pop, hip-hop, R & B, and country.[6] Major labels, popular magazines, and commercial radio do not have an idealistic commitment to supporting unprofitable genres (cf. Negus 1999, 49–50). Comparing a popular genre such as country music with one that largely resides outside the corporate industry, as jazz already did in the 1950s, will illustrate some implications of these conditions.

Before we close in on country music and jazz, let us recognize a few general aspects of the reactions to rock and roll in Tin Pan Alley, R & B, and the folk revival:

Tin Pan Alley had a large audience of white urban and suburban middle-class adults, and they generally resented rock and roll. Many of the people involved in the production shared the public opinion that rock was vulgar and destructive (Garofalo 1997/2002, chapter 5). Smoother versions of rock and roll such as so-called schlock rock and the Brill Building output resulted from the corporate industry's attempt to move into the teenage market and can be seen as compromises. Tin Pan Alley continued to dominate Hollywood film music for another decade. *The Graduate* (1967), with music by Simon and Garfunkel, was a turning point in this history (Gabbard 1996, 136).

African American artists did not benefit from the rock and roll boom, and some felt alienated by it (Keil 1966/1991, 44). The big market, the white market, was still relatively closed to blacks, and urbanization provided part of the background for a shift in tastes toward young soul singers. Motown and Stax popularized blues and gospel traditions and developed standardized production methods. In these respects, soul music paralleled the Nashville Sound in country music, but racial inequality should be taken into account: Soul artists still struggled with segregation, and major labels were initially more eager to produce country-pop (Gillett 1983, chapter 10). Racial boundaries generally add a significant layer of complexity to genre relations and pose challenges to comparative thinking about music categories. Segregated histories have identified African Americans with the 1950s' R & B and the 1960s' electric blues, not with rock music, which became a white-dominated culture. Bob Dylan and Eric Clapton, for instance, who were deeply influenced by black artists, became rock icons in a way that no black artist could have, with the possible exception of Jimi Hendrix. The reductionism persists, despite the criticisms voiced by Dave Marsh and others.

The culture of folk music represented by Leadbelly, Woody Guthrie, the Seegers, and others was not close to rock and roll to begin with. The first generation of rock and rollers did not have a background in the folk revival, which was based in the urban middle class and was not particularly oriented toward teenagers. The revival had connections with the political Left, and like the nineteenth-century folk movement in Germany, it articulated discontents with modernity. Goldsmith sums up: "Folk music enabled college students to ground themselves in a value-rich past while resisting the transitory, expendable mass culture they had inherited from their parents" (1998, 295). Rock and roll articulated a different kind of youth identity and was viewed by youngsters such as Guralnick as an alternative to folk music. It was harder to keep pop influences out, and the distinction between the authentic and the popular was a major issue, especially after the Kingston Trio took folk music to the *Billboard* pop charts with "Tom Dooley" in 1958. In effect, the boundaries of folk music started to become quite complicated as its social network expanded and the industry began exploring folk music as a marketing label. The opposition to electric instruments and the rock rhythm section dominated well into the 1960s, when it was amplified by anxieties about rock's commercial expansion. When folk rock emerged, folk music was falling off the popular music charts, and rock became the prime music genre of middle-class youths and the counterculture movement (ibid., 298 and 327).

The case studies in chapters 3–4 explore the mechanisms underlying these reactions in greater detail. To add a bit more conceptual substance, I present the following model for understanding reactions to rock and its role in genre transformations. These *genre transformations in processes of modernization* are open to a wide range of theorizations. My model is primarily developed in relation to country music and jazz, and it specifically focuses on mechanisms that regulate genre boundaries in processes of change. It would be problematic to aim for an exhaustive theoretical scheme because the situation was unique in each genre. One indication of this is that the reactions culminated at different points in time and cannot be adequately explained by a sequential model. I work from the assumption that at every major stage the reactions and transformations involved three different but interconnected processes or modes of activity:

1. *Disruption*
Rock and roll had great youth appeal and caused greater competition in the field of popular music. The resources of existing genre cultures were drained, and the balance between ages, places, and styles within each genre network changed. Boundaries were simultaneously intensified and destabilized. The reactions were conditioned by general social changes, by the social status of the individual genre and its cultural distance to the new competitor.

2. *Outreach*
The disruption provoked attempts at integrating outside influences from rock and roll or mainstream pop. Some of these attempts coalesced into a hyphenated style, a genre fusion. This fusion primarily appealed to

younger generations but not to specialists with a solid grounding in the tradition. Commercial interests among producers were strong because a musical blend with popular styles has the potential to cross over and thus reach a large market.

3. *Resistance*

Resistance appeared as skepticism and protectionism in the name of tradition and purity. One form of protectionism was revivalism. Resistance has resulted in more or less voluntary exile and marginalization whereby people maintain their views and identities in marginal spaces.

This outline could easily be expanded, but I have kept it brief in order to focus on the core ideas in a general perspective. More elaborate versions can productively be developed from more specific perspectives. The reader is welcome to expand and adjust the model to other contexts and case studies. The wish for flexibility also explains why the model is not framed in a particular theoretical paradigm but rather in general and open-ended terms.

Figure 3 Patsy Cline, mid-1950s. Courtesy of the Country Music Hall of Fame and Museum.

Figure 4 Patsy Cline, ca. 1962. Courtesy of the Country Music Hall of Fame and Museum.

CHAPTER THREE

Country Music and the Nashville Sound

To a high degree, country music has been defined publicly by media products that are aimed at a mass market and tell popular stories about popular things. Academics have been very slow to engage critically with the music and recognize its social and cultural significance. Country music is one of the most popular genres of music in America. It is a vital component in the lives of millions of working-class people and functions as *the* vernacular musical tradition in some rural areas where the variety of musics has been relatively small. But it has always had an urban existence, too, and more research could be done on the diversity of country music cultures across the country.

In a chapter-length case study of broad changes in a genre, however, it is useful to focus on one of the centers. By the 1950s, Nashville had become the biggest center for country music. The Grand Ole Opry's radio show was a magnet for talent, and an industry network of publishers and record labels was developing there (cf. Malone 1968/2002a, chapters 6–7). Interestingly, though, Nashville was also a central site of encounters between country and rock and roll. The Nashville country scene has been shaped by insiders as well as by outsiders, by executives in New York policing the business, and by its relationships with cities that have a different country scene, such as Bakersfield, California, in the 1960s or cities identified with other musics such as New Orleans and Memphis. The wider popular music scene in Nashville was and is characterized by a flux of artists coming to town to record with local session musicians and then going out on tour. Its emerging role as a recording center for various kinds of music created a complex relationship between media and local practice: A small team of session musicians recorded country, pop, and some rock and roll with a number of star vocalists who had little or no involvement with each other, and the rock and roll recordings, for instance, never became identified with Nashville. The rockabilly stars from Memphis came over to record because Nashville was the capital of the music business in the South, but they remained identified with Memphis.

The musical diversity on the recording scene was important to the country field, as the story of RCA Studio B illustrates. It was Elvis's success that instigated the head of RCA's country division to have RCA build the studio in 1957 (Rumble 1998, 431). (Some insiders of the business told me that the reason so much money went there was that the studio was essentially paid for by Elvis's first number 1 hit, "Heartbreak Hotel," which had been published and recorded in Nashville the previous year.) The studio then became a legend in country music and the home of the Nashville Sound. Elvis frequently returned from Memphis to record rock and pop music in the studio. It should be added that the Everly Brothers were also important to the growth of the local rock and roll field because they lived in Nashville and worked with the local publishing and recording industry.

Nashville and Rock and Roll

Rockabilly stars (born 1932–35, except where noted otherwise)
Elvis Presley, Jerry Lee Lewis, Johnny Cash, and Carl Perkins recorded for Sam Phillips's (b. 1923) Sun Records in Memphis and recorded in Nashville on and off from around 1956.
Wanda Jackson (b. 1937) recorded in Nashville from 1960.

Pop-oriented rock and roll in Nashville
The Everly Brothers and Brenda Lee were based in Nashville and were not really rockabilly artists.

Influential rock and roll recordings made in Nashville
"Be-Bop-a-Lula" (Gene Vincent 1956), "Heartbreak Hotel" (Elvis Presley 1956), "Bye Bye Love" (Everly Brothers 1957), "Sweet Nothing" (Brenda Lee 1959).

(Based on information in Kingsbury 1998)

The historically tense relationship between country music and national mainstream popular culture constitutes a broader background for understanding how country reacted to rock and roll. When the so-called hillbilly market in the South was developed by major record labels in the early 1920s, most executives disliked the music (Peterson 1997, chapters 1–2). Their corporate culture was built around Tin Pan Alley and white popular jazz, which at the time formed the center of mainstream tastes in urban and national mass-mediated spaces. National media defined country music as distinct from popular music (ibid., esp. chapters 1–3). Country music was, in a word, "othered" from the beginning by influential social groups and institutions in the metropolitan areas on the two coasts. Artists had very little control over the production and distribution of their music, and, like black songwriters, country music songwriters were excluded from ASCAP membership into the 1940s. They were not represented by an organization until BMI broke the monopoly in 1939 (ibid., 13; Jensen 1998, 44).

These inequities were reflective of the status of southern, rural, working-class people in the national cultural hierarchy. Country music has always suffered from stereotyping, and this has created distorted views of the relation between country music and other musics.[1] Moreover, country artists and blues artists have been easy victims because they value simplicity and relatively straightforward genre schemes. To insiders, the music usually has different and richer meanings than many outsiders perceive.

The historical embeddedness of traditional, rural working-class values in hard-core country music is itself an important background for understanding how country music people responded to cultural change in the 1950s and what their conditions were. Old-time and hillbilly images had embodied such values during the 1920s and 1930s. Family bands and brother duos, for instance, were associated with home-centered values and the domestic sphere of the log cabin or similar mythical locales with a premodern aura. Even the honky-tonk style of the late 1940s, which brought the music into the urban tavern, represented what Malone calls "displaced ruralities" (1982, 121), typified by the troubled life of the newly urbanized male subject. Western swing in the 1930s integrated elements of mainstream pop, but it remained distinct and was associated with the Southwest. Eddy Arnold was a pioneer of pop-oriented country in the late 1940s, but it was not yet a collective trend.

The corporate music industry became more interested in country music during the 1940s. The new interest was motivated by the declining popularity of jazz and the recent successes of country songs performed by pop artists. *Billboard* launched its country music charts in 1944 and began to discuss and promote the music. Articles about the music's history outlined a canon, and debates about the name contributed to the crucial change from "country & western" and "hillbilly" to "country music" (Peterson 1997, chapters 12–13; Pugh 1997). *Billboard* did not have as much competition in country music as in jazz which was the subject of more magazines and books. As a trade magazine *Billboard* reached radio deejays, booking agencies, and writers for national newspapers.

The years around 1950 were a formative period in which the development of country music as a genre and as a major sector of the corporate industry went hand in hand. Major labels expanded their roster of artists and began operating in Nashville; most of them had studios and permanent offices in the city by the early 1960s. The growing industry engagement was not questioned before the rock and roll boom. Honky-tonk music thrived, and record label executives were not trying to change the direction of the genre.

Rockabilly and Cultural Blending

The optimism following the growth of country music was soon challenged by the emergence of a new outside musical formation called rock and roll. It changed the agenda in country music—but not because audiences felt country music had gone in the wrong direction or because established artists became more interested in other kinds of music.

Rock and roll was not wholly external to country music. In fact, a major reason country music was the first genre (in addition to Tin Pan Alley) that was greatly affected by rock and roll is that the two were so close and actually overlapped. The rockabilly stars on Sun Records were key figures in the rock and roll wave, but they also had one foot in country music and in black R & B, which was easily available to whites over the airwaves. Their seminal recordings were made in Memphis between 1954 and 1956 (see box, p. 64), and it is symptomatic of the market dynamics that Sun's production of R & B and country music dropped as rock and roll exploded in popularity.

R & B, country, and rock and roll were not as distinct as one might expect. Above all, the boundaries of commercially distributed music were defined largely through marketing practices and charts in trade magazines. In the pre–rock and roll era such crude divisions were made that a record store selling "popular music" would generally not have "race" or "hillbilly" records (Ackerman 1958, 36). Moreover, these relatively new categories were pushed into an old system of racial segregation that violated a more complex reality. In fact, rock and roll was a product of particular forms of cultural blending across musical cultures. Artists such as Chuck Berry and Ray Charles were deeply influenced by country music, and many country artists were influenced by African American styles before rock and roll came along. Moon Mullican, recording for King Records in Cincinnati, did several covers of R & B recordings. Some of them were so close that they were in the same key and tempo and based on the same boogie rhythm and arrangement. This kind of border crossing is illustrated by Mullican's 1946 retitled cover of the Louis Jordan hit "Is You Is or Is You Ain't My Baby?" (Decca, 1943), which made it into a few movies and soon was recorded by popular jazz singers such as Bing Crosby, Louis Armstrong, and the Andrews Sisters.[2] New interest in music across the boundaries of segregated record catalogs was also generated by Harry Smith's *Anthology of American Folk Music* (1952). Smith anticipated today's culture of American roots music by anthologizing commercial recordings of the 1920s and 1930s as early historical documents in a canon of vernacular American music (see pp. 38–41 and 157).

It is impossible to make absolute distinctions between country and rockabilly, but it does make sense to track how individuals were positioned. Elvis and Jerry Lee Lewis performed on the *Louisiana Hayride*, a big country radio show, in 1954 before they became really famous, and live recordings from the *Hayride* suggest that Elvis performed in a more country-oriented style than he did on his recordings in Memphis. He was also nicknamed "the Hillbilly Cat" on his first tours, and as late as February 1955 he appeared in a concert in Memphis together with a handful of country stars.[3] Virtually all of the rockabillies came from southern working-class families who loved country music, and they started out in the milder tributaries of mainstream country music (Malone 2002b, 135). It was Elvis, of course, who first exploded the established boundaries of country music, and he was never a core country act. Many immediately recognized that his music was different and that it crossed over to the pop market. When he shared the bill with country artists in 1954 and 1955, they complained that he stole the show.[4]

It was hard for Sam Phillips to get Elvis on the Grand Ole Opry because it did not welcome electric instruments and drums, and we shall see that rockabilly had limited circulation in the country network.[5] Also, few rockabillies committed themselves exclusively to country music. Elvis was not inducted into the Country Music Hall of Fame until 1998 and remains most closely identified with rock and roll. No one calls him the king of country music.

Changes and Reactions on the Nashville Country Scene

There is no comprehensive empirical study of reactions to rock and roll in country music. While my research on this, in the field and in archives, has been qualitative and limited in scope, it has nonetheless generated evidence for what is hopefully a more complete understanding of this history. First of all, the general anxieties described above (p. 53–54) were also common in Nashville. The cultural establishment invested in the elitist notion of Nashville as the "Athens of the South" and had no interest in rock or country. In the country field, many professionals felt that rock and roll was an immediate threat to their business and their values:

Ernest Tubb's manager in 1955 and 1956, Gabe Tucker, said, "Rock and roll was eatin' our damn lunch. They damn near put us out of business." These were the days, remembers Wesley Rose of Hickory Records and Acuff-Rose Publishing, that his staff had so little business to transact they whiled away much of the good weather months playing softball or golf. Ernest Tubb, Stonewall Jackson says, was hurt by the decline of traditional country music's appeal and his own pulling power on the road. "I've seen it at the Ryman where you'd only have a few rows of people up front." (Pugh 1996, 217)

Among my informants in contemporary Nashville, memories of the time were still imbued with a sense of disruption, crisis, theft, and in some cases even violence. An experienced journalist had been told by legendary Bill Anderson that "after rock and roll hit, you could have shot a cannon off in the Ryman and not hit a person!" (Anderson, quoted by Robert Oermann, conversation with author, Nashville, 12 November 2004). This statement has special meaning considering that the Ryman Auditorium had the status of the "mother church" of country music. Another informant, the session musician Harold Bradley, explained to me that his community of top professional producers "felt they had to do something 'cause we were getting killed." Joli Jensen has questioned this view, suggesting that the crisis narrative was fictitious and used as an excuse for pushing the genre toward pop and, in effect, maximizing profits (1998, 47, 61, and chapters 5–6). Some producers surely adopted the survival motif to naturalize and defend their strategy, but there was a crisis. This was not some kind of mass hypnosis. The audience shrank, artists began doing package shows to save touring expenses and attract a greater audience, and country dropped off the radio. Top 40 format radio was taking over the radio market and put country into tough competition with other genres because very few country records made it to the lists of the forty most popular records (Jim Sloan, conversation with author, Tucson, Arizona, 4 November 2004). To get airplay, the pivotal link in the commercial circuit, country music now had to cross over to the pop market, and that rarely happened in the mid 1950s.

By all accounts, the country market shrank around 1954, but it had already recovered by around 1958, and it skyrocketed in the early 1960s (Jensen 1998; Malone 1968/2002a, chap. 8; Peterson 1997, 224; Rosenberg 1985, 132–134). To understand the situation in more depth, we need to recognize that the Nashville country scene was affected unequally by rock and roll. Paul Kingsbury made a point about this when I interviewed him in November 2004:

It didn't really matter to RCA that there were rockabillies now because they had the number one. They had Elvis. They were making as much money. They would put out whatever kind of record. The same for Decca, Capitol, Columbia. . . . I think many of the publishing companies were just as happy publishing rockabilly songs and rock and roll songs as country songs. . . . So my point is that Nashville was affected unequally. Some businesses, record companies, most publishers, many of the session musicians, drummers, bass players, and guitar players did fine. Guys like Grady Martin, Buddy Harmon, Boots Randolph, Chet Atkins—those guys continued to get a lot of work. On the other hand, you hear that there was a period when fiddle players and steel guitar players were getting less work in the recording sessions and that continued into the Nashville Sound era. And then there were performers like Roy Acuff, Eddy Arnold, Lefty Frizell—their records sold less for a while and they were able to tour less, and touring was the bulk of their income. (Kingsbury, conversation with author, Nashville, 9 November 2004)

In a word, the more traditional country music performers were losing ground, while those who were adjusting to pop were gaining ground. It is therefore not surprising that the strongest resistance to rock and roll came from people who were established in country music before rock and roll came along. More than a few "old-timers" have said that they hated rock and roll and what it did to country.[6] In June 1958, the editor of *Billboard*, Paul Ackerman, wrote an article titled "What Has Happened to Popular Music?" about the broad changes following the rock and roll boom. He described the situation in country music:

Presley's success was such that he quickly displaced the leading country singers on the best-selling record charts. Well-entrenched artists, talent managers, and other members of the trade resented him fiercely. . . . More and more, the so-called traditional country singer has become a victim of the rockabilly—the archetype of which is Presley. For several years, country disc jockeys and performers fought the rockabilly trend; but it finally overpowered them. Today, most of the better-known country stars . . . make recordings with "pop-styled" arrangements. (Ackerman 1958, 37 and 108)[7]

The resistance to rock and roll is reflected in the recorded output from Nashville. It was largely kept out of the country music production at major labels up to about 1958 when the first wave of rock began to fade. Buddy

Holly's single session in 1956 was not very successful, and Elvis only did two sessions there before he went into the army in 1958. Incidentally, Elvis worked a lot as an actor and recording artist in Los Angeles during those years. Executives were interested in copying the success of Elvis and had artists do covers of rock and roll hits, but the production network as a whole did not integrate rock and roll to any significant extent. Moreover, a lot of the rock that was produced in Nashville was relatively pop oriented, including the work of the Everly Brothers, Brenda Lee, Roy Orbison, and Elvis when he came back from the army. Harold Bradley agreed with me on this:

> Yeah, yeah, I mean my brother [Owen] never did wanna mix rock and roll and country. When I went over to work with Elvis or Roy Orbison or Jerry Lee Lewis ... that was a different thing, you know. We just rocked the best we could 'cause rock and roll was new, and we were all just trying to learn it. But that was separate. When you came in to play for my brother or Chet or Don Law, Ken Nelson, then they basically kept it kind of country, with the exception of Nelson, who brought Gene Vincent in and did "Be-Bop-a-Lula" in our studio. We never tried to mix them. (Bradley, conversation with author, Nashville, 12 November 2004)

What these executives tried to do and did do with country was make it appeal to a broader audience by mixing it with pop and downplaying rustic and traditional elements. Malone observes that styles such as honky-tonk and bluegrass and core genre instruments (steel guitar, fiddle, and banjo) disappeared from recordings and jukeboxes for a period in the mid 1950s, but rather than vanishing they went underground, and honky-tonk thrived in Texas and southern California (Malone 1982, 124). There was no mystique about the changing politics. Columbia's vice president, Hal Cook, who was based in New York City, talked openly in the *Country Music Reporter* in 1956 about efforts to improve sales and "modernize":

> We determined that in 1956 we were going to find out what country business there is, where it is, and what we should do about it.... When Goddard Lieberson took over as president of Columbia, it was his opinion ... that we could make better records with our own country artists by steering away from some past conceptions—use a little modernization— primarily because people who liked country music were being exposed to the same entertainment as other people." With this thought in mind, Hal explained, Don Law, Country and western A & R [Artist & Repertoire] man for Columbia, studied the field and learned that preferences

had swung over—listeners had changed their views—toward a new sound
and style. ("Columbia Modernizes CW" 1956)

Country Music in Nashville

Singers of hard-core country styles, including honky-tonk
George Jones (b. 1931), Webb Pierce (b. 1921), Ernest Tubb (b. 1914), Porter
Wagoner (b. 1927), Kitty Wells (b. 1919), Hank Williams (1923–1953).

Nashville Sound producers and A & R men at major labels
Chet Atkins (b. 1924) at RCA, Owen Bradley (b. 1915) at Decca, Don Law (b.
1902) at Columbia.

Nashville Sound star vocalists
Patsy Cline (b. 1932), Don Gibson (b. 1928), Ferlin Husky (b. 1927), Jim Reeves
(b. 1923), Marty Robbins (b. 1925), Faron Young (b. 1932).

**A-team session artists (born 1926–33, with the exception of some chorus
singers)**
The Anita Kerr Singers, Harold Bradley, Floyd Cramer, Ray Edenton, Hank
Garland, Buddy Harman, the Jordanaires, Grady Martin, Bob Moore, Boots
Randolph.

The development of the Nashville music industry
1946–1956 The Castle Studio, Nashville's first professional recording service.
1955 Music Row is "founded" with the opening of the Bradley Studio.
1956 Columbia makes efforts to "modernize" country music.
1957 Ferlin Husky's "Gone" (Capitol, 1956), the first Nashville Sound hit.
1957 RCA is the first major label to open offices on Music Row.
1957 RCA Studio B opens.
1958 The Country Music Association (CMA) is founded.
1961 The Country Music Hall of Fame is founded.
1962 Columbia buys the Bradley Studio
1963 All major labels have offices in Nashville. A trade magazine reports that
half of all American recordings are made in Nashville

(Based on information contained elsewhere in this chapter and in Kingsbury 1998)

If this sounds calculated and cynical to you, the rhetoric of the Country
Music Association and its magazine, *CMA Close Up*, would not be any
easier to digest. The formation of this trade association in 1958 was the
biggest organizational effort that the music business made to recover from
the crisis. CMA's purpose was to promote country music to broadcasters
and advertisers. It commissioned marketing research, developed sales kits,

and even produced a promotional short aimed at radio station managers. As the Nashville business grew over the course of the decade, emphasis shifted from the down-home ambience of the barn dance show at the Opry to the recording and publishing area known as Music Row.

The Nashville Sound(s) and Beyond

The big musical change occurred in the recording studio. The industry's network and production were not as organized in the mid 1950s as they were later. Harold Bradley remembered: "Well, the community wasn't that big. We were just playing kind of scattered sessions. There wouldn't have been much continuity to it. So we didn't have a trend of thought. We were just trying to stay alive and play sessions and play whatever came along" (Bradley, conversation with author, Nashville, 12 December 2004). It did become more organized, with a small team of regular session musicians (the A-team), regular session hours, and a particular division of labor between star vocalists, session artists, and producers. This meant that vocalists as diverse as Ernest Tubb, Patsy Cline, and Elvis worked with the same session musicians and producers. Some standardization inevitably resulted from this continuity in personnel and musical practice.

All country artists were not produced in exactly the same way, though. It is possible to distinguish between a retooling of hard-core country in which some traditional instruments were eliminated and the sound was smoothed with strings, for instance, and a later, more thoroughly pop-influenced style that was labeled country-pop. This hyphenated word appeared as early as February 1957 in an ad for Ferlin Husky's "Gone," and it was more or less replaced in the early 1960s with the term Nashville Sound, which later, in the mid 1970s, was defined as a style and time period (ca. 1957–72) (Ivey 1998, 371).[8] Some of the people involved in making this music have preferred to pluralize the term into Nashville Sounds because they produced more than one kind of country music, and each artist was different. That does not mean that the singular form of the term cannot be meaningfully applied to the country-pop that came out of Nashville. Many musicians and fans defined themselves in relation to the Nashville Sound because it was popular and because it pushed the boundaries of the genre.

The Nashville Sound style is known not only for the absence of certain traditional instruments, but also for its smooth character, created by strings; a subdued rhythmic feeling; influences from pop jazz in harmony and arrangement; and finally the overall impression of professional craft and high-quality studio sound. Although the musicians were famous for making music on the spot without a score, their playing is highly disciplined. They create a balanced texture and a discreet background. Fills are played only in the spaces between phrases so that they do not draw attention from the singing when the music is heard on the radio. In comparison with rockabilly, the tempos are generally slower, the emotional style softer, and there is less influence from African American musics. The producers did not say that they wanted to keep country music "white," but they recorded white artists almost exclusively and never expressed a strong interest in black popular music, although some of them appreciated jazz. The producers brought country music closer to white pop, and because they were working for major labels with rigid ideas about segregated markets, it is unlikely that there could have been substantial space for black music. Charlie Pride had a fairly straight-ahead country style, and the country music establishment in Nashville never produced anything as steeped in African American culture as the country music stylings of Ray Charles. Charles did a cover version of Hank Snow's "Movin' On" (Atlantic, 1959), the album *Modern Sounds in Country and Western Music* (ABC-Paramount, 1962), and returned to country many times later. His country recordings contrast with the Nashville Sound, with his improvisatory, gospel-derived vocal style, swing and shuffle rhythms, hard-driving big bands and electric pianos, and advanced jazz harmony.

The Nashville Sound was a move toward (white) mainstream pop. Singers lost some of their southern accent and moved away from the hard-core, nasal styles of singing and closer to smooth Tin Pan Alley–derived styles. The music's smooth and relaxed character is also conditioned by the generally slow and moderate tempos. A common complaint among people with a pop ear was that hard-core country singing and fiddle playing was "whiny" and "sour." In contrast, the Nashville Sound was described as "smooth" and "lush."[9] Moreover, artists adjusted or dropped their cowboy image in favor of standard middle-class fashion. For Patsy Cline, for instance, who had identified with honky-tonk music, these conditions were not ideal but were gradually accepted (Jensen 1998, chapter 5).[10]

At twenty-five to thirty-five years of age, the star vocalists of the Nashville Sound were older than the rockabillies, who were between nineteen and twenty-three when they hit the scene, and five years can make a big difference at this stage in life. The new Nashville stars also appealed to a broader age demographic than did rock and roll artists. Patsy Cline, Faron Young, and others expressed the feelings of people younger than middle-aged, but older people could still identify with them. The looks and voices of the stars were important age indicators, and age was less specific in the song lyrics, just as the lyrics were less specific about time and place and less autobiographical than in hard-core country.

I have suggested that one of the main reasons mainstream country music moved toward pop and not rock was that mainstream country had become integrated in the corporate world of middle-aged executives who grew up with white popular music in the 1930s and 1940s. It should be noted that the legacy of this continues to shape mainstream country. Robert Oermann comments:

> I don't know why that is, but it seems that every time an artist has come along who's a little over on the rock side of things, they have a really much more difficult time as when someone comes in who's basically a pop artist like Olivia Newton John, you know, or John Denver. That's okay. But God help you if you wanna rock a little bit! It's an unwritten law and it's definitely there. Waylon [Jennings] is a great example. (Oermann, conversation with author, 12 November 2004)

The British Invasion, jump-started by the Beatles' appearance on *The Ed Sullivan Show* in February 1964, was another blow to country. Rock influences nonetheless became more acceptable in the mid 1960s, in part because rock was becoming more popular and more accepted in society. Still, it was California and not Nashville that became the home of country rock. The omnipresence of distorted guitars in contemporary Nashville productions indicates that boundaries and individual genre rules have changed, while some of the broader discursive structures in the relationship with rock persist.

Did Country Lose Its Identity?

Reactions to the Nashville Sound outside the small sphere of professional production and commerce remain largely undocumented.[11] Important sites of consumption were private homes and bars with jukeboxes because the music was closely tied to recordings. Star vocalists would usually tour with a different band and without the same high-quality studio sound. In bars around Nashville on a Saturday night, one would likely have heard some country-pop songs performed by local bands because audiences expected to hear some of the hits of the day. To many listeners, it did not make a big difference if the star vocalist was not backed by A-team musicians, and local bands necessarily reduced the complexity of the music to make it workable. To A-team musicians, Harold Bradley told me, there was a huge difference because they were keenly aware of the subtleties in texture and performance that defined the style and were generally lost in live contexts.

Let me try to discern a few musical and discursive reactions with system character. The infrastructure of the genre changed in two important ways. Firstly, there was the emergence of the spatial boundary between country-pop in Nashville and more traditional country in the Southwest. This boundary was reinforced when Waylon Jennings and other "outlaws" left Nashville in protest against the assembly-line system and pop hegemony. Secondly, the genre network went through a process of fragmentation when bluegrass went into exile. Major labels lost interest in bluegrass, and bluegrass people frustrated with the new terrain of country music created their own distinct network based on grassroots and small labels (Rosenberg 1985, chapter 5).[12] Bluegrass artists only used acoustic instruments and identified the music with the past and the rural, drawing on a series of dichotomies known in other genres (acoustic vs. electric, traditional vs. modern, rural vs. urban).

There was virtually no country music criticism at the time. Popular and trade magazines celebrated the successes of stars and the business without much discussion of the broader changes in the genre. A few magazines provided a public forum for discussion in the "Letters to the Editor" section. I shall focus on the debate in the Nashville-based *Music City News* in 1964–65. It reveals fundamental disagreements about the definition of the genre and a deep frustration among some fans with how the genre was changing. It began with a March 1964 editorial that tried to calm down the fans who "loudly and frequently" said, "Let's keep the Country in Country Music" (Scutt 1964). The editor, Roger Scutt, suggested that innovation was necessary and that even the CMA did not have a definition of country music. His argument shows whose side he was on and what its logic was: expand the boundaries to expand the market. In the ensuing debate, readers roughly divided themselves into two camps: critics and supporters of this view. Support came in the July issue from the CMA's president, Tex Ritter, who adopted the concepts of progress and experimentation in a quasi-capitalist-modernist fashion, but that only generated more criticisms, some of which were acrimonious (Ritter 1964).

Critics argued that the genre has certain values, and central to those values are notions of tradition and authenticity. A typical example: "Country Music is country people. It's their life their up and downs, about sad times and the happy times expressed in the only way they know how" (Hubbard 1964). Critics operated according to a core-periphery scheme that guided them in acts of inclusion and exclusion. They asserted that the Nashville Sound was not country music, and in December 1964, for the first time, a fan declared he would no longer subscribe to the magazine (Barone 1964b; see also Barone 1964a). He later said that it was painful to realize that he had lost the battle (Barone 1965). Critics felt somewhat marginal as a minority of individuals against larger forces, and the decision not to renew the subscription can be seen as a form of voluntary exile. When the debate was still intense and the British Invasion added further pressure, Buck Owens placed a full-page ad in March 1965 with a personal manifesto saying that he would always stay true to country music, and that he was proud to be a country artist (Owens 1965).[13] His appreciation of country music as a beloved person and his commitment to a monogeneric ethic are typical aspects of the simple and existential language of genre identification among hard-core country people. I have met several fans who are familiar with this ad and adopt a similar rhetoric when they describe their relationship with country.

Stories of Individuals

A few stories from individuals who experienced the Nashville Sound at a distance from both Nashville and the business should add more nuance to this picture. The overall picture that emerges from the following recollections and observations, made in 2004, indicates that age and the experience of time are essential aspects of genre transformation. My informants are core country music fans and musicians who are either amateurs or have not worked professionally with music for a long time. Most of them were regulars on a small country music message board in which I participated daily throughout 2004. I also had extensive private correspondences with the ten or fifteen most active members.

A man whose nickname I shall paraphrase as "Cuz George T-Bone" (b. 1939) and who grew up in Atlanta, explained to me that he "always played with traditional country bluegrass bands" and listened to WSB (personal correspondence throughout September 2004). This station presented leading Nashville stars as well as minor figures. From the Erlanger Theater it broadcast a barn dance show as well as a "headliner show" featuring more famous artists. Right below the theater was a drugstore with a lunch counter where George spent a lot of time—his mother was the manager—and he met many artists there.

Another participant on the board, "Cuz Caroline" (b. 1947), grew up on a farm in a remote rural community in Canada (personal correspondence throughout September 2004). The nearest city, Lloydminster, was about thirty miles away on the provincial line between Alberta and Saskatchewan. Although there were no professional musicians in her family, there was always country music around the house, either from family members playing or on the radio. They listened to CKSA in Lloydminster and, for the most part, CFCW in Camrose, Alberta, which had a strictly country music format. Like WSB in Atlanta, these stations presented a variety of music, but obviously with fewer live performances by American artists. Caroline remembers that there was a great deal of diversity at the talent shows in which she participated as a singer and guitarist. Some acts were more pop oriented than others, and she leaned toward the traditional styles. She recalls that, like many other youngsters, she also liked rock and roll and had fun dancing twist and jive. In her view, the Nashville Sound appealed mostly to urban middle-class people older than thirty. She was never able to sing or play much of it because the material was demanding. Harmonically, for instance, she felt that it was harder to play because there were more minor chords, an indication of how the complexity of the style limited its vernacular circulation.

These accounts were echoed by other members of the message board who grew up in other areas. "Cuz Nick" (b. 1956) started listening seriously to country music in the mid 1960s on Seattle's KAYO, which covered "a wide spectrum of country music from the 1940s to the current hits of the day." Nick continues:

> Perhaps because of my age, I can understand both sides of the controversy concerning the Nashville Sound. I can see how "purists" who grew up in the 30s, 40s and early 50s could see the Nashville Sound as not being country, but I also think that the Nashville Sound produced some of the all-time country classics and a lot of my favorite country music is from that era (late 50s to mid 70s). By the same token, I don't like most of today's country music, nor do I consider it even "country." (Nick, e-mail to author, 1 September 2004)

Country music did not change in the same way for everyone, and, again, age-related divisions in the genre culture are important. Many of those who had invested their identities in earlier country music had powerful memories of where they had come from and what they had believed in. This tells us that identity, taste, and other habitus elements that define a genre culture on a generic and collective level are shaped by individuals with particular experiences. Different fractions of a genre culture have different histories, and historical discourses surrounding the music continue to have great power in the present. In chapter 2 I noted how the film O Brother, Where Art Thou? fed a discourse on bluegrass that made it authentic and cool to certain youths, and that discourse contrasts with the traditionalism of the Bean Blossom festival. The message board I write about is a close-knit community of fans who communicate daily about country music of the past, especially the 1950s. They feel that mass-media privileges contemporary country, and the Internet allows them to create a virtual space in which they share feelings about the music they have loved for decades. They center on the past in their discussions, their trivia games about history, and their prayer circles for dying friends. Several of them came to country music around 1960 and were enculturated to the Nashville Sound as the norm because it was the mainstream at the time. They say that they later discovered it was controversial, but repeatedly add that the situation in country music was much better in the past than it is today.

Conclusion

Institutional and social forces have continued to bring country music into close competition with pop and rock, as the careers of Garth Brooks, Shania Twain, and the Dixie Chicks illustrate. In this sense, the genre has taken a further step on the path initiated by the Nashville Sound. Today, more than 90 percent of commercial country radio stations are owned by a few media conglomerates, and the business has become more corporate than it was in the 1960s. Nashville now parallels Hollywood in its countless wannabe artists, unapproachable corporate offices, lawyers, and celebrities who arrive in limousines at the CMA Awards show dressed like Hollywood film stars. The two major TV networks, Country Music Television and the Nashville Network (both launched in 1983), target their mainstream product to people between about fifteen and forty.[14] As in the food and travel industries, TV has given more weight to the visual and to the standards of beauty in mainstream popular culture. The stars are typically in their thirties and urban in orientation. Oftentimes, a cowboy hat is one of the few things that immediately set them apart from rock and pop stars. Continuing negotiations with contemporary rock and pop are a form of modernization that serves a particular cosmopolitanism through which southern and rural subjects cross the boundaries of the local and traditional rural imagination and deal with national fashions and politics.

One of the most obvious rules of the mainstream ideology is the systematic exclusion of elders. Many have commented on the exclusion of "gray hair." The Nashville veteran Billy Grammer explained to me that he has discussed this problem with Waylon Jennings, Willie Nelson, and others, but that they have not been organized in their efforts (Grammer, conversation with author, Sesser, Illinois, 6 May 2004). In the mid 1990s, one veteran

CHAPTER FOUR

Jazz and Jazz-Rock Fusion

Paris 1954

One of the foundational books of modernist jazz criticism was published in Paris just before the rock and roll explosion. The author, André Hodeir (b. 1921), had studied violin and composition at the Conservatoire de Paris and started writing about jazz in the early 1940s. Some of the essays had previously been published in the magazine *Jazz Hot*, of which he became the editor in 1947 after a serious fight with the traditionalist camp in the offices. Paris was a cultural metropolis in Europe and became a center for jazz, too, when it spread across the world as an international fashion in the 1920s. Various kinds of primitivism proliferated on the local scene, and Hodeir fronted a reaction against the conservative primitivism of the hard-core fan cult, which was opposed to the new sounds of bebop. In his magnum opus, *Hommes et problèmes du jazz* (1954), he conducts a systematic analysis of various musical parameters of jazz, with pioneering research on concepts such as swing and improvisation. He also develops an evolutionary historical narrative and refutes racial determinism. Typical of white modernist discourse is the tendency to downplay the music's connection to the African diaspora and steal ownership under the guise of musical autonomy and musicological rationalism. The book got a broader readership in other countries when it was translated into English in 1956. Among its American admirers were Gunther Schuller and Martin Williams. They, too, would praise jazz for the formal sophistication associated with Western art music.

The growing diversification of jazz in the mid twentieth century into cultures of traditional, modern, pop, and art jazz makes it difficult to represent the genre in the singular and increases the need to specify which culture of jazz one refers to. Another general point illustrated by Hodeir's legacy is that jazz has a complex transatlantic geography. Jazz has appealed to cosmopolitan sensibilities and had shifting centers throughout its history, whereas country music, for instance, has remained more tied to its home regions in the American South. Jazz communities around the world have followed the situation in America so closely, however, that by the time of the rock and roll explosion, the core of the global jazz network had gravitated toward the concept of art jazz. The art emphasis dominated among specialized jazz labels and publications in American metropolises. Many artists and fans did not consider jazz a genre of popular music, and the situation was further polarized by the mass-culture debates in the national public sphere. Henry Pleasants reported in his essay "What Is This Thing Called Jazz?" that there were disparate concepts of jazz, but that there seemed to be general agreement about the exclusion of Paul Whiteman, the king of early popular jazz (Pleasants 1955, 177). The boundaries with popular music were discussed, but popular music usually meant Tin Pan Alley and not more recent styles.

Miles from Rock and Roll

Jazz people paid little attention to rock and roll in the 1950s. The two moved along rather separate paths, as if they had little relevance to each other and were incompatible. Hard boppers such as Art Blakey and Horace Silver drew on African American folk and popular musics, but not so much on contemporary R & B.

Very little has been written about the limited contact between jazz and rock and roll in the period up to the mid 1960s, but the relative silence is worth exploring in order to understand genre boundaries. A few contemporary reports were written by broad-minded critics. In 1956, Nat Hentoff (b. 1925), the associate editor of *Down Beat* from 1953 to 1957, did a one-page article in the magazine titled "Musicians Argue Values of Rock and Roll." It is basically a collage of excerpts from interviews with a handful of jazz musicians, and I suspect the deadline did not permit time for more than short phone calls, because the structure is a bit loose. Time pressures may have generated more direct responses and questions (e.g., "What about the alleged monotony of the rhythm and blues beat?"). The swing veteran Benny Goodman is the only white interviewee, and Hentoff focuses on black R & B. The term rock and roll is used only in the title. Goodman clearly dislikes rock and roll but does not want to make any statements for publication. He had no reason to feel threatened by rock and roll financially, but it must have hurt to see fewer and fewer young people taking an interest in his music.

The article also shows that age was an issue from early on and that it was cast in terms of a simple opposition between parents and their teenage kids. Thad Jones says that he wants his son "to have a musical background so that he'll know what's happening and so that he doesn't get sidetracked by rhythm and blues." Milt Hinton and a tenor player named Sam Taylor both say that R & B is "simple" and appeals to "kids." They suggest that education is important and that musical craft in R & B should be improved. This echoes Booker T. Washington's old philosophy of education as a means by which African Americans can improve their social conditions and fight stereotypes. It is not hard to understand why African Americans would have anxieties about being associated with a new form of popular culture that was criticized for being simple, repetitive, and unrefined. Teddy Wilson, another swing veteran, grew up on the campus of Alabama's Tuskegee University, which had been founded by Washington, and he voiced similar sentiments in the 1970s: "It's an absolute farce to hear intelligent Englishmen [the Beatles and Rolling Stones] trying to imitate the vernacular of ignorant Southern Negroes in the US who haven't been to school" (Wilson, Lighart, and van Loo 1996, 96).[1] Hentoff's interviewees generally judge by their own taste when they criticize the music. Billy Taylor, for instance, describes the melodies as "repetitive" and adds that "harmonically, a lot of it is incorrectly written and... played." Taylor is also frustrated that R & B is more heavily promoted than jazz. John Lewis is one of those who admit that they judge the music without listening much to it: "Most of what I've heard has been of very poor quality musically. I haven't heard very much because I don't care to." The music is "so limited in scope" and the dancing is "the worst dancing I've ever seen. Again, I haven't seen much."

Another informative source is the essay "Rhythm and Blues (and Rock 'n Roll) Makes the Grade" that Ralph Gleason (b. 1917) wrote in 1957 or 1958 for the *San Francisco Chronicle* and included in his anthology *Jam Session* (1958). This was the only discussion of the subject in the book, and few jazz books would even say that much about rock. Whereas Hentoff was based in New York City, Gleason was in San Francisco, and although he was associated with *Down Beat* from 1948 to 1961, his remoteness from the jazz capital and his job at the *San Francisco Chronicle* might have made him more receptive to the rock boom that transformed the city's cultural space. This early piece on R & B is interesting because it tells us something about how Gleason approaches the music as a jazz specialist. After a historical survey of the blues based on books and recordings, he reports from a field excursion to Fillmore, the city's main African American neighborhood, where he has interviewed the manager of a local record chain store. The manager tells him that jazz does not fit the dancing and lifestyles of the new youth generation. He explains that a recent Count Basie record was a hit, but not among "the kids," because they could not dance to it (Gleason 1958, 279–80). Here, jazz has grown old and resides on the parents' side of the generational gap. It is significant that Gleason does not report from his own firsthand experience and does not act as a mediating interlocutor, as someone explaining R & B to his readers from his own perspective. Like Hentoff, he primarily writes about African American musicians. Elvis is briefly mentioned as a "country and western" artist in a way that indicates that there was a great distance between Gleason's San Francisco and the rockabillies in the South.

These two reports illustrate general aspects of the relationship between jazz and rock and roll in the late 1950s. Above all, the relationship was characterized by limited contact and interest. A number of jazz musicians supplemented their income by working as sidemen and session musicians for rock artists, but genre mixing was limited by musical and social divisions. Artists such as Louis Jordan and Ray Charles crossed the boundaries of jazz and R & B but were based in the R & B circuit. Let me point to five important dimensions of the distance between jazz and rock and roll:

(1) *Music*. Rock and roll was singable and danceable; art jazz was advanced instrumental music.

(2) *Age*. Rock and roll was younger than jazz and located on the other side of the generational divide.

(3) *Place*. Rock and roll emerged in the South; jazz was now concentrated in the urban North.

(4) *Class*. Rock and roll had a lower status than jazz; jazz was dominated by a high-art orientation.

(5) *Race*. Rock and roll became dominated by whites; blacks continued to have a central position in jazz. Abiding cultural racism caused anxiety about rock and roll among black jazz musicians.

This situation was a defining moment with long-term effects. Even after jazz and rock approached each other in the late 1960s, older and conservative jazz people would feel that total separation was natural, and the stereotype of rock as superficial and vulgar music for white teenagers has not entirely disappeared.

One of the big differences between jazz and country music in this situation is the standards of popularity. Although dominant forces in country music struggled to keep it in the popular culture mainstream, jazz people had generally accepted the music's loss of popularity in the 1940s, and the jazz production network was largely based on independent labels. The world of popular jazz, with artists such as Louis Armstrong, Frank Sinatra, and Dave

Brubeck, shunned rock and roll like the rest of the adult pop world, and the corporate industry did not try to push these artists in the direction of rock and roll.

Interlude, 1958–66

Rock and roll of the 1950s slipped into the background with the British Invasion, which marked the musical and terminological change to "rock music." Rock immediately reached a mass audience and affected many music cultures, culturally, financially, or both. Perhaps no other music has had such a central and powerful role in transforming contemporary society and its cultural hierarchies. Age was important in defining its boundaries with other musics because rock was strongly identified with youth. In a musical tradition with an older audience, such as jazz, the struggle for survival was a prime force in a transformation that resembles the modernization process in country music in the late 1950s.

The diversification of jazz continued after 1958, even within art jazz, where explorations of musical styles and concepts were leading in different directions. Third Stream, free jazz, and modal jazz all appeared around this time, and African American musicians in particular became more interested in musics of the non-Western world. Among the many recordings of this period of extraordinary artistic achievements are Miles Davis's *Kind of Blue* (Columbia, 1959), Bill Evans's *Sunday at the Village Vanguard* (Riverside, 1961), and John Coltrane's *A Love Supreme* (Impulse! 1964).

When Hentoff portrayed jazz culture in his 1961 book *The Jazz Life*, jazz was not in deep crisis, and there was not a word about rock and roll. He complained a bit in the epilogue about "the suspicious insularity of many jazzmen" and admitted that he had been happy to write more about non-jazz subjects since 1957 (1961/1975, 251). He also complained that the business "is relentlessly cruel for most jazzmen past forty" (he was thirty-seven): "To the audiences, the booking agents, and even some of the critics, jazz is still a music for the young and by the young" (ibid., 253). That statement would have been odd ten years later. When the book was published again in 1975, Hentoff felt the situation had changed so much that a new introduction was needed. The big issue in that introduction was rock music. There he observes that rock established its "hegemony over popular music" soon after the book was first published, and that the result was "a bleak decade for jazz. . . . many of those young listeners—who might in earlier decades, have certified their hipness by joining the auditors and spectators of the jazz life—were lost instead to rock." There was, he continues, "a decided recession in the jazz life until the early 1970s" when fusion and "vintage jazz" attracted a larger audience (ibid., vii–viii).

The folk revival took a share of the market away from various kinds of music, including jazz. Some folk genres and performers enjoyed popular success in the 1960s in a way that jazz did not.[2] Jazz was not very important to the civil rights and counterculture movements, for instance. Although jazz was challenged economically by the folk revival, there was an audience overlap, and jazz people had been interested in the African American folk roots of jazz since at least the late 1930s (see Ramsey and Smith 1939; Stearns 1956). Jazz magazines occasionally published record reviews and feature articles on folk music. However, folk music was approached from the perspective of the modernist jazz canon. If jazz was becoming "an historical artifact," as Hentoff feared in 1975, it was not only because rock was eating up the jazz world, as he suggested, but also because jazz people had distanced themselves from contemporary popular culture (Hentoff 1961/1975, xiii). The first signs of a crisis appeared around 1963:

> The death of jazz has been predicted countless times since its birth.... Now in the year 1963, when for the first time the prophecy is likely to be fulfilled, no one will believe it—no one, that is, except those who are close to the jazz scene and conscious of the very great problems that are plaguing the art and its practitioners.
>
> During the past few weeks, two of the outstanding jazz critics in the United States and Britain, Nat Hentoff (in the *New York Herald-Tribune*) and Francis Newton [Eric Hobsbawm's pseudonym] (in the *New Statesman*), have described the depressed condition of the New York scene and endeavored to explain its causes. Returning to the city after a two-year absence, Newton was shocked to find the clubs dark or half-empty, the musicians without work or gigging behind counters, and the much publicized avant-garde the victim of a club owner's lockout.... Hentoff finds great irony in the present jazz "boom," which he views as largely the work of publicists and image-makers, and as merely a hollow thud for the dozens of musicians who have had to take demeaning "day jobs" just to survive. (Goldman 1971a, 265–66)

This was a time when the public face of jazz was widely associated with Armstrong, Duke Ellington, and Goodman, who were over fifty, and soon afterward John Lennon proclaimed that "jazz is dead," one of his many catchy aphorisms (Lake 1974).[3] The jazz economy took a steep dive in the

1960s and reached a low point around 1972 with a share of 1.3 percent of total record sales (rock/pop had about 75 percent). Jazz clubs around the country also closed as a consequence of urban renewal projects. In Manhattan alone, the number of clubs was reduced from almost thirty to six (Hobsbawm 1998, 282; Nicholson 1998, 58; Porter, Ullman, and Hazlett 1993, 357; see also Strongin 1970, 31). Hentoff and Hobsbawm were the preeminent sociologists of jazz, and their diagnosis proved to be correct. Albert Goldman, in the passage quoted above, was questioning the reason for being skeptical of the present simply because the music was not as popular as before. He felt it was natural for jazz culture to adjust to a more underground existence.

Facing symbolic and financial death is a structure of feeling in modern jazz history. It appeared in different forms at the moments of recession and transition in the 1940s and 1960s where narratives of continuity were compromised. In each case, old styles suffered and new ones were born, but there was also a transformation of the genre and its historical matrix. The evolutionary paradigm of the 1950s, for instance, could not account for the influx of rock in the late 1960s. People like Hobsbawm argued that it was a "wrong" turn. He, and doubtless many other older fans, felt that rock "almost killed jazz" and that rock-influences at best gave jazz "a certain public presence in the years of isolation" (Hobsbawm 1998, 281–82). They disregarded rock-influenced jazz and therefore much of the music that had begun to circulate in the jazz network after 1967. The evolutionary paradigm was embedded in a monolithic notion of tradition according to which innovation can come only from within. Rock challenged the boundary and the core of the genre and created the illusion that the gates to popular music were opening, whereas in fact they had already been open until recently.

Goldman was not a core jazz writer working for the mainstream jazz press, so he was less dependent than many other jazz writers on the business and its need for positive stories. Whereas Hentoff and Hobsbawm primarily pointed to causes of decline that lay outside of jazz, Goldman was more critical of internal affairs. In a 1963 article he wrote about "all the faults of modern jazz—the eclecticism, the attitudinizing, the forced-draft experimentation, the general atmosphere of confusion" (1971a, 269; cf. Goldman 1971b).

Enthusiasm declined even among insiders such as Miles Davis. Miles had "very few jazz records" and listened a lot to Duke Ellington and Maurice Ravel in the early 1960s, and by the middle of the decade he was tired of playing jazz clubs. He later recalled that in 1964 a lot of people were talking about the death of jazz and that some blamed free jazz for driving audiences away (Davis and Troupe 1989, 271; Szwed 2002, 223–25, 246).

With our model of genre transformation in mind, we can understand the crisis as constituted by a series of interlocking mechanisms. The immediate problem was the recession, which put pressure on many aspects of the genre network. At the same time, the recession was both cause and symptom of the disintegration and weakened focus of the network. As with country music in the late 1950s, the recession cannot be explained only in terms of competition from rock, and its financial and cultural aspects are inseparable. Avant-garde jazz musicians in Chicago and later New York and elsewhere built their own network on a grassroots level outside the established jazz business (see chapter 5). In country, something similar was happening with bluegrass, but the general economy of country music grew with the formation of country-pop.

Unlike with country music, the dominant genre discourse distanced itself from popular music. There was still jazz-pop singing and the bossa nova fad in the early 1960s, but there was no broad collective effort to approach popular music until the 1970s. The record producer Creed Taylor was an important figure in renewing the old model of mixing jazz and pop by having a jazz soloist play against pop arrangements. He developed it into the form of jazz-pop that would be termed smooth jazz and included contemporary pop styles, not only older Tin Pan Alley styles. Taylor organized the bossa nova sessions with Stan Getz and worked with Wes Montgomery, and he would later work with George Benson and Grover Washington, Jr. He also did less polished productions with the organist Jimmy Smith, who had a background in R & B and was associated with soul jazz. The term soul jazz came into widespread use beginning in 1960, when the Riverside label used it to promote the Cannonball Adderley quintet (Kernfeld 2002b, 635). Musically and culturally, however, soul jazz remained much closer to hard bop and other forms of modern jazz than to the sounds of Motown or Stax.

In short, jazz artists had crossed boundaries to popular music in many ways before rock sounds emerged in full force around 1969. Until the late 1960s, artists primarily integrated pop in familiar borderlands with R & B and Tin Pan Alley, and jazz was essentially acoustic and centered on live performance. Indicative of the somewhat traditional outlook of the early approaches to rock was the use of the old practice of doing instrumental jazz versions of pop songs. Covering Beatles songs was a novelty that even Basie and Ellington tried out, but it soon wore off (cf. Gendron 2002, chapter 8).

Another loose end was Gary Burton's 1966 recording project, which blended jazz and country music. Burton grew up in the Midwest and lived in Nashville for some time beginning in 1960, when he was seventeen. He discovered country music, met country artists, and played jazz with the guitarist Hank Garland in one of the city's nightclubs. In 1966, he returned with three other prominent jazz musicians, including Roy Haynes, to make the album *Tennessee Firebird* in collaboration with local studio musicians. Burton subsequently wrote a piece in *Jazz* magazine in which he described the sessions and reflected on the encounter (Burton 1967). He felt that boundaries were eroding around the world and that there were obvious connections between jazz and country music. In the studio, his team had tried to combine their art jazz conceptions with different styles of country music, and Chet Atkins had served as "interpreter" (ibid., 12). They also did two Bob Dylan tunes, and Burton proudly notes that several of the musicians also participated in a recent Dylan session in Nashville. *Tennessee Firebird* integrates the various genre elements with great sensibility. It contains ballads with improvisatory, floating passages and Burton's characteristic restraint and harmonic subtlety. The tracks with country- and rock-based rhythms are well crafted but sound a bit tame. Various genre audiences may have felt that something was lost, but it is certain that country radio did not play the album because there was no singing, and art jazz people generally looked down on country music. A subgenre of country-jazz never developed. However, country influences can be heard later in the music of Burton and one of his guitarists, Pat Metheny, another midwesterner. Burton may also have inspired Bill Frisell, one of the few contemporary art jazz musicians with a country-influenced style. On *Good Dog, Happy Man* (Nonesuch, 1999) and other albums since the mid 1990s, Frisell has generally moved closer to a country-tinged roots music sound similar to that of *Tennessee Firebird* and with some of the same relaxed atmosphere.

Festivals on the Two Coasts, 1967–71

Summer and love or, rather, some of the accompanying activities widened the spaces of contact between jazz and rock in 1967. The first small wave of rock-influenced jazz started around 1966 and expanded the following year with predominantly white bands such as those led by Larry Coryell and Gary Burton. They had relatively little impact on the jazz world, however, and the watershed in 1967 was discursive rather than musical. An important event was the Monterey International Pop Festival, held on 16–18 June, about a year after a rock audience had discovered the mellow, soulful sound of Charles Lloyd's quartet at the annual Monterey Jazz Festival. One of the organizers had been there and purportedly got the idea of a rock festival equivalent to the jazz festival. He felt that rock had become "a more serious art form," and although the festival was not focused on prestige, it happened at a time when rock was becoming more accepted, and that reduced the distance to jazz a bit ("Music Festival Homepage" 1996; Thurman 2001).[4] Pop was a broader category than rock, and the festival illustrates that rock was part of eclectic cultural formations, with elements of folk and various popular musics. Ravi Shankar performed, and a few of the rock-based acts were influenced by jazz (Hugh Masakela and Electric Flag). However, rock mythology is not entirely wrong when it tells us that this was the first big rock festival. Several acts played the new, high-powered psychedelic rock that embodied some of the excitement and spirit of the colorful counterculture. Among them were the Jefferson Airplane, Janis Joplin, the Who, and Jimi Hendrix.

Less than two weeks after the festival, *Down Beat* declared that "rock-and-roll has come of age" and that the magazine would "expand its editorial perspective to include the musically valid aspects of the rock scene" (Morgenstern 1967). The magazine's editor, Dan Morgenstern, hinted that "the future paths of jazz and rock may converge." The general tone was positive, and he tried to soothe the segment of the jazz audience that did not like rock by promising that the magazine would not reduce its coverage of jazz and would stay true to its high artistic standards. Morgenstern later told me that the magazine was forced to include rock by advertisers in the musical instrument trade (not the recording industry), and that the magazine basically remained the same except that something new was added (Morgenstern, e-mail to author, 25 April 2003).

About two months after the festival, the magazine *Jazz* changed its name to *Jazz and Pop*. Here the editor, Pauline Rivelli, signals a full integration of jazz and popular music in the magazine and refers to the Monterey festival: "1967 has witnessed the birth of a serious American pop music which encompasses jazz, rock, folk and blues," she writes, and rejects the word rock and roll as a "tired cliché" (Rivelli 1967, 5). Rivelli had a hippie-influenced approach to categories, and she did not have a strong grounding in jazz modernism.[5] *Jazz and Pop* was the only magazine to embrace jazz and rock in equal measure. However, the latter dominated within two years, and consequently the magazine was named *Pop* in 1971. There were clear divisions between jazz and rock writers, and the discourses on two musics were more juxtaposed than integrated. The magazine was less organized than *Down Beat* and *Rolling Stone*, for instance, and it included things that they would likely have censored. One example is the African American voices expressing frustration with the white dominance in the rock world. Herbie Hancock was quoted for saying that part of reason for the mass success of rock bands is that "the white audience can identify with them, because they both have long hair that they can shake, and they both have white skin and hair on their chest and all these things" (Strongin 1970, 32; see also Kofsky 1967, 24).

In jazz, the dominance of rock resulted in strong generic and racial dichotomies that have worked reductively in discourse on the music's complex relations with other musics, including popular musics, non-Western music, and classical music. I have researched the terminology in jazz magazines and the *New York Times* and found that the term jazz-rock was established in 1968 and that "jazz-rock fusion" or just "fusion" became common only in the second half of the 1970s. "Jazz-rock" was still the norm as late as 1975 (Feather 1975; Lake 1974). Fusion is not a hyphenated term and does more justice to the somewhat hybrid character of this field of jazz, which draws heavily not only on rock but also on soul and funk. "Jazz-rock" gained currency because of the dominance of rock and was the result of a somewhat colorblind culture: virtually every editor, journalist, producer, manager, and executive was white and served the big white market. Trade magazines and major record labels directly and indirectly enforced racial boundaries. Most jazz journalists were diplomatic for commercial reasons when they wrote about racial issues (often ignored) and rock music (often disliked).[6]

Gleason reported from the Monterey Pop Festival for the *San Francisco Chronicle* and from the Monterey Jazz Festival in September for *Jazz and Pop*. For the first time, the jazz festival included artists based in folk and rock. Gleason was pleased with the change. He was getting more into rock and co-founded *Rolling Stone* in November 1967. To him, Gary Burton's quartet was "a pallid interlude" before Richie Havens and Janis Joplin, who "received a standing ovation when she finished her wildly exciting version of Big Mama Thornton's blues, *Ball and Chain*" (Gleason 1967b, 16 and 18).[7] She also brought dancing to the jazz festival experience as "the arena . . . filled with seething clusters of dancers" during her performance. "An old-line jazz critic was outraged at the rock bands' presence but I think it's reasonable to say he was only suffering from cultural shock," noted Gleason. In his regular column, Gleason talked about "the merger of jazz and rock" as a familiar issue and said that jazz fans were less open-minded than rock fans (1967a). He referred to a recent show at the local Fillmore Auditorium, where jazz fans rejected Charles Lloyd and rock fans liked him. This was one of the earliest examples of jazz making its entry into large rock venues, and rock venues were actually less open to jazz when Bill Graham closed his two Fillmores in 1971 in frustration over the escalating mass-market orientation of the rock business (Graham 1971).

Jazz was generally absent from big rock festivals and rock venues in the late 1960s and early 1970s. A Sunday night jazz series at the Fillmore East

was discontinued in the summer of 1969 "due to lack of attendance" ("Interview with George Wein" 1969, 44), and even Miles Davis only appeared
at one rock festival (the Isle of Wight in 1970). Rock, soul, and urban blues,
on the other hand, became a fixture of jazz festivals and some jazz clubs.
The motivation was profit, and that was necessary for some clubs. Others
switched to popular music entirely, sometimes in the form of a discotheque.

The opening up of jazz to popular music on the festival scene in Monterey
in 1967 was followed in 1969 by the major jazz festival on the East Coast,
the Newport Festival. "Rock is what's selling the festival," said the festival's
producer, George Wein, whose thematic organization of the program reflects
typical distinctions among jazz and pop audiences. The first night was called
"For the Jazz Aficionado" and presented modern art jazz (see figure 6). The
second night was called "An Evening of Jazz Rock" and essentially presented
white rock bands and two black jazz soloists. Of them, only Steve Marcus
and Blood, Sweat, and Tears crossed the boundaries a little bit. Incidentally,
Marcus had connections to the circle around Gary Burton, and Blood, Sweat,
and Tears had connections to that of another vibraphonist, Mike Manieri.
These are some of the circles of white, East Coast–based instrumentalists in
their early and mid twenties who engaged in mixing jazz and rock.[8] They
adopted cultural codes strongly identified with their generation and with
youth: rock music and hippie fashion. "I'm young and want to relate to
young people," said Burton in 1967, as if this were a right that needed to
be claimed in jazz. In 1969–70 he appeared in magazine ads saying, "The
sound is young. The vibist is Gary Burton. The vibes are Musser" ("Pop
Talk" 1967).[9]

The remainder of the festival program alternated loosely between jazz
and popular musics such as rock, soul, and blues. Rock stars in particular
drew a historically large crowd and changed the outlook of the modern jazz
festival, which had evolved since the mid 1950s. John Wilson's daily reports
in the New York Times are informative here. In the first, he briefly turns to
the question of whether the name jazz would be dropped from the festival's
name now that there is so much rock. Wein responds that the term jazz
has "taken on a broader meaning" and that rock artists like to be associated
with the more prestigious world of jazz. "Rock groups were so anxious to
play here at the jazz festival that most of them came at their lowest rate," he
says ("Sixteenth Newport Jazz Festival Opens to Sounds of Rain," New York
Times, 4 July 1969).[10] The first big surprise for Wilson was the turnout of
34,000 people on the second day and the disorder that made Wein plead with
the audience for self-restraint (Wilson, "Sun Ra Plays at Newport," New
York Times, 5 July 1969, and "34,000 Hear Rock at Newport Fete," New

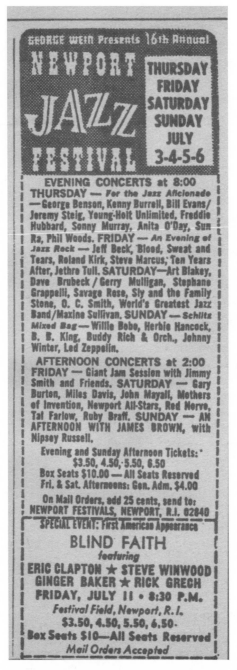

Figure 6 Ad for Newport Jazz Festival, 1969. The ad was printed in the *New York Times* on 11 May and a couple more times before the festival.

York Times, 6 July 1969). A fence was broken, and the following day the festival was "invaded by several hundred young people," so the main gates were opened to prevent further damage. Wein was disappointed with the consequences of adding rock music to the festival and canceled the evening's Led Zeppelin show at the request of a local city councilman, who urged him to eliminate rock from the festival (Wilson, "Unruly Rock Fans Upset Newport Jazz Festival," *New York Times*, 7 July 1969). Two years later, things got so out of hand that the festival closed two days early. "These are the same kids who invaded the festival in 1969," said Wein, and trespassers were now reportedly in the thousands. "Their purpose in being here was to get stoned and raise hell. They had no concern for jazz, no concern for the festival. They are America's disgrace" (Wilson, "Newport Closes Festival Early," *New York Times*, 5 July 1971).

In short, these jazz festivals drew a larger audience by including rock, but the space of jazz was reduced and compromised. Problems at rock festivals such as Altamont also encumbered the alliances with the jazz world. Wein was much more skeptical of rock in 1971 than in 1969, and so were Keith Jarrett and Dave Holland, who split off from Miles Davis's band and from fusion around the same time. The belief in a convergence of jazz and rock culture that a few younger jazz people had held in 1967–69 seemed less realistic in the early 1970s.

Bitches Brew

Recording sessions for the album that shook up the jazz world and set an example for how jazz musicians would integrate contemporary pop began on 19 August 1969. It was the day after the end of the Woodstock festival, and by that time rock had a strong foothold in society. Miles and other jazz musicians had approached soul and rock, but this time he did not do it in a silent way.

Bitches Brew was the full entry into the rock era of a canonical jazz artist. Miles moved to the edge of jazz from an established position in the core of modern art jazz, and he took with him a dozen of the top young acoustic jazz players. Because of his position in the genre, one might say that *Bitches* changed jazz from within, and it was harder for the jazz world to ignore the album than it would have been if he had been a newcomer. For many experienced jazz listeners, this was viewed not just as the fall of a great figure, but also as the deterioration of jazz itself, of that sacred space, however small, where pure jazz was perceived to survive. If Dylan was the Judas of the folk revival, Miles may very well have been the Judas of jazz. People had begun to blame him for "selling out," and jazz fans and musicians fell into camps.

Most of them were offended, including old friends such as Dizzy Gillespie, Clark Terry, and Charles Mingus (Szwed 2002, 282, 290, and 313).[11] Tensions would only increase after *Bitches* when he moved closer to free jazz and began using wa-wa effects or even switching to keyboards so that the instrumental sound with which the public had identified him for decades would disappear. In the fall of 1970, Keith Jarrett was his only band member with a background in jazz.

Bitches Brew quickly sold over 500,000 copies and became the first big commercial success of rock-influenced jazz (Szwed 2002, 297). Many of the young musicians in Miles's band were not initially keen on doing rock-influenced jazz, but this album made fusion seem financially attractive, and they would soon adopt his model and form their own fusion bands. Ever since, fusion has been a way for jazz artists to reach a broader audience, and during the 1970s fusion stole attention from straight-ahead jazz at major labels (Keepnews 1979, 63). Miles survived the purge of jazz artists at Columbia because he was able to reach a wider market. Columbia's president, Clive Davis, had worked to expand the label's share of the pop and rock market since his appointment in 1967 (Albertson 1971, 196; Szwed 2002, 260–61), and the four big fusion bands in the 1970s would record for Columbia and be led by musicians that played with Miles between 1968 and 1971: the Headhunters, the Mahavishnu Orchestra, Weather Report, and Return to Forever. Though much of the seminal fusion was produced in New York City, it was not strongly grounded in the local scene and was never really identified with this city. The spatial boundaries of fusion were further complicated by influences from abroad and the conspicuous number of foreign-born musicians, such as Joe Zawinul, John McLaughlin, Airto Moreira, and Michael Urbaniak. Moreover, the production methods were not as standardized as in Nashville country music, so it was unlikely that something like a New York sound would emerge. Jazz purists have always perceived fusion as commercial music, and rather than becoming the mainstream of jazz, it became something core jazz musicians did on the side.

Another aspect of the album was the presentation of the music in word and image, which signaled the beginning of a new era. Ralph Gleason's liner notes, typed in beatnik-underground fashion without capitals, were as programmatic and ambitious as the music:

> electric music is the music of this culture...so we have to reach out
> to the new world with new ideas and new forms and in music this
> has meant leaving the traditional forms...and playing something else
> altogether which maybe you can't identify and classify yet...

look. miles has changed the world. more than once. . . . it will never be
the same again now, after in a silent way and after BITCHES BREW.
(Gleason 1969/1999)[12]

Central to this statement is the association of innovation and newness
with contemporary popular culture and hybridity. In part, this is a familiar
form of modernization in which elements of tradition are lost and new elements imported, with popular culture as the chief signifier of youth and
contemporaneity. It differs from our previous examples of modernization,
however, because of the modernist emphasis on boundary transgression and
its capacity to unleash powerful cultural energies. The music on *Bitches* has
this sort of modernist sentiment in the way it mixes jazz and popular music
with head-on rock guitar, aggressive rhythms, experimental studio practices,
and seriousness of tone. Previous jazz and pop projects can sound a bit tame
and modest when compared to *Bitches*. Rather than flirting with rock, on
this album Miles confronts it like a boxer without gloves, with sheer volume and spiritual power conveyed through his majestic trumpet playing. In
the beginning of the title track a simple repeated one-note pattern invokes
the sound of a human call. It is followed by a dramatic response from the
whole band in suspended time, like an extended caesura. The band then
makes a single-stroke gesture, dwelling on a complex harmonic cluster with
a touch of contemporary classical music. Such elements of disruption introduced a new form of discontinuity that can be heard as a sonic metaphor for
the historical moment of disruption in jazz.

The album cover was a painting by Mati Klarwein, whose psychedelic
hippie surrealism played with notions of spirituality, primeval forces, time-
lessness, and utopia, as did the song titles in their references to witchcraft
and ancient Egyptian mythology. Connections to rock culture were further
established intertextually through the covers that Klarwein did for Jimi
Hendrix and Santana. Miles had met Klarwein in a Moroccan clothing bou-
tique in New York where these and other rock artists also came. He had
married the twenty-three-year-old Betty Mabry in 1967, and she brought
him into contact with Hendrix, Sly Stone, and parts of the New York rock
and dance club scene.[13] The concept of discotheque had just been imported
from France, and a new culture of deejaying and dancing emerged in the
late 1960s at places such as Arthur, the Sanctuary, Salvation, and the Loft
where rock stars and other celebrities hung out. Deejays discovered how to
build intensity and spiritual communion among young urbanites in these
new and heavily amplified social spaces (Lawrence 2003, chap. 1). Moreover,

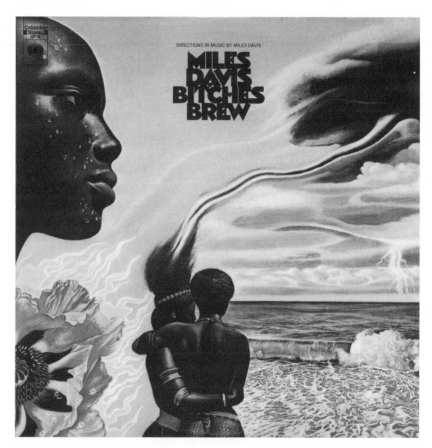

Figure 7 Cover of Miles Davis's *Bitches Brew* (Columbia, 1969). Courtesy of Mati Klarwein.

Mabry encouraged Miles to switch from black suits to funky clothing from Greenwich Village. But he did not fully embrace hippie culture and retained his cool modernist attitude. The cover of the 13 December 1969 *Rolling Stone* showed him wearing haute couture sunglasses and looking serious (see figure 5).

The music on *Bitches Brew* articulated a new and more complex relation with popular music. It did more than just use more pop "elements." The album was the culmination of a series of changes in Miles's music that began in 1967. Miles's album *Nefertiti*, which had come out in the summer of 1967, was wholly situated within the paradigm of modern art jazz and represented a mature statement at a late stage in its development. His famous quintet

had experimented with jazz for years, but it was not yet moving in the direction of pop. This move occurred in the following years and involved a deep
musical transformation.

The first of three interconnected aspects of this transformation is the
reduction of harmonic complexity, which can be linked to the development
of forms of musical communication and interaction based more on simple
rhythmic and melodic grooves (cf. pp. 137–40). On the album *Filles de
Kilimanjaro* ([June–September] Columbia, 1968), walking bass and swing
rhythm had disappeared, and modal elements emerged. The modal was tied
to soul-influenced ostinatos and less to jazz harmony than to the type of
modal jazz that developed from albums such as *Kind of Blue* (Columbia,
1959). The second aspect of the transformation is the shift from chorus form
and constant rhythm group playing toward larger sections with different
tempos, rhythms, and moods. This tendency is clear on *In a Silent Way*
(recorded February 1969), where both of the album's two long pieces move
between extended meditative passages and energetic passages that define the
overall architecture of the piece. Before, overall form had been characterized
by the somewhat abstract character of long solos over a steady rhythmic
flow, and the new focus on continuity within larger contrasting sections allowed for other narratives in the music. Miles increasingly used simple
rhetorical gestures and processual narratives to shape the form of his music.

The third aspect of the transformation is sound. With *Bitches*, Miles
began using the studio facilities in new ways by doing relatively improvised
sessions while the tapes kept rolling for hours. The producer, Teo Macero,
looped recorded passages and moved them around like a film editor, and he
used reverb to design the musical space. In Brian Eno's words, Macero put
the musicians miles apart in a soundscape where "you have the conga player
three streets down the road here" and "the trumpet player on a mountain
over there" (Szwed 2002, 298). This was a technological intervention that
deviated from previous practices of performing and recording jazz. It changed
the material existence of the music and the spatial boundaries that had
defined the sensuous epistemologies of the jazz experience. Miles said that
he had to get used to electric instruments. No wonder core jazz listeners such
as Williams and Hobsbawm were offended and alienated. The skepticism
about fusion has perhaps been most evident in the enduring opposition to
electrification.

Miles had approached rock music slowly and expanded his stylistic range
from soul jazz and electric blues, which he encountered on the Chicago
South Side in 1966–67, to funk and psychedelic rock in 1968 (Davis 1989,
288–94). *In a Silent Way* of early 1969 had a spacious, meditative sound and

introduced the British rock guitarist John McLaughlin. It was also the first of Miles's albums to get a long and enthusiastic review in *Rolling Stone*: Lester Bangs found it very authentic and called Miles a timeless genius. He concluded: "I believe there is a new music in the air, a total art which knows no boundaries or categories, a new school run by geniuses indifferent to fashion" (Bangs 1969). This is strikingly reminiscent of Gleason's liner notes for *Bitches* and draws on the same countercultural optimism and utopianism. Miles did cross over with *Bitches* in terms of record sales and appearances at rock arenas, and his band looked like a rock band on stage, with electric gear and hippie-inspired fashion. Like many other rock bands at the time, he bought his own sound system and a Volkswagen minivan. He also shared the bill with Santana on a tour in the summer of 1970 and continued to be an opening act for white rock bands (Albertson 1971, 195; Szwed 2002, 288 and 312). Nonetheless, his opinions about rock were invariably harsh and cast in racial terms. It was the height of black nationalism, and though he said he was not a Black Panther, his attitude toward whites was frequently hostile. He had white musicians in his band and did not boycott the rock world, but he said that he would rather be popular among black youths and drew attention to his influences from such black artists as Sly Stone, Jimi Hendrix, and James Brown. In some situations, his position was particularly ambiguous, such as when he expressed contempt for the rock world when interviewed by *Melody Maker* right before his appearance at the Isle of Wight Festival (Szwed 2002, 315–18).[14] It was only reasonable for a black artist, however, to be skeptical of the white press and music industry. White representation and ownership had long produced racial inequality and ignorance of black voices. In this context, Miles's remark that "I don't play rock, I play *black*" (ibid., 287) makes perfect sense.

Conclusion

There is no evidence that rock and roll affected jazz in any substantial way in the 1950s. Jazz was affected to some extent by the folk revival and gradually became a more insular and elitist music as experimentation within art jazz escalated. The situation changed in the mid 1960s with the recession in jazz, the sense of exhaustion, and the British Invasion. After the Monterey Pop Festival in 1967, when rock had become more accepted and the pressures on the jazz business were greater, some jazz writers saw the possibility of a convergence of jazz and rock. Jazz magazines and festivals opened the door to contemporary styles of popular music of which rock dominated, and younger jazz musicians, mostly whites, began experimenting with rock influences. This music was termed jazz-rock and created divisions between younger and older jazz people, with the particular exception of Miles who changed his established position in jazz. In retrospect, the term fusion more adequately represents the plurality and hybridity of the phenomenon.

In the early 1970s, it was clear that there would be no convergence of jazz and pop. Jazz and pop artists continued to influence each other, but they have largely fallen into different camps because they work from different concepts and in distinct networks. The jazz-influenced music by artists such as (in more or less chronological order) Frank Zappa, Santana, Steely Dan, Tom Waits, Joni Mitchell, and Elvis Costello is not difficult to distinguish from the pop-influenced music of Miles Davis, Weather Report, Steps Ahead, and John Scofield. There is some audience overlap, but the degree of specialization that some genres require creates boundaries for the musicians and their music. One of the residual areas that should be mentioned is the mass-media world of film, TV, and commercials, in which the music's functions and the ideologies of the industry allow for certain forms of genre blending, such as the commercial strain of fusion known as smooth jazz or Muzak. Quincy Jones, Jan Hammer, and thousands of lesser figures have produced volumes of music in this large and diverse area of jazz-derived music, which has a much wider circulation than "pure" jazz.

Like the previous chapter, this one ends with the basic transformation and modernization of the genre. Another study could say more about the further differentiation of the network in the 1970s and about later moments of modernization where artists connected with salsa, hip-hop, roots music, the jam band scene, and techno. Obvious examples are the Bad Plus, John Scofield, and Cassandra Wilson. Chapters 5 and 6 discuss examples from the contemporary Chicago scene. For the most part, we have seen minor tendencies; nothing has come close to the deep transformations of the early fusion period around 1970. The situation is similar in rock, where artists have borrowed from some of the same musics as jazz musicians without causing major changes in the genre. A major difference is that rock has become a component in a larger culture of pop genres.

It should be noted that the reactions to rock in jazz were less systemic than in country music, and that part of the reason is that jazz had a more complex geography and was mainly in the hands of independent labels. There was not the same top-down control and concentration of major labels as with country music in Nashville. The division between traditional country and modern country-pop had a parallel in jazz between acoustic art jazz and fusion, but the situation was different in that art jazz was a divided culture with a major boundary between neo-bop and avant-garde jazz. The transformation also had different geographical dynamics. Whereas the coun-terreaction in country was mobilized in the American West, in jazz it was mobilized less in the United States than in Europe, where countless small labels emerged in the 1960s and 1970s. One of the most influential was the German ECM label, which became a refuge for many American artists in and provided a space in between the commercial conditions of fusion and the precarious economy and radicalism of avant-garde jazz.

Urban Boundaries

Figure 8 Front door of the Thrill Jockey offices, 2003. Photo by the author.

CHAPTER FIVE

Jeff Parker and the Chicago Jazz Scene

I am standing in the Chicago Cultural Center in late January 2003. It is the first night of the annual Chicago Jazz Fair, an event that introduces many newcomers to local artists. One of the first bands I hear is Ernest Dawkins's New Horizons Ensemble. I am immediately attracted by the spiritual power of the music. A fascinating play between the familiar and the unfamiliar unfolds in long, thoughtful dialogues. The music speaks of a troubled world but not a world without soul, tradition, and community. There is a warm atmosphere, a sense of shared joy. I am listening somewhat impressionistically as a private person, and my experience is further conditioned by the fact that I have never heard these musicians before. I have never even heard of them. Then a guitarist picks up a solo. He plays a few notes and stops for a second. Looks uncertain, as if he is searching for an answer. Another phrase takes shape. It evolves unexpectedly and does not follow classic jazz models. In a distinctive way, he is playing as a listener, and I find it very musical.

One of the things I did not immediately recognize during my first encounter with these musicians is that they do not have a genre-centered identity. This is especially true of the guitarist, Jeff Parker. His pathways provide fascinating perspectives on the hybrid spaces across jazz and popular music scenes in Chicago. I had no idea that the show in the Cultural Center was a step toward a study of any kind. I had just arrived from Denmark and was immersing myself in the intellectual life of the University of Chicago as a visiting scholar. If the purpose of my trip had been fieldwork on jazz, any scholar would have considered New York, but Chicago proved to be a rich site of inquiry. Indeed, I found it a valuable alternative to the New York scene, which is marked by the powerful presence of star soloists and by touristy upscale Manhattan clubs. It does not take a Marxist to spot the commoditization of jazz in contemporary society; a process that has been sustained by Woody Allen movies and episodes of *Seinfeld* and *Sex and the City* in which the jazz club is a place to eat and talk rather than actually hear music. The Chicago scene is generally less touristy and more grassroots based.

Ideology and Reality

I started doing fieldwork as a somewhat detached analyst, but questions about genre continuously brought up ideological issues, and the interaction with my subjects in a world that is quite different from Denmark transformed my perspective on many things. I was active in the field for more than one year and seized the opportunity to discuss drafts of the present ethnography with my informants at various stages. This brought us closer and created a new layer of dialogical reflexivity. Knowledge does not eliminate ideology, though, and there are a few general issues that I should like to address.

My field research focused on Jeff Parker and some of his many collaborators, including Josh Abrams, Ted Sirota, and Tortoise, and their connections with local record labels and clubs. Their music can be identified broadly in the space between jazz and contemporary popular musics, but the boundaries are particular to the social and ideological context of the local network in which they operate. They work in a small-scale economy, usually recording for independent labels and earning between $40 and $120 per gig, sometimes more, sometimes nothing at all. Their music falls outside the radar of major record labels and commercial radio for the sole reason that it is instrumental and has a small market. The musicians value artistic freedom highly and do not consider corporate production an option. They have slightly romanticized notions of small-scale production, but I was wrong when I in typical academic fashion approached these ideologies of production as more or less fictitious constructs. That made it difficult for me to take their subjectivities seriously in the beginning. The boundary between majors and indies is blurred, but it has very concrete and tangible implications for these particular musicians. It is also certain that their small local network would not exist without the grassroots efforts of a number of core artists and producers that can be described as organic intellectuals, to use a Gramscian term.

Ideology also shapes the boundaries of jazz discourse in the city, though some gatekeepers pretend to be neutral. The influential voices of the Chicago-based *Down Beat* and Chicago Public Radio favor mainstream jazz over experimental jazz and do not provide a broad perspective on jazz culture and the life-worlds of individual artists and listeners. Magazines and textbooks generally ignore politically engaged music such as Ed Wilkerson's "jazz opera" about Harold Washington (Chicago's first African American mayor) and Ernest Dawkins's large-scale work about a 1968 trial of antiwar activists.[1] These are just two examples of a Chicago tradition of politically engaged jazz. It has beauty and spiritual power, and musically it belongs to the core of jazz, so why is it ignored? The fact remains that the systematic repression of politics in dominant jazz discourse has implications for how people define jazz.[2]

Locating the Local

When I discovered how rich the jazz scene is, I wondered why I had not heard more about it. My curiosity increased as I met jazz fans in Chicago who were largely unfamiliar with the local jazz scene. Those who were familiar with more than a few local artists usually knew the scene quite well, which indicates that it is a specialized culture with a small but intense network. Many insiders are involved in or have a personal relation to someone who is creating or mediating the music. A long-term insider at one of the important local record labels described the label's audience as "active listeners": "Our consumers are not kids, they are a little bit more experienced listeners. And for that reason, I think we have a pretty steady consumer relationship. We don't get as huge booms, and we don't get those huge drop-offs either, because it's the hard-core music fan, the obsessive fan, if you will" (Bettina Richards, conversation with author, Chicago, 17 November 2003).

First of all, Chicago has no big jazz stars, and the scene gets little coverage in international publications. The recordings are produced by local labels with small marketing budgets.[3] Most European jazz scholars know about the avant-garde scene in the 1960s and 1970s but have heard virtually nothing about the contemporary scene. The scene is also somewhat self-sufficient in that musicians do not tour as much as musicians in New York. It is easier for Chicago musicians to make a living playing within the city, and their market outside is smaller because they are not as famous. Jazz stars in New York get more press coverage and generally rely more on income from recordings and big festivals in Europe. There is thus a self-sustaining differentiation within the jazz network that helps maintain New York's status as the global center.

To my knowledge, the only Chicago-based jazz artist signed to a major label is Kurt Elling (b. 1967), who is on Blue Note, a subsidiary of EMI. Patricia Barber (b. 1955) has been on a major label and is now distributed by Blue Note, but she has chosen to be on a local indie called Premonition and has said that independent production "might be our only hope in this corporate vortex of a culture" (Friedman 1998). The Art Ensemble of Chicago has recorded several times for ECM, which has a distribution deal with BMG, but this is unusual for jazz artists in Chicago. Elling and Barber are arguably the only two artists with broad appeal in the international jazz market, and their singing is a key factor here. Compared with local colleagues, they are featured more often on National Public Radio and in cover stories in jazz magazines. It is striking that Elling in particular is frequently identified as an international artist ("Blue Note recording artist," "Grammy winner," "winner of *Down Beat*'s readers' poll") rather than a local artist. He has performed at the Green Mill, for instance, on a weekly basis for more than ten years, and it was in this club that Blue Note's president, while visiting from New York, discovered him.

The presentation of the Green Mill in tourist guidebooks draws on the mythology of the Prohibition era, when the club was owned by Al Capone, and the legend of this golden era of "Chicago jazz" in public memory keeps discourse on jazz in Chicago fixed in the past. This is also reflected in popular histories (e.g., Ciccone 1999) and films such as *Chicago* (Miramax, 2002), which was shot almost entirely in Seattle, the exception being one scene at the Green Mill. None of the tourist guidebooks really gives a sense of the city's contemporary live music scenes.[4] The historical asymmetry also exists in jazz studies, as evidenced by *The New Grove Dictionary of Jazz* (Kernfeld 2002). This dictionary features many musicians of the 1920s and virtually none of the 1990s, although the second edition (2002) was promoted for its addition of fifteen hundred biographies of artists that emerged in the 1980s and 1990s.[5] It has entries on Barber, Elling, and Ken Vandermark, whose reputation grew when he was awarded a MacArthur Fellowship in 1999. But it has no entries on Josh Abrams, Jim Baker, Jeb Bishop, David Boykin, the Chicago Underground, Dana Hall, Isotope 217, Robert Mazurek, Nicole Mitchell, Jeff Parker, Liz Payne, Avreeayl Ra, Ted Sirota, Chad Taylor, or Michael Zerang.

Contemporary jazz by local artists (in 2003–5) is strikingly absent from Chicago Public Radio, which broadcasts a great deal of jazz.[6] It covers the annual jazz festival and new albums from Elling and Barber, but that's about it. Out of the station's list of twenty-one "best albums of 2003," only three involved Chicago-based musicians, and the avant-garde was not represented. Three full hours every Sunday afternoon are allocated to "Jazz with Dick Buckley," celebrating classic recordings of traditional jazz and swing music. On National Public Radio, Marian McPartland hosts the program "Piano Jazz," and it generally features New York–based musicians. Buckley and McPartland are both over well over seventy years old and have hosted their shows since 1977 and 1978, respectively. There are a couple of younger jazz hosts on these two public radio stations, but they, too, present little or no avant-garde jazz. The only stations that play contemporary and avant-garde jazz by Chicago-based artists are three college radio stations and a community station. WNUR at Northwestern University occasionally broadcasts from local clubs and bring musicians to the studio for interview or performance, and it receives promotional copies from local labels. The station's jazz music director, Mark Cartwright, informed me by e-mail that he asks his deejays "to make 1/3 of the music they play on their show be from Chicago... this doesn't always happen since we get a lot more non-Chicago recordings than Chicago ones, but we try" (Cartwright, e-mail to author, 18 February 2004)." He added that "all of our music is nonmainstream." This statement relied on a commonsense distinction between "mainstream," which is identified with styles such as swing and hard bop, and "nonmainstream," identified with experimental styles and nonconformist aesthetics. WHPK at the University of Chicago and WZRD at Northeastern University do not have quite the same editorial emphasis on the local scene (Daniel Groll, e-mail to author, 19 February 2004).[7]

The two major daily newspapers, the *Chicago Tribune* and the *Chicago Sun-Times,* and the weekly *Chicago Reader* have a small but regular and broad coverage of the scene. Core jazz writers such as Peter Margasak, Howard Reich, Neil Tesser, and Kevin Whitehead are open to many kinds of jazz, except smooth jazz and Dixieland. Margasak, Whitehead, and John Corbett have been enthusiastic about fusions with indie rock and experimental music and have made efforts to bring national attention to these activities in Chicago.[8]

At the *Tribune,* Reich writes from the perspective of the art jazz canon. Having covered a variety of musics in the 1970s, he devoted himself exclusively to jazz when he was appointed staff writer in 1983. He is now one of the two or three full-time jazz writers in the country, and that says something about the presence of jazz in the national public sphere.[9] Reich has written enthusiastically about Jeff Parker but has not dealt with his eclecticism, and Parker's work on the rock scene is covered by the rock critic Greg Kot.[10] When I asked Reich about meeting him and Kot at the *Tribune* on the same day, he responded: "I must say that I almost never see Greg Kot, as we operate in very different worlds," which is surprising considering that they are office neighbors (Reich, e-mail to author, 4 March 2004). The worlds he is referring to are the small jazz scene and the much larger world of rock and pop. At one point he simply stated that "Greg Kot writes about popular music, and I write about unpopular music" (Reich, conversation with author, Chicago, 29 March 2004).

Chicago and New York

Chicago's cultural life is defined in relation to larger cities, especially New York and Los Angeles. Because the real estate prices are lower and there is much less corporate culture industry, Chicago has come to be viewed as a good place for experimentation in grassroots settings, not only in jazz and experimental popular music, but also in other arts. In theater, for instance, there is also a broad independent scene compared to the small off-Broadway scene in Manhattan. Film follows the same pattern, but this art form requires larger production teams, and film production is more centralized nationally.

As we explore how various people make sense of the situation, it gets harder to separate myth and reality. This is evidenced by the so-called second-city syndrome associated with Chicago's perceived inferiority complex with respect to New York. It sustains narratives of absence and deficiency, and it tends to obscure the fact that Chicago, like all other places, has its own unique culture. An illustrative example is the series of radio shows with the title "Should I Stay or Should I Go?" that was broadcast over a week in early 2004 on Chicago Public Radio (Chicago Public Radio, 30 January 2004),[11] Each day was devoted to a different art form, and the focus on weaknesses was most apparent among filmmakers: "The theatrical film industry is not a local business, it's a national business, and whoever controls distribution controls the power, and all the distributors are either in Los Angeles or New York, so without viable distribution our film goes nowhere," said a local producer of independent film. A filmmaker involved in a Hollywood production in Chicago reported that her producers would not even consider casting the main characters in Chicago "because they think if you're an actor, you should be in New York or L.A."[12]

Some of the same logic governs the pages of *Down Beat*, which is run out of an office in the Chicago suburb Elmhurst. The editor, Jason Koransky (b. 1974), came to the magazine in 1999 from a job as editor of the Web site "Chicago Center Stage," which concentrates on the rock scene. (Incidentally, this illustrates that gatekeepers of a genre are not necessarily purists.) He has lived in Chicago for more than ten years and daily negotiates the balance between coverage of Chicago and the rest of the world. "We're based here, but we're distributed in more than 100 countries," he says, talking about how he is careful not to let Chicago dominate.[13] He has no reservations about New York–centricity, though: "If you really want to know what's happening on the jazz scene, you got to go to New York." His goal is not so much to represent all countries as to follow the dominant values of the global market. This has implications for the representation of jazz as a genre in the magazine:

> Well, you know... *Down Beat* is... We try to reach a large audience. Peter Brötzmann will never be on the cover of *Down Beat*. Unfortunately, he is a good musician but we are on newsstands around the world and we try to compete with other newsstand publications, so we got to be good to recognize faces. Also if someone really wants to get into the avant-garde scene, they'll pick up *Signal to Noise* or the *Wire*, you know, something that is maybe more focused on that, because right now, at this stage of *Down Beat*'s history, it's something we cover, and we cover it consistently, but it's not the major focus of the magazine. We focus more on the straight-ahead side, and we're expanding more on the world music side. World music, blues, and the jam band type scene. (Koransky, conversation with author, Elmhurst, Illinois, 5 December 2003)

Koransky has been great for *Down Beat*'s business and has attracted many young readers, and one of his great initiatives is having musicians write for the magazine. He is running a business, however, that privileges big names and popular taste. He continuously applauds Chicago for the few local musicians that have a national reputation and emphasizes how well they have mastered their craft and are grounded in "the tradition."[14] Koransky's statements are typical of the national mainstream jazz discourse that tells us that Elling is of international interest and Dawkins is not. One could hope that there was room for greater diversity in the marketplace. The two big international magazines, *Down Beat* and *Jazz Times*, dominate the genre discourse and sustain a hierarchy between different jazz cultures. The more eclectic magazines to which Koransky refers only represent some of the marginal spaces, and not even the most eclectic magazines are all-embracing.

A contrasting perspective is provided by Bettina Richards (b. 1965), who worked for major record labels in New York before she started her own label, Thrill Jockey, in 1992. Richards "didn't like that corporate treatment of music... the way they treat artists as commodity" (Richards, conversation with author, 17 November 2003).[15] The Chicago indie label Touch and Go was a source of inspiration, and in 1995 she moved her business to Chicago. Many of her artists were based there, and the costs of operation were lower.

She also found that musicians have more freedom in a city with fewer industry agents. Her label became the prime outlet for the wave of Chicago indie
rock (a.k.a. "post-rock") that came to national attention around the time the
Seattle grunge scene was fading in the mid 1990s. Richards has a unique perspective on genre in local cultural production because of her experience in
New York and her contact with influential artists on various scenes:

> I think Chicago is outside of the main media spotlights. New York and
> L.A., there is much more industry there, either publishing magazines
> and stuff or actual record labels. I think of Chicago as a sort of wood-
> shedder's paradise. People can really practice and work on the craft of
> their music. I don't know if I can encapsulate the sound or anything but
> there is an attitude, an ethic for musicians who stay in Chicago. They
> stay here because it's a really healthy city to work and create in. It's
> more affordable, there are lots of places to play, labels . . . But if you're
> looking for the limelight, you would probably go to L.A. or New York. So
> I think there's commonality to the approach, and that attracts all kinds
> of musicians. Certainly, for free music for example, the history of the
> AACM in this town, just like there's a history of experimental theater,
> there's a history of adventuresome[ness] that I think feeds on itself and
> gives people a network and a history to draw upon. (Conversation with
> author, Chicago, 17 November 2003)

Talking about "those who stay" is common in Chicago, and many artists
think about leaving. There has been a pattern, at least since Louis Armstrong's departure in 1929, of artists moving to New York once they have
reached a certain level of fame, not to mention the many who have moved
in the hope of becoming famous. Although New York's magnetic power can
be registered all over America, it is particularly strong in Chicago's cultural
life because the competition is stronger. This adds complexity to the notion
of Chicago as an alternative with local traditions. Richards goes on to talk
about the relation between social conditions and musical practice:

> Collaborations come easier. . . . Also, the purely financial, you know, if
> you live in New York, getting your gear from your apartment to the
> place of the gig is extremely difficult because people don't have cars. You
> usually share a practice space. You have very fixed amount of time. . . .
> Compared to Chicago, where it's much easier to rent practice space,
> have [a] home studio, all this kind of stuff. . . . I don't necessarily think
> the musicians [in Los Angeles or New York City] are less inclined, I just

think it's a lot more difficult. The rent is so much higher. You got to work so much more to pay your rent. How are you going to join five other groups?! There are many people who do it in New York. I mean, Jim O'Rourke lives in New York, and he plays in a lot of stuff, it's just much more difficult to do, and he's fortunate to have Sonic Youth... to have financial means to allow him more time. It's not that the musicians here are in some way entirely different from there, but the environment fosters an attitude. (Conversation with author, 17 November 2003)

If the elite in New York have the means to collaborate, is Chicago merely a cul-de-sac for those who cannot make it in New York, or does it have something else to offer? This question looms over the city, and the answers are full of contradictions. At the heart of the matter is the contingency of cultural value to particular places. There is general agreement, for instance, that New York has the largest group of elite artists, but how does one measure differences in the musical and social atmosphere? Moreover, attempts to measure two different places have reductive implications because they presuppose common standards. Jeff Parker is familiar with this problematic, both as a local artist and as a collaborator with New York musicians. At one of the formal interviews I conducted in his home, he first responded by describing advantages and disadvantages of being in Chicago:

> Some of the advantages are that it's not as expensive.... I can think of Chicago, New Orleans, and Austin, Texas, as the only three cities in the U.S., generally, where musicians can make a living only working within the city and the suburbs.... Another great thing is the independent labels....
>
> The disadvantages: A lot of the musicians, myself included, don't really have the confidence, don't play with the authority that a lot of the musicians out in New York do. Probably without a doubt, jazzwise, the best musicians in the world live in New York, man. Definitely. I wouldn't say the most creative because... I think I'm getting off the subject here... yeah, I think a lot of the musicians here, they don't play with the assertiveness as musicians in New York.... Ah, it's so complex! I have talked and talked about this so much, man. (Conversation with author, Chicago, 4 November 2003)

This statement goes beyond the usual complaints about being in Chicago. Parker focuses on how the urban hierarchy shapes musical practice and subjectivity (notice his use of the words confidence, authority, and assertiveness).

A few minutes later, he returns to the problematic with a more personal perspective:

> So this is my take on it—and it's a total outsider's view because I've never lived in New York.
>
> So much of the music industry is in New York City—major labels, A & R guys—and that coupled with a big overhead, somebody who's living there, paying a $1,000 or $1,500 a month for the rent, they don't really have time to experiment. They're trying to work, they're always dealing with that industry standard, you know. Like if X such-and-such musician is hot, then everybody gotta sound like them, and you can hear it in the records, man. Every guitar player playing like so-and-so. A lot of saxophone players playing like one guy and then piano players play like this dude, and all the bass players and drummers they just follow that industry standard because they gotta work. They gotta eat. They don't want to hear someone up there who's trying to work out their own stuff. They gotta get the gig—they gotta keep it. That's a social condition and it affects the music. Here, cats don't have to deal with that. They can be, "I wanna do this," you know, and they can afford to play like six $40 gigs in a week, and they can still pay their rent. They can experiment. Find your niche. For better or worse, it's more freedom. That's really important, man. (Conversation with author, 4 November 2003)

This says something about what Chicago has to offer musicians and what some of them are looking for. It is typical that Chicago's difference from New York is articulated mainly through the opposition between those who identify with non-mainstream music and those who gravitate toward the national mainstream. The latter group does not have positive views of Chicago's difference, which explains why they are less ambivalent about the second-city syndrome. Parker is talking about the freedom of working in an environment with room for diversity and experimentation, and about the fact that the independent labels in Chicago generally give musicians the freedom to produce their own music. It is also easier to survive with a small market because the costs of operation are lower. Parker may have generalized a bit in this conversation, but that does not disqualify the truth of his basic message.

The value problem extends into the distinction between mainstream and non-mainstream music. A typical argument in the mainstream camp is that avant-garde artists are not more creative but less professional, so they cannot save Chicago's national reputation. Most mainstream jazz people are diplomatic enough not to say this publicly, and I got the sense that I was touching on a delicate issue when I asked them about this. (They would usually not articulate this view in formal interviews, and I shall therefore not reveal their identities.) The concept of mainstream jazz is difficult to pin down. In addition to its identification with swing and hard bop, perhaps with a few modal elements and occasional outside playing, its critics describe it as commercially safe, somewhat predictable, and, more negatively, as narrow-minded and slick. Some of the artists associated with the term include tenor sax players such as Hank Mobley and Dexter Gordon of the 1960s, contemporary New York stars such as Wynton Marsalis, Roy Hargrove, and Christian McBride, and smaller fish such as Jim Rotundi, Mike LeDonne, Eric Alexander, Dave Hazeltine, and Steve Davis. Elling and Barber have been identified with mainstream because of their pop and rock influence and the smoothness of their music.

The term non-mainstream is centered on what jazz historians call free jazz or avant-garde, but the musicians instead use the terms free improv, improvised music, and creative music. These terms were used synonymously and as alternatives to dominant jazz discourse and genre categories. Jeff Parker and his collaborators all dissociated themselves from mainstream jazz, even though they sometimes played mainstream gigs. Their concept of non-mainstream is informed by a skepticism of commercialism and standardization, as indicated by Parker's critique of the formulaic jazz sound in the Blue Note productions of the late 1980s and early 1990s; a sound appreciated by many as an essential jazz sound. The output from the indie jazz labels in Chicago has some homogeneity, too, but it is not standardized and industry-regulated to as great a degree.

The distinction between "experimental Chicago" and "mainstream New York" is a simplification sustained by the power of the Manhattan mainstream scene and the notion of Chicago as an alternative. Howard Reich has played with this imagery by calling New York "the undisputed capital of slick, mainstream forms of [jazz]" and describing Chicago as superior in "indie jazz," a term he associates with "provocative innovations," "idiosyncratic talent," and independent labels (Reich, "Sonic Boom: Chicago's Independent Jazz Artists Improvise Their Own Riffs on Success," *Chicago Tribune*, 8 April 2001, Magazine, 12). This carries an element of local patriotism that may appeal to some readers of the *Tribune*. With Richards and Parker, the positive image of Chicago is related to their success in this city. People who have been unluckier are usually less optimistic, and some of those who have relocated to New York feel that Chicago is provincial. An infamous example is the Jim O'Rourke cover story in *Wire* (November

2001) in which O'Rourke says that Chicago's "improv and electronic music" scene is very overrated (Keenan 2001a, 40), but he is not impartial and
sounds a bit self-righteous in this part of the interview.

Genre and Scene

My musician informants did not talk much about generic concepts in everyday conversations. They seemed to have little time for talking about what
they played, and their ordinary language was expectedly vernacular rather
than academic. I was prepared for musicians to question the validity of the
genre concept when I introduced it, and I tried to do so when they were in
a reflective mood. They associated the category with educators and writers,
but with few exceptions they felt that it was relevant and felt no doubt that
music categories had had important consequences for their careers. The following statement, made by Parker upon reading a project description for my
genre research, is illustrative: "I went to your Web site, and your project
sounds really interesting to me. The whole issue of genre/classification with
regard to music is something I've been interested in for a long time, especially in recent years, mostly because it's something I've been forced to confront (by default) because of certain artistic, professional paths I've chosen
to take" (Parker, e-mail to author, 18 February 2003).[16] Parker's musical education (see p. 132–33) has influenced his thinking about genre in musical
practice, as an excerpt from a conversation with another interviewer shows:
"I feel that I play both jazz and improvised music. To me, there are specific
parameters that inform the genre of jazz improvisation. To me, it is having a
certain harmonic conception, rhythmic conception, in order for you to deal
with the most obvious characteristics of that music. But as far as improvisation, that is a very broad term that applies to many genres, inside and
around art and music" (Jung 2002).

More frequent in everyday discourse was the term scene. This term became common in jazz terminology in the 1950s and has also been used
in discourses of other musics and of other art forms.[17] In the late 1980s,
"scene" became a central concept in popular music studies, in which it was
positioned by some as an alternative to the concept of subculture. Hesmondhalgh critiques scene theory in this field and doubts that it can become a
useful academic concept (2005, 27–30). I cannot reach the same conclusion
because the term is still central to many people, and I find it striking that
he does not deal with its vernacular basis, except to mention in passing that
it can be a source of further confusion. It is not particularly confusing when
used as a commonsense term for a particular music culture in a city. Nor do

I agree with Hesmondhalgh that the concept of scene should be replaced by genre. I think they are complementary concepts. The concept of scene provides a local perspective on genre. It creates a close and fairly straightforward connection between the abstract notion of genre and its concrete relation with practices occurring in a particular place. Because it is common to think about musical life in terms of scenes, we can assume that it forms a ground in many people's understanding of generic categories. It represents the immediate social space and network in which a music is experienced and articulated locally. Genres have their own local life, embodied in the clubs, artists, and audiences that continue to bring the music alive and form a scene. There is also a translocal level of interaction between local scenes and scenes in other cities. Scenes struggle in the national urban hierarchy, as we have seen.

Like the concept of culture, the concept of scene has been plagued by holistic views that create a false sense of unity. To be sure, jazz culture in Chicago cannot be understood as a singular and clearly bounded entity, but it still makes sense to speak of a Chicago jazz scene, of an overall jazz scene in the city. Musician networks are structured by identity categories such as age and race and by differences in musical style and level of professionalism. Many musicians also work outside their immediate circle, and the various forms of collaboration resemble a spiderweb rather than a simple system.

Chicago and Its Jazz Scene

Chicago's jazz scene has been divided between the black South Side and the white North Side since the 1920s, when Chicago was the main destination of the Great Migration. The South Side is no longer a thriving cultural center, though. It suffered disproportionably from the deindustrialization process that began in the 1960s and culminated in the 1970s.[18] In the 1960s, a vibrant black avant-garde community organized itself independently of the jazz establishment, but even this community almost died out in the late 1970s. A lot of business disappeared from the South Side, and new entertainment districts emerged in Lincoln Park on the North Side (Grazian 2003, chapter 5). Today, there are very few places with live jazz performances more than once a week on the South Side and West Side (west of West Town). To my knowledge, the Velvet Lounge is the only such place on the South Side, and it almost ceased to exist when the landlord sold the property to developers in 2005.[19]

Apart from a few mainstream-oriented downtown venues that cater to businesspeople and tourists, most of the venues for live jazz are small clubs on the North Side that feature more experimental jazz and attract students and aspiring musicians who can afford the typical cover charge, usually of $5 to $12. In this respect, it is paradoxical that the flagship of jazz in the heart of the city, the Jazz Showcase, does not present many local artists but instead focuses on international mainstream stars that other clubs cannot afford.[20] During my time in the city, very few of the non-mainstream artists performed there. The owner of the place laments that his club is the only club for "national jazz" (Mandel 1999, 205), and let me remind you that this does not include the music of the Art Ensemble of Chicago.[21] It is similarly striking that the jazz series organized by the Chicago Symphony Center in the 2003–5 seasons was a showcase for stars such as Wynton Marsalis, Cassandra Wilson, Herbie Hancock, and Keith Jarrett, none of whom are based in Chicago.

A restructuring of Chicago's economy began in the 1990s under the influence of changes in the global economy. Sassen (2001) describes a new global economy emerging from a massive increase in the volume of transactions in the transnational financial industry and the concentration of power in a small number of "global cities," while production moves to lower-wage regions. The Chicago metropolitan area is still the third largest city in the country, with 8.6 million people, and it is a financial center with the functions of a global city. Its distance from New York, however, has increased in terms of population, major business sectors, and concentration of foreign finance.[22] The growth in advanced service and finance sectors generates a small group of high-income consumers who sustain the waves of gentrification on the North Side. Gentrification creates unstable conditions for small artist communities such as the indie jazz community in the neighborhood of Wicker Park in West Town. The conditions are shaped by larger social forces, among which race is crucial. Chicago is still one of the most racially divided cities in the United States. Abu-Lughod (1999, 331–32) locates three main types of residential zones according to racial and ethnic categories: white zones concentrated on the North Side, African American zones concentrated on the South and West Sides, and Hispanic zones concentrated on the Near Southwest and Northwest Sides. About 42 percent of the city's population is white, 36 percent African American, and 25 percent Hispanic (of any race), so this typology involves large segments of the population.[23] Abu-Lughod argues that some of the Hispanic zones function as "buffer zones" between white and black areas. This notion of buffer zones can be extended to the zones of rapid transformation in Pilzen and West Town in which older residents are being priced out of ethnic neighborhoods and younger white yuppies are moving in. The indie jazz community represents one of the momentary formations in the changing and diverse cultural space of

West Town. It emerged in the early 1990s, and although it is now somewhat splintered, it is a component of the area's heterogeneous soundscape characterized by disjunctures that are typical in a big city. Many of the musicians came from other parts of the country and created a neighborhood scene that is only loosely connected to Chicago's jazz traditions. This is an important context for understanding how these musicians cross genre boundaries.

Parker and the Scene

From about 1994 to 2002 Jeff Parker's primary home on the scene was this Wicker Park community. He has always played in various jazz contexts on a more casual basis, and since 2000 or so his work has mainly been divided between the group Tortoise, his solo albums, and various pickup gigs and collaborations in jazz. Before describing Parker's routes within and beyond the jazz scene, I should mention that among the few areas he does not work in are the smooth jazz scene downtown and the "trad jazz" scene, where the majority is white and over fifty.[24] Parker is African American, and his main interests are modern jazz since the late 1950s and various forms of art-oriented and experimental popular music and world music. Let us look at his position on the scene before exploring his individuality in more detail in chapter 6.

Within one year after his arrival in Chicago in 1991, Parker began to work with members of the Association for the Advancement of Creative Musicians (AACM). His connection with this community helped establish his reputation as a local artist. Parker played in the New Horizons Ensemble, one of the lasting AACM bands, like the Art Ensemble of Chicago and Eight Bold Souls. The AACM did not become his home community, however. Parker does not live on the South Side, like most of the organization's members, and most of his long-term collaborations have been based elsewhere. He is technically an "associate member" and has never committed himself exclusively to this community. He collaborates closely with white musicians and is involved in rock music. Since its inception in 1965 the AACM has been an all-black organization with an identity core in free jazz and in notions of artistic and political freedom rooted in the African diaspora (cf. Lewis in press). Several key figures migrated to New York in the late 1970s, and its glory days seem to be over. By 2004, several of the founding members had died, the weekly jam session at Nu Beginnings at 7051 South Crandon Avenue had ended, and the younger musicians were not as politically engaged as the older ones. There were few professional musicians between twenty-five and forty-five, which is the age demographic of Parker's principal collaborators. The Velvet Lounge is the main local club for AACM members, but they also play regularly at places like the HotHouse and the Candlestick Maker. The latter eventually closed in 2006.

It took a while before I discovered that Parker also plays mainstream jazz, a side of him that is unknown to many. It is remarkable to think that he was a mainstream guitarist when he came to Chicago and eventually became an insider of non-mainstream jazz and indie rock circles. During the 1980s he specialized in mainstream jazz as a student and performer in Boston, where he performed with musicians such as Geoffrey Keezer, Antonio Hart, and Roy Hargrove.

Parker plays pickup gigs at various bars and restaurants where jazz is background music to eating and drinking. In 2004, for instance, he had played weekly at Andy's on Hubbard Street for more than a year. Andy's is a bar and restaurant devoted to mainstream jazz as represented by local hard bop tenor sax players such as Marcus Wolfe and Eric Schneider and by the soft soul jazz of the guitarist Bobby Broom. A large part of the audience is middle-aged tourists and businessmen. Parker works there as a sideman with Ari Brown, who is a longtime AACM member but also enjoys playing mainstream.

Parker also crosses the boundaries between mainstream and non-mainstream in other ways. As a member of Ted Sirota's Rebel Souls, he has worked in the space between hard bop and free jazz and performed at mainstream-oriented clubs. One of them is the Green Mill, a bastion of mainstream with some room for free jazz elements. Free jazz is featured periodically on Sunday afternoons and someone like Vandermark may appear on a weeknight, for example, when he has made a new album. The club tends to showcase younger musicians and have a younger audience. The owner, Dave Jemilo, prefers not to have fusion and smooth jazz in his club, and electric bass players and synthesizers are not welcome (Jemilo, conversation with author, Chicago, 16 March 2004). Still, many of the musicians who perform there have integrated elements of rock and other popular genres in their performance styles and compositions, and one occasionally hears the sound of a screaming saxophone and a guitar with a rock edge. Elling draws on pop jazz, Tin Pan Alley, and fusion, and Barber contrasts smooth and traditional singers with her leanings toward rock. Her label, Premonition, generally has mainstream-oriented artists, including Broom, John McLean, Von Freeman, and others. The particular culture at the Green Mill depends on Jemilo's close contact with local artists and his decision to feature the same artists each night of the week except Friday and Saturday. The predominantly local audience comes for the music and the vibrant atmosphere in the historical aura of the largely intact 1920s interior. It is the only jazz club in Chicago at which there is a long line on the street after nine o'clock a couple of nights a week, even in the freezing Chicago winter.

The history of broad-minded mainstream musicians goes back at least to Von Freeman (b. 1923), who has been a mentor to several free jazz musicians.[25] Other mainstream communities have little contact with free jazz. A small circle of older African American musicians on the South Side, including Jimmy Ellis and Charles Walton, spent some of their formative years in the area's large black entertainment world in the 1940s and 1950s. They have kept their distance from the South Side avant-garde. Walton, who died in 2005, did not think of the AACM as a central part of the scene. He told me that this "abstract music" comes "from the sessions and the black people that hung [out] in Chicago University" in the 1960s. His view of the AACM was underpinned by cultural barriers: To him, music had always been a business rather than high art. Musicians were "supposed to play in all idioms" to satisfy the needs of audiences at social affairs and dances. Being a black drummer on the South Side the 1950s, it was only natural for him to play with the blues players Willie Dixon and Jimmy Reed as well as some early rock and roll singers. He played in the house bands at the rock shows at the Regal Theater and wrote the script for a documentary on the deejay Al Benson, who played various kinds of black popular music and had a huge following on the South Side (Walton, conversation with author, Chicago, 17 March 2004).[26] It should be mentioned that Parker has even less contact with the middle-aged white mainstream community represented by the Chicago Jazz Orchestra, a repertory band formed by Bill Russo.

The Indie Jazz Community

The musicians in the indie jazz community share an eclectic aesthetic of which avant-garde jazz as an important component. They have a solid training in post-bebop jazz but grew up listening to many different kinds of music and developed a more eclectic and experimental taste while in their twenties. They borrow from rock, hip-hop, soul, reggae, and avant-garde classical music, and several of them are active on other scenes. Judging from his main projects, Ted Sirota is one of the more straight-ahead-oriented musicians. He is from Chicago and regularly attended the Jazz Showcase in his mid teens to hear such icons as Tony Williams, Max Roach, Milt Jackson, and Benny Golson (Sirota, conversation with author, Chicago, 10 November 2003). There was also a time, before he went to Boston to study jazz at Berklee, when he also attended punk rock shows with the Dead Kennedys and Youth Brigade at the Metro. Although he focused on jazz, he always listened to new wave rock and other popular musics, and he has worked on the blues, reggae, and hip-hop scenes.

Josh Abrams is more experimental and lives a somewhat bohemian lifestyle in Wicker Park. Abrams described his activities in March 2003:

> The main things I'm involved in are this band Sticks and Stones with Matana Roberts and Chad Taylor, but they both live in New York now, so we play tours and stuff, but we don't play all the time around Chicago. I play in this band called Town and Country, which is kind of an acoustic chamber group. It focuses a lot on minimalist music. We write all our own music, and that's a bit different because there is jazz influence, but in a much less direct way. And then I play with David Boykin's band and Nikki Mitchell's band. I play with Jeff in a bunch of different things, and there are random gigs, too. Like tomorrow night I'm playing at the Smoke Daddy—it's a more straight-ahead gig—and on Wednesday night there's a peace benefit, where I think I'm going to play with Oscar Brown, Jr. He's a kind of older famous singer. So it changes from week to week, and then there are certain things like what I mentioned first—those are more constant things, you know. (Abrams, conversation with author, Chicago, 3 March 2003)

Note how Abrams describes his various areas of activity. The regular bands are more specialized than the pick-up bands; only some of the bands make recordings, and deejaying brings him out in front of a dancing audience. Abrams works with like-minded musicians from different parts of the jazz scene and from other scenes, so it is not surprising that he does not experience deep divisions between communities and scenes. Nor is it surprising that his approach to categorization is inclusive and plural. Abrams is also typical in that he does not subscribe to jazz magazines and more often reads the *Wire*. Their eclecticism notwithstanding, he and his peers consider themselves jazz musicians. Jazz "forms a kind of center," he says, "it's the tradition I learned from," suggesting that his jazz training enables him to play other kinds of music, too.

This community emerged in the broader atmosphere of hipster- and bohemian-inflected culture across different art scenes in Chicago, and especially in the neighborhoods of West Town. The bohemianism I am referring to is connected with underground and alternative fashions inspired by the 1960s counterculture and by punk. These fashions manifest themselves in some of the neighborhood stores, such as Earwax (an eatery), Reckless Records (a record store), and Myopic and Quimby's (bookstores). There is a heightened sense of identity making in the social life in this neighborhood, involving everything from food to clothes and body language. The musicians share with others a skepticism about gentrification, yuppies, and national chain stores, and like many others in the neighborhood, they are being priced out of their homes and driven into neighborhoods farther west.[27] Rising real estate prices have led to the closing of clubs and lofts that were used for galleries and rehearsal spaces. "Now it's just like west Lincoln Park," said Sirota in November 2003.

I call this the indie jazz community because it is influenced by indie rock and has some of the same underground identity, age profile, and small-scale economy. The music is produced by and identified with independent labels, and the radio situation is similar, although more local: the music is played little on college radio stations outside of Chicago, and none of the artists have gone to major labels. Several of the musicians collaborate with indie rock musicians, typically for a Thrill Jockey album.

The core musicians are in their thirties (in 2004) and primarily live and perform in West Town, with the area between Pulaski, Chicago Avenue, and Devon as a wider radius whose boundaries are currently expanding. There are a few African American musicians, and it is probably the community with the most interracial collaborations on the generally segregated scene.[28] Ken Vandermark (b. 1964) is at the center of one circle of musicians; the other main circle is that around the Chicago Underground, a flexible unit ranging from duo to quintet. The Underground circle shrank when Chad Taylor (b. 1973) moved back to New York in 2001 and Robert Mazurek (b. 1965) moved to Brazil in 2002, though both are still active in Chicago. Other musicians are Josh Abrams (b. 1973), Jeb Bishop (b. 1962), Jeff Parker (b. 1967), and Ted Sirota (b. 1969).[29] They are very active, and few of them need to teach or have a second job.

Out of Vandermark's bands has emerged a new circle of musicians who are generally in their late twenties; some are still on the learning curve. This circle includes Jason Ajemian, Josh Berman, Tim Daisy, Brian Dibblee, Aram Shelton, and Karl Siegfried, and the members often perform at places such as the Hungry Brain and 3030 (at 3030 West Cortland Street; the place closed in 2005).[30] Berman and Dibblee explained to me that there was very little free jazz when Vandermark came to Chicago in 1989 and that Vandermark and the Chicago Underground created a small scene. These younger musicians were attracted to that scene, and this resulted in a minor influx of musicians from other parts of the country in 1999 and 2000 (Berman and Dibblee, conversation with author, the Hungry Brain, 2 May 2004). Some of them were also attracted to Tortoise, but they generally play in acoustic settings

and are less interested in mixing jazz with popular musics. Dibblee added,
"We're young and trying to find our own voices. The tradition to us is what
Miles, Coltrane, and others did, but we do not try to sound like them. We
don't try to canonize jazz." He feels that the past is sometimes an oppressive
force in jazz culture and admits that "there's a division between us and the
traditional jazz scene." Parker has not played much with these musicians,
but he plays with younger musicians, and his Wicker Park circle also works
with a couple of musicians who are ten or twenty years older, including Jim
Baker, Guillermo Gregorio, and Michael Zerang.

Most jazz people in Chicago think of Vandermark's circle as the core
of contemporary white avant-garde jazz in this city, a view that has been
sustained by Corbett's promotion of these musicians under the flexible term
improvised music in his "Critic's Choice" articles in the *Chicago Reader*,
his radio shows, and engagement in the Wednesday night jazz series at the
Empty Bottle.[31] However, there are also rock-influences in the music of the
Vandermark circle. Some of the sounds Vandermark makes on his horn resemble a distorted punk-rock guitar sound, and there are rock elements in
the character and volume of expression in some of his music. "It's that same
kind of energy," says Bettina Richards, talking about "the rock and roll experience" in relation to Vandermark's shows at the Empty Bottle (Richards,
conversation with author, 17 November 2003). He has a core audience of
white college kids at this rock club, where some fans occasionally make energetic moves associated with rock culture. The influence of and crossover
to rock culture can be found in other bands identified with avant-garde jazz.
There are two main reasons the rock influence does not cause much trou-
ble. One is that it happens outside the center of purist jazz culture. Another
is that the dominant distinction between avant-garde and mainstream jazz
cuts across genre boundaries, even when some musical and social aspects
suggest something else.

Local record labels construct their own musical and cultural identities
in close contact with local musician communities. The musicians tend to
think more about generic codes when they represent themselves on recordings because they know that the recording shapes their public image. Their
recordings are more carefully coded "texts" than are live performances, and
the conditions of production are very different. The four most important labels to this community are the jazz and blues label Delmark, the experimental music labels Atavistic and Okka Disk (in Milwaukee), and Thrill Jockey.

Thrill Jockey brings recordings by these jazz musicians to audiences in
other genre networks. The label also encourages jazz musicians to collaborate with musicians based in the city's rock, folk, and electronic music

scenes. Probably every musician on the label has some experience playing rock music, and the artists are in their thirties or early forties, roughly within the same generation as the president of the label. Richards is reluctant to talk about the label's identity and its musical boundaries. She feels that "the musicians create the identity for us" and points to the fact that the label has no logo and lets the musicians produce their own music. It may be true that the label is not "consciously creating an image," as she says, but the productions and the roster do form a territory in dialogue within existing genre cultures.

AUTHOR: So you don't have the same genre-based production system as major labels. You don't say, "This is going to be a rock record so let's follow this scheme of production and marketing"?

BETTINA RICHARDS: No, no . . . we really try not to. . . . We think of the music as the music on a record and not like, "Okay, we're gonna to put it into this category and do that now." I think categories are like barriers. Once you name it as something, certain people say, "Oh, I don't like that!" It's a barrier. If you just present it as what it is and not name it as such, then I think . . . and this is where you're getting into the blurred line. Completely blurred. Naming it as a genre only limits it. (Richards, conversation with author, Chicago, 17 November 2003)

This resistance to categories is underpinned by the opposition to corporate production. The indie market is small and operates outside the big media channels, so Thrill Jockey tries to appeal to avenues outside conventional genre cultures, including skateboarding and inter-art magazines. These conditions shape the particular rhetorics of hybridity in the self-representation of Richards and many others in this community. However, even this emphatically hybrid culture does not transcend genre categories. Rock culture is a common point of reference for musicians on the label, and jazz is one of the other important domains (the label put out a brochure in 2003 entitled "Jazz on Thrill Jockey"). Richards recognizes that the musicians come from different scenes and that they are trying to push genre boundaries. She feels that the musicians have great freedom to do so in the process of making a record, but that genre becomes an issue in the distribution process:

I think the practical ways that happens is, for example, if there's a magazine that's a folk music magazine, no matter whether we really want them to write about Isotope, for instance, there's some point that I know . . . jazz is maybe too wide to cross, and we're not going to force that record on

a very specialized magazine. Similarly there are certain stores . . . if it's a
store that sells all hip-hop and it's a great store, something that we might
think has blurred the line, that we think, "Oh, Tortoise fans might appeal
to hip-hop fans," there is a little crossover there, we might try but there's
going to be records like Bobby Conn, which is a pretty glam rock and roll
record which we wouldn't try to push into that store, because it's not
gonna. . . . As much as I wish that was the reality, you can't force your
reality on somebody else! I mean there are certain practical things that
we have to think of the music, like "Okay, this is a singer-songwriter,
this will probably work in this magazine, and I'm not going to send it
to *Jazz Times.*" But they do have a very open column in *Jazz Times,*
and you can get an amazing amount of stuff in there, or in *Down Beat,*
but there are limits to that gray area. We keep trying to stretch them a
little bit but in practical nature you have to be aware of them. Because
you don't want to be sending out hundreds of records of your bands that
cost money if the magazine or the stores are just going to stock them. At
certain points you're forced to focus your attention—for practical means.
(Richards, conversation with author, Chicago, 17 November 2003)

The *Wire* is perhaps the most important magazine for this label and
its musicians. The magazine functions as a feedback loop between the local and the international, because its representation of Chicago feeds the
cosmopolitan imagination of readers in Chicago and elsewhere.[32] The musicians read the *Wire* and are represented in articles and ads for Thrill Jockey,
for instance. Moreover, since 2003 the magazine has held an annual festival
at the Empty Bottle titled "Adventures in Modern Music."[33] The Chicago
Underground circle and Tortoise have been featured in two cover stories
in late 2000 and early 2001 that contributed to their growing international
recognition. Typically for the *Wire,* they were represented as a group of
serious young artists in a vibrant cosmopolitan space. The November 2000
cover story situates the Underground circle historically with reference to the
AACM. The reporter, David Keenan, enthusiastically argues that the first
album, *Playground* (Delmark, 1996), is "every bit as woozily sunstroked and
timeless as Dylan's *Basement Tapes*" (Keenan 2000, 39). The February 2001
cover story on Tortoise, also by Keenan, starts off at Earwax in Wicker Park,
where the band's frustration with the course of the 2000 presidential election
is linked to the album *Standards* (Thrill Jockey, 2000) and its cover photo of
a shattered American flag. Keenan describes Tortoise's origins in the 1980s
punk and art rock scenes in Chicago and London, and he points to influences
from a wider range of avant-garde jazz and classical music (Keenan 2001b).

Since its inception in 1982, *Wire* has become a leading voice in experimental music cultures with a hip cosmopolitan identity. The core age demographic is roughly twenty-five to forty. As the *Wire* became more important in the early 1990s, its editorial attitude became more self-conscious, and a canon began to take shape. Clearly, the content is not quite as broad and unlimited as the editorial rhetoric suggests. There is an emphasis on eclectic musics in the spaces between contemporary avant-garde forms of jazz, popular, and classical music. In terms of place, the magazine centers on metropolitan areas and on transnational rather than local culture. There are plenty of reports from different places, but they basically present variations of the same type of culture. One does not get the sense that there are musics that can only be understood if moves out of the Western or Westernized metropolis.

Crossing borders in a large but far from global space is also characteristic of the magazine's approach to musical boundaries. Its universalisms and globalisms are characterized by a preference for plural eclecticism rather than simple hyphenated concepts implying a mix of two genres. The magazine is also more difficult to read for a newcomer because it uses generic labels less frequently than one might expect and in a somewhat esoteric fashion. From talking to core readers in the United States, Denmark, and Germany, I have learned that they in fact invest a lot in music categories.[34] The headings and the descriptive language suggest that names of artists and record labels to some extent substitute for music categories. Categories, however, are used in the main headings in the review section: "Avant Rock," "Critical Beats," "Dub," "Electronica," "Hip Hop," "Jazz & Improv," "Outer Limits," "Modern Composition," and "Soundtracks." These categories reflect a strong emphasis on contemporary music with a self-consciously progressive attitude. The dogma that everything transcends categories is a weak postmodern idea, and it is refreshing when someone such as John McEntire of Tortoise critiques many writers for not understanding that his band belongs to a genre, that it is a rock band grounded in rock traditions (Keenan 2001a, 28 and 32).

Figure 9 Jeff Parker, ca. 2002. Photo courtesy of Saverio Truglia.

CHAPTER SIX

A Closer Look at Jeff Parker and His Music

Life-World and Subjectivity

Jeff Parker is in many ways an ordinary guy, balanced and generally in a good mood. He grew up in a suburb in Virginia, went to college in Boston, and has been working as a professional musician since he came to Chicago in 1991. He became a father in 2002 and enjoys family life in his house in West Town. Parker's interests have centered on experimental and underground culture, especially jazz and popular music but also film and literature. He reads magazines such as the *Wire* and, when time permits, also scholarly writings on music. Albert Camus and Franz Kafka made a big impression on him. Parker is commonly perceived to be a kind, reliable, versatile, and perceptive musician, and it is therefore unsurprising that he is a sought-after collaborator.

Parker's interest in many kinds of music has led to the accumulation of thousands of records in his living room. The collection has been trimmed and rearranged a couple of times. When he introduced me to his collection in 2004, he briefly described the major sections as being "R & B, rock, pop, and soul" (6.5 boxes), "hip-hop" (3 boxes), "electro (= house and techno)" (1 box), "reggae, Brazilian, and African" (1 box), "jazz" (7.5 boxes), and "classical," (1.5 boxes) (Parker, conversation with author, Chicago, 3 April 2004). Parker explained that this genre-based system is convenient when he deejays, which he does about four or five times a month.

Like his close collaborators, he feels that dominant jazz discourse is somewhat narrow-minded, and he does not identify himself exclusively with jazz. He prefers not to define jazz, although he makes some defining gestures when he talks about it. This reluctance to define is related to his modest attitude and his sensitivity to generic complexity. He is not a leader type or a dominating personality. His style of self-representation signifies discreet sophistication. He does not dress in a suit, as many mainstream performers do, or in the flashy or provocative styles associated with certain rock cultures.

Instead, Parker usually wears dark pants or jeans and a shirt, some of which are bought in the hip stores in West Town where students, yuppies, artists, and other people of his age go. He does not identify strongly with the dress codes of a particular social group or music genre and could easily pass for a writer, actor, or academic. This, too, makes it easier for him to work in different contexts without adopting different identities. He usually sits down when he plays, even in front of a rock audience of more than two hundred people. Except for a smile, his only bodily movements are some tensing of the face during passages of particular excitement or difficulty. So his body language displays an affinity with the quiet and introverted attitudes typical of jazz rather than rock guitarists. Down to the smallest detail of his finger movements, it is evident that he has internalized the practices and values of jazz musicians.

This informal attitude is shaped by folk impulses in the AACM and indie communities. Many of them are skeptical of the way that expressive culture is reified and standardized in mass-market culture. Josh Abrams says that "in the making of superstars, the corporate industry removes some of the social aspects of music." He values music for "a whole community" rather than "music that's just heard by musicians" (Abrams, conversation with author, Chicago, 3 March 2003.). Parker shares these views and adopts the perspective of the audience when describing the listening modes he had in mind for his first solo album, *Like-Coping* (Delmark, 2003): "I wanted to make a record that people would like, that my mom would like, and that my family will enjoy. That they can invite friends over to the house and put it on. And it sounds good, you know, creates a nice space in the home." Parker hopes that this is an album that "you can just put on and relax if you're around the house." These ideas about music for pleasure and relaxation in the family are far from the dominant attitudes in cultures of art jazz.

"It was a great time," says Parker, telling me how much enjoyed Wicker Park in the late 1990s. He and his colleagues have vividly described to me how they worked and hung out in the same galleries, clubs, rehearsal spaces, and bars in this neighborhood. The indie jazz community thrived there, together with musicians based in other genre cultures. Parker first got into contact with Tortoise at the Rainbo Club, for instance. The club started out in the 1930s as a polka dance hall. Today it is a bar that caters to urban bohemians with sophisticated tastes in contemporary genres such as rock and hip-hop, and this is indicative of cultural changes in the neighborhood.

This neighborhood scene began to splinter around 2000 as gentrification accelerated. Parker's life also changed in others ways around that time. Becoming a father has reduced his time for socializing, and he has consciously made recordings a larger part of his income in order not to be forced to gig every day. Family and house also motivated his decision to position himself in the realm of mainstream jazz with *Like-Coping* (Delmark, 2003); a decision that was also a reaction against the marginalization of his non-mainstream projects:

JEFF PARKER: I think professionally, it [*Like-Coping*] puts me in a different place. You know, like I was telling you [in February 2003], I've kind of come to terms that I am a jazz musician, and I'm doing what jazz musicians do—put out a record. That was kind of a conscious effort. I could have made a record for other labels, but I wanted to do a record for a jazz label, and I wanted it to be "jazz." Assert my identity publicly as a jazz musician. Basically, that's where I come from, even though with bands like Chicago Underground and even New Horizons Ensemble, they're more avant-garde tradition, and the Chicago Underground has never really gotten, and it doesn't really get, any respect in the mainstream jazz community, you know. They just look at us as weirdoes. Not even weirdoes, just hacks or trendy hacks or something. So I just wanted to put myself out there: "jazz guitar player" or "jazz musician, composer, whatever...conceptualist..." [*laughs*].

AUTHOR: I thought the Chicago Underground was recognized here in Chicago?

PARKER: In Chicago it is.

AUTHOR: But not in the national press?

PARKER: No. I can actually assert that point 'cause I was just talking to Rob [Mazurek] the other night. They did this big cover story in *Jazz Times*, probably two months ago, on jazz-tronica, and you know there was absolutely no mentioning of the Chicago Underground projects at all, as far as people that are mixing jazz and electronic elements in an artful way. I don't mean a band like the Yellow Jackets or something. But you know they mentioned all the people, Dave Douglas, Matthew Ship—guys who are just starting to do it now, man. We were doing it seven or eight years ago. They didn't mention it, and they got this huge backlash from the readers: "How come you guys didn't mention the Chicago Underground?!" And the editor had to apologize: "Oh yeah, we know that they're leaders in their field but...," and that was in *Jazz Times*, man! It's kind of super weird, and I knew that about the Underground, so I decided when I was going to put my own thing out that I wanted to identify more with the mainstream jazz community. (Parker, conversation with author, Chicago, 4 November 2003)

One of the points illustrated by these statements is that magazines shape the practices and identities of individual musicians. This is particularly clear in a situation where an artist defines his or her subject position in relation to mass-media discourse. In order to make a living, Parker is trying to obtain a position in a genre culture by adopting the classical soloist/bandleader role and making an album of a type of music preferred by this culture. Parker is no less active in non-mainstream than before he made the album, and he is still playing rock; his strategy is to give higher priority to one of many avenues rather than focusing exclusively on one. Old friends from the indie jazz community still constitute a part of his immediate network. They share some intimacy and have made a lasting impact on each other during their formative years in the early 1990s.

A Reaction against the Marsalisization of Jazz

The first formative period in Parker's career was his years at Berklee College of Music in Boston. In the past three decades, it has become common for jazz musicians to go to music high schools, and this has implications for jazz culture. Schools such as Berklee teach more than one kind of music, but their programs, faculty, and methods are organized in a system of genres, and students are grouped in genre divisions. Berklee operates this way not only because students wish to specialize, but also because the school tries to prepare students for the world of commerce. It is a kind of trade school. Professional studio musicians and sidemen are usually expected to master genre conventions and emulate the styles of others, no matter if they perform film music or commercials, play in a wedding band, teach, or tour with star vocalists such as Shania Twain or Diana Krall. Parker became skeptical of the conditions at Berklee, and his reaction made him appreciate his Chicago environment more:

PARKER: After high school, I went to Berklee for four years [1985–90, taking 1988–89 off]. But I didn't graduate.
AUTHOR: Why?
PARKER: Ah, man. I just felt that I was done, you know. Like I have learned enough . . . like I had gotten what I needed to get out of it. I actually stayed there too long, because I got really bitter! [laughs]
AUTHOR: Were you tired of the place, or did you feel that the school restrained your creative development?
PARKER: I just felt—well, this is an interesting point. I wanted to be a jazz musician from when I was really young, from when I first started playing. I was attracted to the mystique. And plus, the music, I listened to it from my parents' house. I knew that it was art music, you know. And when I went

to Berklee, I wanted to explore that. Of course, when you are in school, you learn technique and theory. You concentrate on practical skills and the more technical side of music. It was just the way that they were approaching it at Berklee. And after a point, it seemed really wrong, you know. I met a lot of musicians; they all sounded alike, and they had a narrow perspective of what music is about. . . . It seems like it's not really alive. And that's the thing: When I was a kid, jazz music seemed really alive to me, and then when I got to school, in Berklee, a lot of the musicians were more concerned with this certain level, a kind of historical barrier, it seemed really closed off.

AUTHOR: Do you think the schools have a negative impact on jazz?

PARKER: Most definitely. I mean, of course not everyone and everywhere, but for the most part. It's just like my love for jazz music. . . . Just as a fan. . . . Once I realized it, it made me really mad! [laughs] It's not why I came to Chicago, but it definitely has a lot to do with why I ended up staying here. My plan was to live here for a while and then move to New York City. (Parker, conversation with author, Chicago, 20 February 2003)

His recollections of going to college bring up interesting aspects. Above all, his critique of narrow boundaries and standardization is embedded in a declinist narrative of loss modern jazz history. This narrative derives from a critical response to the Marsalisization of jazz (cf. Radano 1993, 269–76) that was going on right at the time Parker was going to college and beginning to work professionally. The response in the indie jazz community forms a context for understanding Parker's thinking about genre and identity:

PARKER: I tried for a long time to cut some of my ties to the jazz establishment. I wouldn't define myself as a jazz musician [laughs]. But now, I can't deny it. I know that in everything I do, I have a jazz aesthetic that I relate it to, always. In the last couple of years I have kind of stopped kidding myself that I'm not a jazz musician.

AUTHOR: Was this part of your reaction against Berklee?

PARKER: That's a big part of it. I feel like, that jazz, as [far as] most nonmusicians are concerned, doesn't really have a social relevance. So I just didn't want to have anything to do with it. . . . I would look at jazz as folk music. It came from the same traditions. It was like these people took it and made something out of nothing. After the Civil War, they picked up old dance instruments, and people started playing and mixed them with these different rhythms. There are certainly intellectual properties to the music that make it appeal to that side of the human psyche, but I think the music has folk roots. In a lot of ways I just think it has become this kind of bourgeois thing. People don't really buy jazz records anymore, nobody goes to see the music, because I think so many musicians are so self-absorbed and the music is so intellectual on many levels: The way that it is perceived by the public as well as the way the musicians look at it, as it's like this elitist thing. I don't think it should be like that.

AUTHOR: So jazz can be folk and art music at the same time?

PARKER: Oh, sure. (Parker, conversation with author, Chicago, 20 February 2003)

This anti-elitist stance also explains why the musicians do not privilege classical music as some jazz musicians did in the Third Stream movement of the 1950s. The binary concept of Third Stream music ("jazz and classical music") is a product of the time when debates about mass culture were raging and the cultural hierarchy was more polarized. Some of Parker's colleagues have performed classical music and have a predilection for minimalism, but they primarily work on jazz and popular music scenes. What is more, the categories of indie and underground culture create divisions within and alliances across genres (between jazz, rock, hip-hop, etc.). In this perspective, the band name of Chicago Underground can be read as a metaphor for a jazz culture influenced by certain attitudes, ideologies, and styles of expression that run through a broader field of popular music.

Genre in Musical Practice

Genre mixing is a central feature of musical practice in the Underground circle. The musicians have collaborated with Jim O'Rourke, Sam Prekop, Tortoise, and other artists that are based in rock and most of them are still affiliated with Thrill Jockey. Parker's main projects in the late 1990s were Tortoise, which is based in rock, and the jazz-oriented bands Chicago Underground and Isotope 217, but they all worked in close proximity. After 2001 he concentrated on Tortoise. Parker has been involved in other long-term projects, among them Dawkin's New Horizons and the experimental trio Tricolor. Then there are infrequent but recurrent gigs with Michael Zerang and Ted Sirota, among others, and finally pickup gigs and occasional studio work. Parker has no manager and transports his guitar and amp around town in his own car. Parker's work across genres is conditioned by the generally collaborative ethos among artists and record labels. Aram Shumavon followed Parker and Tortoise in the 1990s as a fan and did some booking and radio work on the jazz and rock scenes. In a response to a draft of this chapter he attributed much importance to "the collaborative spirit" and suggests that Tortoise was sort of a nexus of encounters between genre cultures:

versation with author, 3 April 2004). Unlike much early fusion, however, Isotope's music tends to be crafted more as compositions with a songlike character and with less display of instrumental virtuosity. Its epic elements are reminiscent of those found in Miles's early fusion recordings and the mid 1970s' Weather Report. Isotope eventually adopted a slightly more aggressive and experimental urban attitude, moving from a post-1980s toward a 1990s sound influenced by the cultures associated with the Empty Bottle and the *Wire*. Again, contemporization is followed by and perhaps consciously indexed via appropriations of genre codes of electronica and hip-hop.

Tortoise adds further complexity to the picture. It is made up of three members of Isotope (Parker, Dan Bitney, and John Herndon) and plays some of the same venues. Musically the two bands are so close that it seems wrong to think of them as belonging to different genre categories. Some have suggested that Isotope is jazz because it has a cornetist and that Tortoise is jazz-rock because it uses vibes, but the musicians themselves obviously find such distinctions simplistic.[4]

If we consider the complexity that we face when studying in detail an urban music culture such as this, it does not make sense to think of generic categories as self-contained entities in a single-layered space. The concept of genre culture allows us to see how the music of the two bands circulates in different networks and multilayered symbolic spaces, while also gravitating toward different centers. Tortoise's music is primarily based in indie rock and is more distantly related to jazz. There is much less solo improvisation than in the music of Isotope, and it also lacks that band's jazz-derived harmonies. Tortoise is also more fully integrated in the social network of rock than Isotope. The band performs in larger venues, and the rock press represents it as if it naturally belongs to its territory. When *Down Beat* contacted Tortoise in early 2004, wanting to do a cover story on the band, the musicians' initial response was something like, "We are a rock band—why would *Down Beat* want do a story on us?"[5] Part of the answer is that *Down Beat* has a young, rock-friendly editor who knows that the band also appeals to some jazz audiences. In short, the two bands do not really belong to a single genre. It is more accurate to say their music circulates with different levels of intensity in various genre cultures.

Multiple Functions of the Groove

For me, studying Jeff Parker's diverse activities was a challenge and only slowly did two important connecting points begin to crystallize in my mind. The first is his guitar playing, which is characterized by a relatively consistent sound and performance style. When he plays in different contexts, he

emphasizes different shades of the same color, so to speak, rather than making categorical changes. His playing has a generic flexibility because it does
not have a strong genre focus. Its jazz foundations are strong, but elements
of various other genres are absorbed in a blend that dissolves rather than
highlights genre boundaries. Parker is also flexible because he is a perceptive listener who finds his place in the common musical space of a group and
does not dominate. His standard sound is clean and works well in different
genres. He usually uses a pedal board between his amp and guitar, but for the
most part it is used only to adjust the volume, and not to create sound effects, which would be a direct way of evoking iconic sounds of particular
artists and musics. Tremolo and flanger are used in rare instances as special effects. Parker's guitar sound changes more in studio productions: On
Like-Coping and other jazz-oriented albums he has a mellow, thick jazz
sound. His sound is brighter and often slightly distorted when he plays with
Tortoise, whose studio work is characterized by carefully crafted sound en-
vironments. Noise-style distortion and long passages of nonmelodic playing
appear only on experimental albums such as *Out Trios Volume Two* with
Kevin Drumm and Michael Zerang (Atavistic, 2003).

The second connecting point in my analysis is the work of the musical
groove, and this aspect deserves more attention because of its broad relevance to genre studies. According to Feld, one of the characteristics of
groove experience is "an ordered sense of something... that is sustained in
a distinctive, regular, and attractive way" (Feld 1994a, 112). In this discussion I work from the concept of groove as a gestalt of interconnected and
regularly sustained rhythmic-melodic patterns that are organized around a
dance beat. At the core of this concrete yet broad definition is a notion of
generic rhythm textures, but any groove theory should recognize that the
articulation of such textures is as important as the textures themselves. I
take the musical groove to be a key component of many popular and vernacular music traditions. In popular music, the groove is usually articulated
by a rhythm section with a drummer and a bass player, which is not always
the case in vernacular traditions such as blues, gospel, and polka. Despite
such differences and the many specificities that can be described in textual
analysis, my inclusive concept of groove provides a way of understanding
popular music as a field of practices of music making that are related to each
other as well as to their roots in folk or vernacular traditions.

The concept of groove has both generic and cross-generic dimensions.
Reggae, bossa nova, and funk grooves, for instance, circulate in many genres
while retaining their original genre identity. This transplantation across genres
reflects a relative independence between basic rhythmic patterns and their

generic musical context. It shows that music categories are embedded in cultural practice such as dancing and cannot be understood only in terms of the stylistic figures, patterns, and models that we conceive of as ideal types.

Grooves function as a ground for music making in many oral traditions and can be viewed as vehicles for genre mixing. A history of the role of grooves in genre mixing could begin by identifying the various styles and genres that were mixed in ragtime practice (what we might call the generic ragtime groove), and continue with the development in the mid 1930s of Count Basie's rhythm section, in which elements of blues, jazz, and Tin Pan Alley were synthesized. The generic swing groove with walking bass was later adopted in other traditions, including western swing and rockabilly. In a similar fashion, the groove practice of the Memphis rockabillies was instrumental in blending white and black popular musics, including R & B and country music. Again, variations emerged in different places—for example, skiffle music in Liverpool. Another story of migrating grooves is that of funk grooves becoming a source of influence on the basic grooves of early hip-hop, which in turn have been subject to many variations in many styles and genres.

The groove is a flexible framework for mixing different things because its simple structural and harmonic framework gives individual layers a certain freedom and allows for various kinds of variation. Patterns in one groove can be rearranged and appropriated into another like multifunctional components. Because many musicians have played the same types of grooves and have similar concepts of them, a groove approach to music making can be useful for musicians with different genre backgrounds. A groove can give musicians a shared framework with space for expressing individuality. The groove concept is also central to understanding the practices of sampling and remixing in contemporary popular music. In world beat, for instance, recordings of traditional music have been spiced up with electronic dance beats, as in the cases of some Bhangra productions by London-based deejays and Moby's sampling of Alan Lomax's field recordings.[6] Grooves can thus become cultural and historical signifiers and constitute an important domain for negotiating identity. When old hits are performed, moreover, the groove is often adjusted to contemporary sensibilities. Two well-known examples of this are Van Halen's 1978 hard rock version of the Kinks' "You Really Got Me" (1964) and the Fugees' 1996 hip-hop-inflected version of "Killing Me Softly with His Song," which is widely known in Roberta Flack's 1973 version. Also illustrative is Cassandra Wilson's cover of Robbie Robertson's 1968 "The Weight" based on a kind of hybrid roots music groove that she has developed with her band, and they play similar grooves in performances of material of different origin.[7] In short, the groove concept is a critical tool for analyzing genre formation, mixing, and transformation in the context of wider cultural processes.

The groove concept is a key to Jeff Parker's work because a lot of the music he plays is based on a groove and because generic differences between his various musical activities are reflected in the work of the groove. Parker has explained to me how he uses grooves and related concepts such as riffs, ostinatos, and vamps, as creative models when he practices and composes. Playing a recurring pattern of motifs and developing them in the context of a groove strengthens his timing and improvisatory skills, and sometimes ideas evolve into compositions. The same processes occur on a collective level when he is working with other musicians. In the following sections I will point to differences in the groove practice in four areas of Parker's work.

Parker's First Solo Album

About half the recordings on *Like-Coping* have substantial groove elements. The musicians primarily work within the tradition of groove-based jazz created by such pioneers as Dizzy Gillespie, Horace Silver, Miles Davis, John Coltrane, and Herbie Hancock, and their influences range from modal harmony to Latin music and the blues. In typical jazz fashion, Parker's trio, with the bassist Chris Lopes and the drummer Chad Taylor, employs grooves as skeletons for improvisation in both group interaction and soloing. The groove, in the strict sense of a repeated harmonic two- or four-bar period with an ostinato, constitutes an alternative to the constant harmonic and thematic progression of Tin Pan Alley songs. It creates a certain stasis and an open-ended flow, giving the improviser much freedom. A practical function of grooves in the production of this album is that they allowed for a relatively improvisatory recording session. The musicians have routine playing jazz grooves and know each other well, so they could record the album in one day without rehearsing much in advance. "Watusi" is a typical track from the album. It alternates between two brief sections, a swing section with walking bass and complex harmony and a groove section based on an African dance rhythm and a chordal riff of two triads (see example 1). In this work I hear echoes of Coltrane's music of the early 1960s, with its modal elements and African influences. The piece also illustrates Parker's sensitivity to groove in his solo improvisations: he improvises with and within the groove rather than using it as a mere background.[8] The musicians retain the eight-bar form of the theme, with its two alternating sections, so that groove and rhythmic difference become central to the overall idea of the piece.

Musical Example 1 Jeff Parker with Chris Lopes and Chad Taylor, "Watusi" (2003), 0:00–0:12 min., theme, mm. 1–8. The piece is in a chorus form based on this theme.

Adding to the complexity are metrical shifts and accents that blur those shifts. Parker says that he and Taylor divide the meter differently and that Dave Douglas had yet another interpretation when he and Parker played the piece together in the summer of 2005. Douglas had learned it on his own and was surprised when he finally saw the lead sheet. There is no clear metrical pattern in the swing section, but it can be viewed as three bars of 4/4 and one of 2/4. The groove section has complicated accents but clearly alternates between 6/4 and 7/4. The beginning of the first phrase is accented and sounds as if it could be the downbeat in the first bar of the section, but it is actually the pickup to that bar. Parker says that he learned this technique from Ernest Dawkins.

The Chicago Underground Quartet

The Underground is also based in a small-group jazz idiom and experiments with textures, meters, and genre. But the Underground emphasizes composition and arrangement and favors light textures with a more imaginary and fragmented sense of groove. It is closer to a sophisticated chamber group than a rock band with a steady drum and bass beat. "Tunnel Chrome," on *Chicago Underground Quartet* (Thrill Jockey, 2001) is typical for its cryptic two-bar guitar pattern of constant triplets, which, together with the calm chordal pattern in the vibraphone and the "cool," near-constant dynamic level and flow of notes, evokes a minimalist soundscape. The influence of minimalism is evident in the static feel, the consciously mechanical patterns, and the layering of short melodic patterns. The contemplative atmosphere also bears traces of contemporary classical music. The refined play with psychological tensions, the sense of mechanical control, and Parker's dwelling on strange dissonances in his solo indicate that another informing context is soundscapes in experimental science-fiction film. The Underground often uses groove elements in textures with cinematic qualities. Incidentally, Parker plays more of the basic groove patterns on this album than on some of the others.

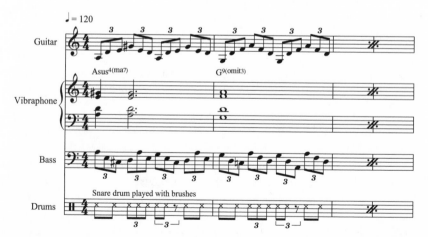

Musical Example 2 Chicago Underground Quartet, "Tunnel Chrome" (2001), 0:42–0:50 min., A section of the theme, mm. 8–12 (the piece is in an AAB chorus form). The upper notes of the vibraphone chords (g#' and a') have a melodic function. This semitone is one of the prime thematic motifs.

A Cushicle

A Cushicle is the trio of Parker, Ajemian, and Tanaka and the video artist Selena Trepp. They describe themselves as an "audiovisual collective" to emphasize that the video art is integrated with the music (Jeff Parker, e-mail to author, 25 February 2006). The musicians frequently improvise without a chord scheme or a set form, and they draw heavily on groove practices in free jazz and contemporary popular genres. Ajemian and Tanaka do not have the same strong background in jazz as Parker does, and their playing is not as structurally and thematically elaborate as that of experienced free jazz players. Their improvisation is based more on variation and repetition of motifs in small-scale structures and on a regular pulsating rhythm. The musicians work a lot with energetic and dissonant flows that have obvious free jazz roots, but they draw on groove practices in such popular musics as funk and punk rock. Those practices help the musicians approach free jazz. In this I see a parallel to the Vandermark circle of which Ajemian is also a member (cf. p. 123–24).

The group was formed in the fall of 2003, when Ajemian was offered a weekly gig at a trendy night spot called Rodan in Wicker Park. I heard them at one of their first gigs, at which Trepp improvised on the wall behind the musicians during the show. They were in the process of building a repertoire and had rehearsed only twice before their first gig. At that point it was not a very integrated group. About four months later, in March 2004, when the musicians performed as part of the Tuesday Chicago Improviser Series at the Empty Bottle, they had literally found the groove. Their timing and general coordination had improved, and one of the reasons was that they were doing more groove-based music. They knew each other better, of course, but the groove concept had clearly been an effective tool for finding a common ground. Reflective of this process, the musicians found a group name in the fall of 2005. As of early 2006 it had continued to have a home base at Rodan, where the weekly gig was still running and its first recording session was scheduled.

Tortoise

Tortoise is a contrasting case because its grooves are carefully crafted over longer periods of time and do not function as vehicles for improvisation. One band member, John McEntire, owns a recording studio, and this gives the band special opportunities for using the studio as a workplace. The band develops grooves in the studio and works intensely on nuances of texture and sound for weeks or months. The activities in McEntire's studio also reveal connections to other artists. Stereolab, Wilco, and several Thrill Jockey artists have recorded there, to name a few.

Tortoise has been identified with the label post-rock, which makes sense insofar as the music is based in rock but leaves out and transforms core rock elements to mark a distance from the rock tradition. There is no singing; the music is instrumental and does not focus on individual instrumentalists. The rhythms and song structures are more complex than in classic rock but not in the fashion of symphonic rock, though they carry traces of art rock. Fans are attracted to the particular sophistication and eclecticism of Tortoise's music, and nowhere are these qualities more evident than in the band's extensive use of grooves. The grooves typically mix elements of rock, funk, and jazz fusion. They have a dance feel, but rhythmic motion is not their only function. They also serve as a platform for thematic and textural variations and for creating a flow in long instrumental pieces with wide open spaces. I have sometimes found myself in an ambiguous position between a sensuous mode of listening, focusing on the rhythmic energy, and a more analytical mode, focusing on the large-scale thematic developments and evocative soundscapes. These aspects of the music cannot be separated because the groove is woven into the larger song architecture. The eclecticism is also reflected in the instrumentation, which is based on that of a rock rhythm group but includes in addition vibraphone, xylophone, and glockenspiel. Listeners with different genre experiences react differently, but there are indications that the generic complexity is mirrored in audience responses: at shows in rock clubs in Chicago in 2003 and Denmark in 2005, I observed that after the first couple of songs many people on the floor went from actual dancing to just swaying their bodies a little bit or tapping their feet. The shows ended up being more like concerts, even as the band continued to play energetic grooves. In Chicago, I noticed that the over-thirty segment of the audience tended to concentrate in the back of the room, and that was also where I encountered people from the jazz scene.

The title track from *It's All Around You* (Thrill Jockey, 2004) is a good example of the band's recent music, with its subtle Latin-rock groove. The basic groove is set in motion by two percussionists and a keyboardist (see example 3). One of the percussionists plays a conventional Brazilian 4/4 rhythm on a drum set, and layered against this, a 3/4 offbeat pattern, which was played later by another person using overdubbing. Much of the groove's energy derives from the tension between those two layers. The other musicians enter gradually and sustain the flow of the groove. They play relatively few notes above the groove, leaving much space open, and the soundscape is

Musical Example 3 Tortoise, "It's All Around You" (2004), 0:26–0:51 min., first ten bars from when the groove sets in. The vibraphonist enters after four bars, introducing the core motif of the song's "chorus." The guitarist and bassist enter shortly after. The basic drum track was played by John McEntire, and John Herndon later overdubbed the 3/4 pattern on the snare drum. The sound editing makes it difficult to do an exact transcription of all drums and percussion. McEntire and Herndon play each their drum set when the piece is performed live.

broadened by floating guitar sounds. Only slowly do individual motifs take shape in a thematic framework. The songlike theme evolves gradually and is repeated throughout with small variations.

The lead guitar carrying the theme is not played by Parker. He is playing the bass, and on other pieces he plays synthesizer, vibes, and glockenspiel. At live shows, Tortoise members occasionally switch instruments between pieces for the fun of changing positions on stage and the experience of having different roles in a groove. This performance ritual has a meta-dimension as a performance of ideas about performance, about making music together in a band. The musicians usually do it in groove-based pieces, and their flexibility reflects a deep familiarity with groove practice. The rotation is related to the egalitarian band ethos in their community and draws the audience into the music and the creative process.

Afterthoughts

From the retrospective of late 2005 I should like to conclude my ethnography by saying a bit more about how my work is a product of my encounter with the University of Chicago and some Chicago neighborhoods at a particular historical moment. It should be no secret that I liked the music I have written about from the first time I heard it, and this experience was influenced by my positive experience at the university. The musicians were not only friendly but also engaged in long discussions and in exchanging ideas. More than once, they asked for my interpretation of things. As I learned more about the tensions on the scene and discovered that other foreigners had written enthusiastic but somewhat naive portraits of the same culture (e.g., Kampmann 2000; Hughes 2004), I felt the need for a more nuanced picture and focused less on defending my subjects and their critique of corporate production and mainstream hegemony, although that, too, is important. One of the insights I gained in this process deserves to be emphasized here: even though a genre always involves a translocal network, it is strongly embedded in local contexts and conceived differently in different places. Local jazz cultures, for instance, cannot be viewed merely as variations of one general jazz culture. Musical experience and musical value, moreover, are particular to cultural locality.

When I arrived in early 2003, the University of Chicago was in the process of building relations with its urban hinterland. Hank Webber, the university's vice president of community affairs and government, tried using music and music venues to connect the university with the immediate South Side as well as the wider Chicago public. The music department was building a jazz program and appointed the young Travis Jackson as its first professor of jazz in the fall of 2003. In 1994 the former AACM president Mwata Bowden became director of the university's jazz ensemble, which gave at least one concert each quarter. The symposium "South Side Aesthetics" was held at the university in April 2004 at the occasion of the Art Ensemble of Chicago's return to Mandel Hall, a university concert hall in which the band had made a memorable live album thirty years earlier. At the symposium, George Lewis, a native South Sider, presented material from his forthcoming book (with the university's press), and prominent AACM members were featured on a panel.

The conscious work on a history of jazz in Chicago was not restricted to campus territories. I have noted the tendency to focus on the era of Al Capone and the contrasting narrative of AACM as the core of Chicago jazz. Then there are the claims that the glory days of the AACM are over and that the current center is the predominantly white musician communities on the North Side. And although Bettina Richards at Thrill Jockey says that Chicago's experimental traditions are unique, Jason Koransky at *Down Beat* claims that mainstream is the thing. Most of the indie jazz musicians are not from Chicago but have contact with older local communities and identify with the experimental traditions in the city. They are also being identified with these traditions by producers and journalists, as evidenced by Richard's statements and the *Wire* cover story on the Chicago Underground.

I have lived most of my life in Denmark, where whites are rarely confronted with their whiteness because they constitute the vast majority of the population. In that part of the world many people have only a dim awareness of racial discourse, and many still use term Negro (*neger* in Danish) without knowing that it has been a pejorative since the late 1960s. I had read a fair amount of literature on race relations in the United States before I did fieldwork in Chicago, but I had no long-term field experience, so I had much to learn about racial issues in everyday life. I learned not only that my own culture is more uninformed about race and racism than is generally believed, but also that my white identity was a barrier in my encounters with African Americans in the field. Because of social conventions, I was perceived as a white citizen, and not as someone who was outside of society's racial system, although technically I was a "non-resident alien."

A few elderly black musicians were skeptical. "When you put this to paper, you'll put it in a white way. You'll lose something," said one musician after telling me about his long career as a musician in a segregated society. He knew that my understanding of him would be distorted by my racial imagination. Interestingly, he used the term "idiom" and considered "genre" a ridiculous novelty. Although I believe his claim that he did not use the term genre, I am also sure his reaction was intensified by his skepticism about white society and the university as a Tower of Babel. The stories he told about his life in the musical culture of the segregated black South Side community suggested that musical boundaries had been superseded by racial boundaries. Another over-seventy African American musician objected to almost every music category I used, and it came to a point where I felt the conversation was about to collapse. He, too, was skeptical about being represented by a white person and voiced his frustrations with racism. When I turned off my recording equipment and focus shifted away from my project, he was as kind as a good friend.

Race did not create significant distortion in my encounters with Jeff Parker. I was reluctant to bring up the issue because I did not want to make him uncomfortable. Once during a break from a formal interview I told him about a recent trip I had made to the South and mentioned southern racism in passing. He quickly added that he hated it and that it was one of the reasons why he had left Virginia. In another interview we talked more about segregation and racism, and this brought up sadness and frustration. Parker explained that he had always lived and worked in interracial contexts and valued this. I think this social ideal is connected to his openness toward musical border crossing. Parker plays in all-black jazz bands and in a predominantly white context with Tortoise in which he is the only black person and most of the audience is white college kids. The Chicago Underground quartet, however, has an equal number of black and white musicians, and the accounts I have of its audiences in the late 1990s, when the quartet was most active, indicate that this was one of the cases where racial integration did happen on the otherwise segregated Chicago jazz scene.

Figure 10 Frances Densmore and Mountain Chief, 1916. Courtesy of the Library of Congress, American Folklife Center, Smithsonian/Densmore Collection, LC-USZ62-67601.

CHAPTER SEVEN

Music at American Borders

When did you last ignore musical sound? You don't have to identify a category, just musical sound. Unless you live in isolation, it probably happens daily, for it is impossible to pay attention to all sounds in the mass-mediated spaces of the modern world. That we use filters is obvious. It is more difficult to explain how they work, because they are regulated by complex cultural processes. If we pay close attention to how individuals choose a station on a radio or respond to a street musician, we quickly learn that such everyday routines are more complex than most people think. Through the acts of identification and negation, our filters define ourselves and others.

Locating music in social space is useful for understanding intersections between music and politics in such a complex category as American music. The term is used every day with the types of casual and intuitive distinctions I just referred to. It is made self-evident by canons, but that does not make it any less ideological. A peculiar aspect of the term American popular music is that it rarely includes all popular musics that are part and parcel of musical life in America. Latin pop, for instance, is a fixture of the domestic scene, but it is exoticized and distinguished from mainstream pop, which is an Anglo-American domain. Other examples I shall return to are zydeco music, which circulates in the sphere of world music, and Mexican American popular music, which has been somewhat ignored by the corporate industry and American music studies. The problem cannot be solved by dumping the category "American" and redefining the subject as popular music in America, because American identities do exist. The blues, for instance, are native to American society in a way that flamenco and gamelan music are not.

The principal question in this chapter is why some musics of the *country* are marginal in discourse on music of the *nation*. In other words, why are some of America's native popular musics considered American while others are considered partially foreign, even though they have existed for just as long in this country and have their main cultural centers here? By "native" I simply refer to music whose central birthplace and home is the United States. Part of the explanation is straightforward: some musics are marginalized as a consequence of the general marginalization of the people with whom they are associated. Native Americans and African Americans have been excluded from and oppressed by the nation for hundreds of years, and their cultures have in many ways been treated similarly.

Inventing Genres of American Music: Art and Folk

The history of ideas about American music and culture in many ways reflects the nation's colonial past. Discourse on American identity continues to be Anglocentric and rooted in the geopolitical space of the White Atlantic (to paraphrase Gilroy) that was established during that era and later crystallized in NATO and the American-led coalition of the second Gulf War. Although race is important, many other things are involved, including tradition, language, religion, and capital.

Musical nationalism developed in the late nineteenth century from European bourgeois models. Their social hierarchy was articulated in generic terms, with art music as the primary domain and folk music as a repository from which composers could appropriate raw materials. Nationalism was used to legitimize the privileged status of art music and advance the belief that America now had its own vibrant and genuine art music tradition. The desire to retain a privileged status also explains why art music people were disinclined to include other genres in their concept of American music.

Edward McDowell was a central composer when the debates about what is authentically American in music began in the 1890s.[1] For him, as for many other composers, European education was a rite of passage at which he confronted differences between the Old and the New Worlds in relation to his own music and career. His first conscious attempt at creating American music was a series of piano pieces titled *Woodland Sketches* (op. 51, 1896) that evoke images of the rural landscape of the New England countryside. Another signifier of America that also appears in the work of other composers is music of Native Americans. The main example is his *Second (Indian) Suite* (op. 48, 1896). McDowell suggested that Antonín Dvořák's choice of African American music as an indigenous source was misguided, and he felt that Native American Indians were a more appropriate signifier of America's difference from Europe.

American composers did not yet have a canon of national folk music to draw on back then, so it was not obvious how American folk culture could be represented musically. A field of American folk song collecting evolved in the early twentieth century and laid some of the foundations for canons of popular music later in the century. Strikingly, Francis Child became a father figure to the field even though his primary interest was not American but British. His monumental five-volume work on English and Scottish ballads (1883–98) set standards for generations of collectors working in America. Among them were Cecil Sharp and the Lomaxes, who are themselves milestones in this history.

Sharp was born in Britain and started collecting in the United States in 1916 in the southern Appalachian Mountains. He believed that British folk traditions had survived in this region and wanted to track their genealogy. Sharp's approach to song lineage has a Darwinian flavor, and one of his goals was to forge a dignified national British culture. This shows the legacy of Child's racially exclusive concept of folk music. Before long, however, Carl Sandburg, Robert Gordon, the Lomaxes, and others began including African American music and claimed that America had a worthy indigenous folk song heritage (Filene 2000, chapter 1).

The first milestone of the Texas-based Lomax family was John Lomax's *Cowboy Songs and other Frontier Ballads* (1910). John felt that "the Anglo-Saxon ballad spirit" had survived in remote areas of the West and that this collection would be a rich document of the pioneer experience (Lomax and Lomax 1938, xxv). His generic concept of cowboy songs is constructed around a mythical figure that is not only regional, but also national, because this character is imagined to have had a foundational role in the nation's history. Nations derive symbolic power from anthropomorphous metaphors. In this case, the nation is implicitly embodied in a white male described as, among other things, young, brave, fearless, and free.

John and his son Alan were more open to cultural difference than most collectors and were encouraged in this through their contacts with Roosevelt's New Deal administration and the American Communist Party. The Lomaxes received federal support for their first joint book, *American Ballads and Folk Songs*, which was published in 1934. They also worked for the Archive of American Folk Song, established in 1928, when the idea of national folk music had gained currency. The 1934 volume is one of their most influential general collections of American folk songs, and it marked the beginning of their use of recording technology in the field. The songs are classified according to various social categories. I identify three thematic cores in its romanticizing mythology: men in dangerous professions (e.g., the cowboy, the miner, the sailor, the soldier), wild and remote nature (e.g., the western plains, the mountains, the sea), and white versus black men (the African American male appears as the racial Other).

The thematic organization was not rigorously systematic, and I am only drawing attention to a few focal points in order to give a sense of the general boundaries. White Anglo-American subjects and the English language obviously predominate; the volume includes only about a dozen songs in French and Spanish. African American genres are strongly represented, however. John had long been seriously interested in and Alan would devote much of his working life to what can be described more specifically as African American vernacular music of the rural South, especially the Mississippi Delta.[2] A couple of introductory pages deal specifically with African American music and culture. The editors have a primitivist gaze and conclude that "the Negro . . . has, in our judgment, created the most distinctive of folk songs—the most interesting, the most appealing, and the greatest in quantity" (Lomax and Lomax 1934, xxxiv). White fascination with African American expressive culture was not new, and it is not surprising that blacks would become the prime racial minority in the field of American folk music because through slavery they had been forced into a role as America's internal racial Other.[3] Native Americans were more external. They did not become an integral part of the workforce, for instance.

This role of blacks has made white society less able to perceive other racial groups. In *Speak It Louder: Asian Americans Making Music* (2004), Deborah Wong addresses this problem and notes that minoritarian approaches have been slow to find a place in American music studies. Of particular interest to us is her chapter on Asian American performers of genres identified as African American. Wong suggests that these performers have been assessed negatively because African Americans dominate the cultural space of these genres. One informant talked about a "stiff" sense of rhythm and did not "attempt to identify an Asian American sound—instead, he was hearing the absence of an African American musicking body" (Wong 2004, 174). I should add that whites have long been charged with being "stiff," but they have had the power to naturalize their presence and appropriate African American musical space. Another important argument in that chapter is that the presence of Asian American performers in this space can disturb the white/black system of difference (ibid., 186). Some of these problems are not particular to music or to Asian Americans but can also be found in discourses surrounding other racial minorities. Lisa Lowe has argued that Americans of Asian descent remain symbolic aliens,[4] and they are not alone. Asian

Figure 11 Columbia "Foreign Records" catalog, 1906. Courtesy of the Library of Congress, American Folklife Center.

Americans can be located near the end of the Americanization continuum that groups of various descents have entered. The use of the term "naturalization" by the Immigration and Naturalization Service authorities indicates that this space is deeply structured by ideological distinctions between self and other.

"Foreign" Recordings and Popular Music

Commercial recordings provide a useful perspective on this history because they have been produced in the interest of a broader population than scholars and institutions. For this reason, recordings and their marketing give some indication of what many people have heard and how it was categorized. Products made for short-term profit, however, are rarely taken very seriously by historians and depend on unstable market forces. In the first half of the twentieth century, the recording industry produced various series for people with a marked identity. Rather than being sold under the name of a genre, this music was named for the presumed ethnic or racial identity of the consumer. The "race" and "hillbilly" series have entered the canon of American music history, and the vaults are being tapped through CD reissues of jazz, blues, and country music.

One market has been nearly forgotten, and that is the one represented by the "foreign" series that major labels ran between about 1906 and 1952. Few of the records are commercially available, and very little has been written about them. Following a conference on this music, the Finnish radio and record producer Pekka Gronow edited the volume *Ethnic Recordings in America* (1982) for the American Folklife Center (Gronow, conversation with author, Copenhagen, 25 October 2005).[5] It shows that the labels were thinking of non-English-speaking immigrants as distinct and somewhat isolated groups of people. The large number of first-generation immigrants early in the century formed the basis of ethnic communities that also had their own native-language theaters and newspapers. During those decades some musics shifted position between domestic and foreign. Irish music, for instance, was placed in the domestic series at Columbia and Victor up to the 1920s, when it, too, began to appear in the foreign series, and Hawaiian music shifted from foreign to domestic (*Ethnic Recordings* 1982, 12). The social basis of the field of foreign-language recordings gradually eroded as immigrant communities adapted to mainstream culture, but the labels' decision to terminate the series in the early 1950s may also have been influenced by conservative cold-war patriotism. Another interesting change is the terminological shift in Columbia's system from "European vs. American" in the years from 1908 to "foreign vs. domestic" after 1923 (ibid., 16 and 36). Most immigrants came from Europe, and the terminology indicates European dominance. Above all, these changes show that the boundaries of American identity change.

The continued existence of the distinctions between American and non-American music as well as Western and non-Western music is indicated by the ubiquity of labels such as "ethnic music," "world music," "world beat," "international," and "tropical." More non-American music gets mainstream distribution now, and this complicates the situation because people move across a greater number of real and virtual borders. It also magnifies the discrepancy between what people in the United States share and what they fabricate discursively as American.

Popular music has been a medium for articulating American identity since the days of Stephen Foster. Paul Whiteman, Bing Crosby, and later

Elvis Presley have at various times enjoyed status as American icons, but nationalism became a more explicit issue in popular music discourse in the wake of the folk revival. Rock musicians were inspired by folk music, and rock critics began integrating popular music into the canons of national art and folk music in the 1970s. In his influential *Mystery Train*, first published in 1975, Greil Marcus strategically associated rock music with national canons and insisted that folk and rock music formed *the* glorious American musical tradition (Marcus 1975/1990).

The notion of roots enjoyed a revival in the culture of American roots music in the 1990s, which shows the lasting influence of the folk song collectors. When Harry Smith edited his *Anthology of American Folk Music* (Folkways, 1952) he listed works of folk song collectors such as Child, Sharp, and the Lomaxes as sources for further study of the individual songs he had chosen. His anthology, in turn, became a major source of inspiration for the folk revival of the late 1950s and early 1960s. The Lomaxes also contributed to the revival by launching the careers of some of its icons, including Leadbelly and Woody Guthrie.

The Lomaxes have also become icons themselves. Magazines and books continue to publish photos of them and their legendary recording equipment, stashed in the trunk of John's car. A significant example is the book accompanying the PBS series *American Roots Music*, in which those photos are printed in the chapter on the folk revival (Santelli, Warren, and Brown 2001, 60). The Lomaxes' legendary status is such that some of their recordings are identified first as Lomax recordings and only secondly by the name of the performer. I have met people who talked about "the Lomax recording" in the opening scene of *O Brother, Where Art Thou?* and journalists have written about "the Lomax recordings" that Moby found in a Tower store in Manhattan and sampled on his album *Play* (BMG, 1999). Another example is the CD *Popular Songbook* (Rounder, 2003), a collection of Alan's recordings of songs that have been covered by artists such as Bob Dylan, Eric Clapton, and Led Zeppelin. Designated "American roots music originals," on a CD whose cover design is reminiscent of a design from the Dust Bowl era, these recordings are presented as the roots of popular music.[6]

Musicologies

Wong's frustration with the canons of American music studies can be extended to a call for a deeper engagement with diversity in the growing body of books on "American popular music." Popular music studies are still dominated by a white-versus-black canon defined by whites, although some

scholars have moved in new directions over the past decade or so. More dialogue between musicology and ethnomusicology would be advantageous,
but there is prejudice on both sides. Major social changes will find their way
to academia sooner or later, but there is no reason to delay an important
process. It would be valuable, for instance, if the ethnomusicological establishment did more to make Western music, including popular music, part
of the field. Similarly, musicologists could do more to integrate ethnomusicological perspectives and methods.[7]

Some musicologists have been optimistic about the recent growth of
interest in "culture." New Musicology, for instance, is proud of its culture-
oriented approach to music, but it remains focused on high-culture theory
and has so far failed to draw on the expertise of ethnomusicologists. A case
in point is the recent performativity fad among art musicologists, who have
shown little interest in the cross-cultural perspectives of the topic and how
it has been studied in areas where scholars have worked with alternatives
to object-centered approaches for a long time.[8] It is also a bit grandiose for
some musicologists to suggest that they have become ethnomusicologists,
too. There is a risk of forcing ethnomusicologists into a passive role in the
popularization of their field. Another risk is that the well-intended focus
on touching surfaces will highlight safe boundary areas and obscure core
differences. The core of art musicology is the textual analysis of canonical
Western pieces, and the core of ethnomusicology is in fieldwork on non-
Western culture. These are some of the big differences that could be confronted more often.

A Poetics of Music In Between Genres

The previous chapters have focused on particular moments, sites, and stories
of genre making. This chapter takes a slightly different approach by using
genre as a tool for understanding aspects of the problem of music and national identity in American cultural history. This way we are not situating
ourselves in a genre discourse from the outset. Our entrance via cultural
history allows us to see how musical categories of all types turn up in discussions in which they are not the primary issue. This also implies that we
are widening our perspective on genre to include other types of categories.

The critique that emerges from my outline calls for new models. To this
end I shall propose a poetics for understanding music in between genres.
Our thematic complex has conceptual and ethical-ideological dimensions
that I seek to integrate rather than separate in order to sustain both analysis
and advocacy. I am foregrounding the agency of the genre scholar a bit

in this chapter. It is helpful to remember that you and I are agents, too, and we can break the false sense of objectivity that third-person narrative tends to create by strategically using first person. Moving between different rhetorical strategies in our "tales of the field" (Van Maanen 1988) can help us recognize that, like the people we study, we choose to look at genres in certain ways and identify with particular genre discourses.

The poetics I propose is consciously built around a decentered concept of genre. My notion of centeredness focuses on conceptual aspects of the core-boundary models with which people organize music into categories, but it also pertains to the related ethical aspects of domination and ethnocentrism in musical culture. Many strategies for dealing with these problems share a commitment to highlighting marginalized groups and cultural formations with a high degree of generic disorder. Typical examples are situations where genre codes are mixed, displaced, or transformed in ways that complicate the conditions in the network of the individual genre.

I employ the notion of music in between genres as a conceptual metaphor in a form of decentered thinking that is structured less by core-boundary models than by models with more chaotic and transformative structures. It is impossible to give a complete account of all models, but suffice it to say that my in-between models are informed by metaphors of transgression and heterogeneity. They are structured by continuums and plural narratives rather than dichotomies, and they embrace polymorphous semantic textures rather than distinct categories. These are properties of basic genre discourse and not exotica, but they go beyond elementary models of everyday thinking about genre. They operate, for instance, in the comparative procedures through which categories are constructed. When people compare categories, they also extrapolate, copy, and transport elements between categories. My in-between poetics emphasizes the cross-generic and processual qualities of music to break the stasis that categories produce. There is a nomadic edge to the ethos of this poetics because it engages in movement and transformation. I encourage comparative explorations of how categories change across time and place, and I encourage a patient search for more than one category and center when studying a particular music. Patience is needed because cultures of categorization are deeply internalized in everyday routines.

The above assumptions can be summed up in six propositions:

1. Core–boundary models of genre should be complemented with decentered models.

2. Music has cross-generic and processual qualities that defy categorical fixity.

3. Spaces between genres are as valid sites of inquiry as are genres themselves.

4. In-between spaces have special significance for understanding diversity and transformation.

5. The metaphor "in between" draws attention to how music is situated.

6. My in-between poetics seeks to unfold connections across borders ad infinitum

A Different Anthology of American Popular Music

Anthologies have played a major role in defining American music and its boundaries with non-American musics. In that spirit, I will conclude by illustrating how my poetics can be used to design a type of anthology that is more sensitive to diversity than anthologies that follow the big canons. I present only three recordings, so what follows can also be described as a couple of related case studies with a heuristic purpose. Obviously, the emphasis is not on the quantity of information or the number of musical examples.

The general theme of national boundaries will be examined within a specific scope of inquiry. The basic idea is to explore some of the diversity of musics in a region of the country that forms a core in national mythology. We therefore need to move beyond essentialist embodiments of genre, ethnicity, and place. The principal core region in American mythology is the South, which is a very large and diverse area defined by social history. Much of its modern mythology was consolidated in the second half of the nineteenth century, including the deep North-South divide and the idea of the South as the backbone of the nation's folk culture. Folk song collecting was centered on the South from the beginning, with Sharp and others creating a cult around southern Appalachia and with the southern odysseys of the Lomaxes. Recording entrepreneurs such as the Lomaxes, Moses Asch, and Harry Smith did relatively little in the United States outside of the South, which is striking considering that they were all very engaged in world music. Contemporary consumers are reminded of Alan Lomax's ties to the region by the CD box set reissue of *Sounds of the South* (1961) and by Rounder's monumental Southern Journey series.

National folk canons have influenced popular music, and the South became a major agent on the national scene in the 1950s and 1960s with rock and roll, the Nashville Sound, and Memphis soul. The South has not dominated mainstream pop, though, and the region's identity as a stable place a bit outside the marketplace has been attractive to roots music people. Their myth of an unbroken continuum of roots music is influenced by the myth of the South as a world of pure and authentic traditions.

A major challenge here is to recognize regional distinctiveness without forfeiting critical distance. There was a need for recognition of the region when Malone wrote *Southern Music/American Music* in 1979, and the foreword to the revised 2003 edition retains the spirit of advocacy present in the first when it claims that "the South has been America's most fertile domain for creative music making" (Malone and Stricklin 2003, xi).[9] In the 2003 edition, prepared with the assistance of David Stricklin, Malone also maintains a certain privileging of the regional over the national. For instance, he sometimes laments that genres have expanded their territories from the regional to the national as a result of their increased popularity.[10] The book follows a familiar narrative of historical growth and coherence. It begins with a chapter on origins and unfolds as a chronological survey of major genres and historical themes such as national recognition and marketing.

Malone's scheme of cultural difference is signaled by his early statement that "the country's two greatest folk music traditions [are] the British and the African" (Malone and Stricklin 2003, 3; see also 5f.). He notes the tendency to view Texas-Mexican music as "foreign" and occasionally touches upon the diversity issue, but the book generally does not give a nuanced sense of diversity and how it is negotiated in the South. The canons of white society dominate, and the few sections on genres associated with minority populations are relatively isolated (ibid., 60). I wish to make it clear that I am primarily using this remarkable book, written by an expert from an insider's perspective, to discuss general problems of mapping the southern musical landscape. Two common problems of regional mappings are that transregional dimensions are reduced and that culture is affixed to particular places and people. Like many others, Malone writes more about genre origins and genealogies than about the areas where their boundaries are blurred.[11] Finally, the concept of mapping makes people search for musics that *belong* to a given area (according to some) rather than the full range of musics that actually *exist* in that area.

I think of the examples in the following anthology as a juxtaposition of difference rather than different shades of the same culture. Each of the three recordings represents a musical culture in an area of the South, a music that has taken root in the area, and at the same time complicates conventional boundaries of "American music" and southern musical geography. It is not hard to find examples because a lot of music is situated in between those identity categories. However, the examples can serve as more than a vehicle for a general model of hybridity. The enthusiasm for hybridity in recent years has led to universalisms that are counterproductive for understanding

Figure 12 Ricky Martin, 1999. Photo courtesy of Photofest.

diversity. Promoting a single model may create a rhetorical flash, but it is
not the best long-term strategy for advancing the cause (cf. Stokes 2004).

Ricky Martin, "The Cup of Life" (Sony, 1998)

He wears a size eleven shoe. His biggest fear is snakes. He can't keep his
hands off junk food.

These details appear on a list of "facts about Ricky" in a 1999 biography (Bergquist 1999, 57–58).[12] The biography begins with his childhood in Puerto Rico and covers his career from his years in the boy band Menudo (1983–88) up to the spring of 1999, by which time he had become a global celebrity. The book is richly illustrated with photos of Martin, typically posturing as joyous, cute, or sexy. His body language appeals to the female gaze, and the author's writing style indicates that many of his fans are young girls. Like other stars, he attracts listeners across genre cultures, and not all of his fans think about his music in terms of genre.

Through music videos and magazines Martin has become known as much for his looks and dancing as for his singing. Sound is only one dimension of the "multi-media Ricky Martin pop text" produced within the Latino culture industry. The corporate conceptualization of one big Latino market (alias U.S. Latinidad) has resulted in more dominance of Mexicans and Cubans in the productions of the TV networks Univisión and Telemundo as well as in the productions of major record labels (Dávila 2002). Miami has been a center of Cuban-oriented productions for about two decades. A Miami sound was developed in the 1980s by the producer Emilo Estefan and others, and several Latino pop stars have lived and recorded in the city over the years, including Martin, Enrique Iglesias, and Jennifer Lopez. Negus has analyzed the complex geography of the corporate salsa industry and conceived the model of a matrix that regulates the production. The centers in this matrix are New York City, Miami, and Puerto Rico, with a wider grid across North America, the Caribbean, and Central and South America. Negus's analysis also reveals that major labels created Latin divisions to capitalize on the growing domestic market but marketed the music as "international" in the United States. The old imperialist pattern of othering non-Anglo populations is a deep structure in corporate music production. It should be noted that though the industry indirectly disconnected Latinos from American space and created exotic images of salsa as "tropical," only a small portion of the music was introduced on the world beat market (Negus 1999, chapter 6; Waxer 2002, 10).

"Do you really want it?! Do you really want it?!" Sung energetically at a high pitch and accompanied by sparkling brass sounds, these lines jumpstart the spectacle of the intro section of "The Cup of Life." The sound of a fanfare and festive drumbeats add further excitement. All this stops after a few bars, when a swirling synthesizer sound comes in and evokes a dreamy soundscape of techno dance music. The synth sound keeps floating, and a percussion groove sets in after two bars. Then the singing returns with another element of the song's refrain ("Go, go, go!"), and its motif is echoed in the brass riffs in the final section of the intro. In short, the intro presents the "hook" of the song in a flow of varied textures and flashy effects. The techno synth and the Latin groove have dramatic qualities, and the juxtaposition of different style elements has a dramatic effect in itself. It adds color to the general atmosphere of a dance club party.

Festivity is also conveyed through the carnival flavor of the percussion groove, with its up-tempo, samba-tinged feel and the large ensemble of timbale drums, congas, and small hand percussion. The instruments are mixed in such a way that it is hard to say exactly which percussion instruments are being used. Certainly, the producers have not attempted to create a real-world live sound or a traditional sound. Another aspect of the indistinct texture is groove, which is usually a good place to look for genre mixing (cf. pp. 137–40). In this case, the groove has been built gradually with overdubs in the studio; unlike more traditional Latin music, it does not follow a particular rhythmic style or genre. The general rhythmic feel is closer to mainstream Anglo pop than to the interlocking patterns of salsa. The generic bonds with Anglo pop are tightened as the song progresses: The overall form follows a conventional verse-refrain scheme, with interspersed instrumental sections that break free of the song progression to zoom in on dance and drama.

0:00 min.	Intro: "Do you really … " (3 bars) → techno sound and groove (4 bars) → "Go, go, go" (8 bars) → riff (8 bars)
0:44 min.	Verse 1 (18 bars) → refrain (8 bars) → riff (4 bars)
1:41 min.	Verse 2 (18 bars) → refrain (8 bars) → interlude (8 bars) → break (4 bars)
2:53 min.	Verse 3 (18 bars) → break (4 bars) → refrain (8 bars) → refrain (8 bars)
4:12 min.	Coda (8 bars +2 bars)

All sections of the song have a simple, symmetrical structure, and the melodic style, too, is pop rather than Latin based, so I was not surprised to learn that one of the two producers has worked with Aerosmith and Bon Jovi (Bergquist 1999, 24).[13] The lyrics are in Spanish in places, but the refrain is mainly in English.

Is this music of a genre? Or are the generic codes so indistinct that the music resides somewhere in between Latin and Anglo mainstream pop? The latter is true if we judge from the music's circulation. Insiders of specialized Latin music scenes around the country prefer core salsa artists to Martin, and if they have a taste for pop they often like Marc Anthony better because his singing is more advanced. Nor have scholars of Latin popular music shown much interest in mainstreamers such as Ricky, J. Lo, and Enrique. I am not arguing for the quality of these artists. My point is simply that their music is absent from certain spheres because their mainstream identity does not appeal to people with a strict genre focus. If one searches for role models in a genre and especially its musically most advanced artists, mainstream stars will likely be of limited interest. J. Lo is a special case because she has a strong Latina identity in the media, but most of her music is based on African American genres, especially R & B and hip-hop.

Martin was invited to contribute this song as the official song of the 1998 World Cup in France, as the lyrics about struggling to accomplish something big suggest. He told a journalist that the French soccer star Michel Platini called him and asked for a song in the vein of "María," a hit from Martin's album *A medio vivir* (Sony, 1995) (Bhawnani 1998).[14] Though this is of course not the whole story about how the music was produced, it provides some context for the song's party sound, as does Martin's comment that he is a fan of Brazilian soccer. To unfold some of the wider cultural connections, we can look at the contexts of three significant performances of the song.

PARIS, 12 JULY 1998: THE SOCCER WORLD CUP FINAL   The first public performance of "The Cup of Life" was in the stadium in Paris at the World Cup final, where France beat Brazil. It was a global moment for Latin pop, broadcast to more than a billion viewers in 187 countries.[15] In this situation, Latin pop was a safe game to play because of its established role in Western culture as a signifier of colorful festivity. Most of the participating countries at the soccer world cups have been Western European countries and some of their former colonies. The neocolonial structure can be identified in the musical production, which for the past decade or so has been regulated by Sony's executives in the West. Each country has had a song performed by its own citizens, possibly creating the illusion that the songs represent indigenous national music. The songs of 1998 and 2002 draw on a variety of styles with local flavors, underscoring the festive "international" character of the event, but most of the songs are rooted in Western pop.[16] So diversity is all right as long as it is digestible to the ear of the White Atlantic, and the concept of world beat serves this neocolonial multiculturalism well.

LOS ANGELES, 24 FEBRUARY 1999: THE FORTY-FIRST GRAMMY AWARDS SHOW   As a result of the commercial success of the song and the album on which it was featured, *Vuelve* (Sony, 1998), Martin was awarded a Grammy for "best Latin pop performance." The Grammy certified his association with this category, and both Latin pop and Martin gained from the attention he got for his performance at the event (cf. Martin 1999).[17] Standing in front of a large band playing this energetic dance music, Martin appeared as the center of a spectacle. He came out of a closet on the stage and moved up a ramp during the performance. Giant stilt walkers waved long colored bands, along with other scenic effects. It was professional entertainment, but looking at how it was fashioned in a wider context raises the question of whether the corporate world keeps Latino artists in the tropical party zone. This image has been nurtured by the use of Latin pop in commercials for tropical drinks and fashion.

For Martin, the event was a step away from an "ethnic" Latino identity toward the Anglo mainstream. He had recently cut his long hair and adapted to mainstream dress codes. Moreover, he was switching to English-language lyrics. About two months later, his first English-language album, *Ricky Martin*, appeared. It included "Livin' la Vida Loca," his biggest hit to date. That song was made by the same producers, and it plays with tropicality, both in the flashy riffs and sexually suggestive singing and in the lyrics, which refer to seduction, voodoo dolls, red lips, and mocha-colored skin, among other things. The accompanying video is set in a dance club with an atmosphere of sex and mystique, and though there are signifiers of Latin pop, there is nothing about the representation of the performing bodies that mark a racial difference from white Anglos. Some of the dancers appear to be Anglos. Gender, on the other hand, is a central structuring force in the sexualized body language and narrative of the whole scene.

WASHINGTON, D.C., 18 JANUARY 2001: THE INAUGURAL FESTIVITIES FOR PRESIDENT GEORGE W. BUSH   The appearance of Martin and George W. Bush on the same stage at this event was a public encounter between two different groups that for a long time have represented the two poles in our story: the privileged Anglo American and the domestic Other. National papers were struck by the encounter, as was Martin's longtime collaborator, Robi Rosa, who issued a press release when he heard about the upcoming performance. Rosa discouraged Martin from doing it. He explained that it would be "a betrayal of everything that every Puerto Rican should stand for" and referred to Bush's handling of civil rights, gun violence, the environment, and other issues.[18] One can understand Rosa's critique on two levels. The first level is the manipulation of the song's meaning by the context of its performance. The message that "you can win if you try hard enough" takes on an unforeseen political meaning when Bush is on the stage. It can be read as a celebration of the conservative ideology that implicitly

Figure 13 Baptist congregation in Louisiana 1934. Photo by Alan Lomax. Courtesy of the Library of Congress, Prints and Photographs Division, Lomax Collection, LOT 7414-B, N46.

accepts poverty and racism. This was not what Rosa had in mind when he collaborated on the song for the World Cup. On another level we have the Puerto Rican celebrating a president who embodies those values. Martin's appearance can hardly be read as a sign of Bush's genuine concern for ethnic minorities. Even if neither Bush nor Martin thought much about the political dimension of this performance, it shows that boundaries are defined in a complex relation between contemporary interests and historical and institutional forces.

Jimmy Peters and Ring Dance Singers, "J'ai fait tout le tour du pays"
([1934] Rounder, 1999)

The lower South comprises transnational border regions that reach into territories south of the United States. These cultural regions are peripheral to the core southern mythology of Texas cowboys, the Mississippi Delta, and southern Appalachia. In this chapter, I move west from Florida to Louisiana and Texas, where transnational music cultures have grown up. Imperial forces have created different patterns of migration and different cultural histories in these regions: Florida, Louisiana, and south Texas have all been Spanish, Florida has also been British, and Louisiana and Texas (for a short time, 1685–90) have also been French.

The connections to pre-twentieth-century history give us a chance to understand that musical and cultural blending is not a new phenomenon, but rather something that has existed under different social and technological conditions. A relatively new concept in the vocabulary of cultural theory, hybridity is in danger of being set off from the past as a signifier of a new and more sophisticated world. Historical inquiry is necessary for developing this critique of contemporary thought.

Histories recorded in the past or for ethnographic purposes are great sources because they are not filtered by dominant canons in the present. In this sense, sound archives are relevant to all areas of musical and cultural scholarship. "J'ai fait tout le tour du pays" (I went all around the country) is an ethnographic field recording made in the town of Jennings, Louisiana, by the Lomaxes on a trip influenced by the New Deal impulse to document diversity in America. John wrote in his 1935 report for the Library of Congress that they had returned to southern Louisiana the previous year and "with headquarters at New Iberia continued the recordings among the French 'Cajuns' of that section" (Lomax 1935, 1). The Lomaxes concentrated on the preservation of French customs among whites of French Canadian descent, but the brief report on this part of their trip concludes with the note that they also recorded interesting "Negro 'shouting' songs." Alan described the event in more detail in his liner notes to the 1987 commercial release of recordings from this trip. He recalled that "some young fellows took me to a Baptist church and with their friends demonstrated the style of sung dances then commonly performed at church socials" (Lomax 1999). Alan never got to know much about the performers. He says a fight started at the peak of their performance, so he decided to leave and did not come back until the early 1980s!

Except for the recorded sound and Alan's liner notes, there are few documents of musical life in this community. There are no interviews, for example, as sources for understanding how they talked about their music and categorized it. Alan assumes that this and one of the other songs are "probably full-blown instances of the *juré* style that is now known to have been widespread in the black Creole communities of western Louisiana" (Lomax 1999).[19] His conjecture may be correct, but little is known about the term *juré*, and what it signified and to whom. It has circulated almost exclusively in oral tradition, and research on *juré* is sparse. Minton defines it as "a localized form of the African American 'ring shout,' consisting of a counterclockwise procession accompanied by antiphonal singing and the shuffling, stamping, and clapping of the dancers, occasionally supplemented by simple percussion such as the ubiquitous metal-on-jawbone scraper or its descendant, the washboard" (Minton 1996, 490).

The ring shout functions similarly to the groove in popular music. Metronome sense (cf. Waterman 1952) and repeated rhythmic patterns help coordinate music and dance as well as integrate various heterogeneous musical elements. However, this recording was made without modern studio facilities, and the performers did not have the vast media library that most people have today. By all accounts, *juré* is not a purely musical category but a ritual that involves music, and it is participatory music rather than music presented for an audience (Minton 1996; Spitzer 1998; Turino 2000, 47–50). One might object that this recording represents folk or traditional music and not popular music, but the participatory ethics and the distance from the world of commerce make this a special case that cannot easily be fully understood in contemporary terms. The term vernacular music is another candidate, but there is no easy way out of the discrepancy between past and present conceptions.

Alan's recollection makes sense in the ritual theory, and his description of the scene hints at relevant aspects of the performance. He says that while he was setting up the equipment, "some of the boys and girls formed couples and began to dance round and round the church, in a shuffling, body-shaking

fashion, very much like the Sea Island shouts" (Lomax 1993).[20] It apparently
started quickly because the record begins in medias res. The tempo is fast,
and the rhythmic feeling conveys a sense of intense physical activity. A
percussionist plays the basic rhythm with his hands on a box or a piece of
wood. It is a constant stream of eighth notes with irregular accents, sometimes improvised in response to the lead singer. The only other nonvocal
sound comes from improvised hand claps.

The whole performance has a processual logic in the improvisatory flow
created within a simple and repetitive structure. There is no large-scale
structural development. The lead singer carries the melody, which is based
on two 4-bar phrases that we can call *a* and *b* (see example 4). They each
have a modal character emerging from a motif of three and four notes,
respectively, and without a strong scale identity. Together they form a pair
of contrasts: *a* appears with relatively few variations and forms a stable
zone, whereas *b* is more challenging and more varied. The two phrases are
generally repeated twice, but there are variations here, too.

0:00 min.	*a b b* (second *b*: 6½ bars)
0:14 min.	*a a b b* (second *b*: 4½ bars)
0:31 min.	*a b b* (second *b*: 4 bars)
0:43 min.	*a a b b* (second *b*: ca. 4½ bars)
0:59 min.	*a a b b* (second *b*: ca. 4¾ bars)
1:16 min.	*a a a b b* (second *b*: almost 5 bars)
1:37 min.	*a a*

The processual character is also identifiable in the way that the thematic
structure loosens up in the *b* sections. This is evident in the mutation of
the motif in the first two bars of *b* sections 1, 2, and 4 (see example 4).

Ring shout poetics and historical change make it difficult to map the
origins of individual musical elements: There are obviously traces of French
traditions in the use of Creole and in the melody, and the raspy growls of the
counter voice can be associated with traditions of the African peoples for-
merly known as bushmen and pygmies. All of these elements, however, had
been transformed into the hybrid African diaspora of the French Caribbean
and southern Louisiana. Other elements, such as the African American blues
sensibility of the lead singer, were closer to contemporary styles. As a whole,
the performance can be located somewhere in between Afro-Caribbean and
African American culture. Above all, it complicates conventional notions of
African American culture as a more or less homogenous ethnic group. The
music represents a form of hybridity that is typical of oral traditions in that

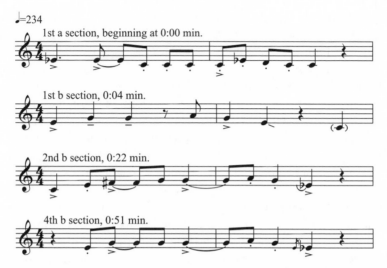

Musical Example 4 Jimmy Peters and ring dance singers, "J'ai fait tout le tours du pays" (1934), 0:00 min., first two bars of four sections. Compare the first *a* and *b* sections for general differences between the first two bars of each phrase. In addition, compare the first, second, and fourth *b* sections for rhythmic changes (again, in the first two bars of each section). Peters negotiates the melodic space between e' and e♭' ambiguously in blueslike fashion.

the performers make music in vernacular idioms of their region. Though the performers are not professionals and have technical limitations, their mastering of the form reveals that they are very familiar with it and were enculturated in local soundscapes rather than approaching them as outsiders. The processual character and the variations of the simple structural units also indicate that structure and code are means of ritual participation, so to explain this music strictly in generic terms would be to miss the point.

The musical tradition of *juré* has virtually disappeared, having never caught the attention of the recording industry. Compared to the major domestic "ethnic" markets of the time such as the hillbilly and race markets, rural Creole music was sung in a different language and had a more limited circulation, and *juré* was not primarily presentational music. When entrepreneurs began organizing hillbilly and race sessions in the 1920s, they wanted immediate profit from radio sponsors and phonograph sales, the potential for which was limited among the Creole population. The big ethnic markets eventually had a major influence on defining American popular music in black and white. Country blues of the same era, for instance, reached a white audience through the folk revival and has been defined as the essence of African American culture.

Creoles have entered the market place of modernity via the popular music genre of zydeco, which emerged in the 1950s and was popularized on the world music market in the 1980s. It is striking that zydeco on one side represents a move toward the American mainstream, with the heavy influence of rock and electric blues and more lyrics in English, and on the other side has attracted a broad audience as a form of world music. Genre has once again been a tool for essentializing connections between ethnicity, place, and music, because zydeco has repeatedly been defined as the music of Creoles in Louisiana. Globalism and Louisiana patriotism are two powerful identity discourses among the more than ten annual festivals in Louisiana dedicated to local traditions. Both discourses appeal to tourists, who constitute a substantial part of the approximately 500,000 visitors at the New Orleans Jazz and Heritage Festival and the approximately 250,000 at the world music– and diaspora-oriented Festival International de Louisiane in Lafayette.[21] Exoticizing stereotypes of Creole and Cajun music as part of an ethnic microcosm that includes food and language customs have been nurtured by coffee-table books, *Rough Guide* products, and Hollywood movies such as *The Big Easy* (1987).[22] In 2001 New York–based Putumayo World Music produced four anthologies of zydeco and other musics associated with Louisiana in collaboration with Louisiana's Office of Tourism, and they promoted the CDs at publicity events in Borders bookstores (Berry 2001).[23]

The representation of zydeco on Paul Simon's *Graceland* (Warner Bros., 1986) gives a fascinating glimpse of its location in contemporary mainstream popular culture. The song "That Was Your Mother" sounds as though Simon has tried to make typical zydeco music. His northeastern, urban, middle-class, Anglo-Jewish accent matches the identity of the narrator, who is telling a story about his experience in Louisiana as a traveling salesman, a kind of tourist, that is. The story paints a familiar picture of drinking and dancing to zydeco music in Lafayette, and joyful music completes the picture, which also includes a quasi-Orientalist romance. This zydeco song about an imagined zydeco experience is a genre pastiche. Simon says in his liner notes that he searched for "a musical connection to home" while working on this African album project and thought of the "accordion and saxophone music I'd heard in South Africa and the Zydeco bands of Cajun Louisiana" (Simon 1986).[24] We can understand the complex location of zydeco in relation to the genre pastiche, Simon's relatively coincidental recognition of the musical connection to Africa, and the song's appearance on an African-style album that fell into the world beat category. He was backed by a Creole zydeco band from Louisiana on "That Was Your Mother," and "All around the World or the Myth of Fingerprints" was done with Los Lobos, a famous Mexican

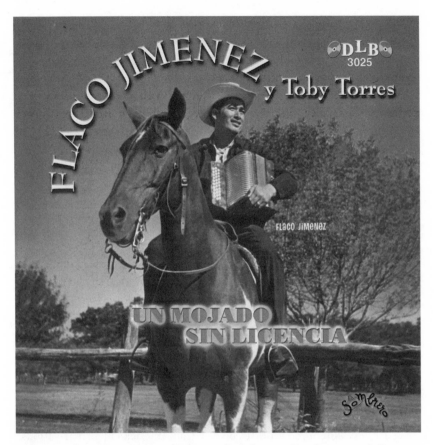

Figure 14 Flaco Jiménez, cover of *Un mojado sin licencia* (Sombrero, 1969). Courtesy of Salome Gutierrez, Del Bravo Records.

American band from Los Angeles. These two songs with American bands are the last tracks on the album, and I am sure they sound just as "African" as the other songs to many listeners in America and elsewhere. Finally, it is important to note how the album's American subject is positioned through the title song. The story is told by a guy from New York and is about his pilgrimage to Elvis's former mansion in Memphis. Graceland might have been a strategic allegory for political reasons, but that does not explain why the story is so deeply anchored in modern American mythology. There is a strong sense of exploring one's own national roots in the lyric about driving to "the cradle of the Civil War" on a pilgrimage to a pop icon of Simon's generation. By going through the Mississippi delta to Graceland, the subject approaches a space associated with African Americans, but the main destination is on white territory, or, to be more specific, the monument of a white southern male who had a close relation with African American music.[25]

Flaco Jiménez: "Indita mia" (Del Bravo Records, 1976)

The national cultures of Mexico and the United States have placed the large Mexican American population in the Southwest in a difficult in-between condition. Mexicanos, as they also call themselves, have been forced to negotiate between national cultures, yet the concept of nationalism eliminates the hybrid experience of these people and forces them to take sides even if they do not have a choice. The two countries have defined their national cultures primarily in the relation between native folk culture and European high culture, and not so much in relation to each other or to other neighboring countries. Differences in prosperity, moreover, have exacerbated the divisions far beyond the geographical borderline. The border is a social fact in the daily life of Mexicanos in the Southwest, where about 20 million people or one-third of the population is Latino, mostly Mexicano.[26] American popular culture has formed a cosmopolitan mainstream in Mexico since the 1920s when nationalists struggled against the "conquest of the Yankee fashion" (Simonett 2001, 148–50). In contrast, Mexican culture has had limited distribution outside of Mexicano communities in the United States, and the Anglo-American media have been much more concerned with Mexican immigration than with Mexican culture. For many of the immigrants, the role of nationhood is registered in their terrible conditions as illegal aliens, so there are very different discourses on Mexican American identity relations.

The musical traditions of Mexicanos in the Southwest witness a long history of transnational contact. *Banda* music evolved from the military brass bands that European colonizers introduced in Mexico in the mid nineteenth century. Polka was introduced by Czechs around the same time and has sunk deeply into the vernacular soundscapes of northern Mexico and the American Southwest. Although polka has lost some of its distinct genre identity and become more absorbed in other genres in the greater transnational region, one can speak of a counterpart in the Southwest to the polka belt in the Upper Midwest. In a similar fashion, jazz and American dance band traditions influenced the Mexicano *orquestas* of the 1930s, but they also fed the regional style of country music called western swing. Country music has had wide influence across ethnic boundaries in the region's major musical traditions. Mexicano musicians have associated themselves with cowboy hats and horses, and country music is big among Navajo people. Navajos have explored the patriotic narratives in this genre as a means

of empowerment against their subaltern existence in official national discourse.

The conjunto tradition in Tejano (Texas-American) culture draws on
many musical cultures, especially Mexican song traditions and polka, but
also jazz and country music. Like much Tejano culture, it is a product of
mestizaje (culture blending), but its canonization and distribution as Tejano
music have created the notion of a self-sufficient category rather than a category in between. Conjunto was first a term for a small, accordion-based
ensemble that existed on both sides of the border; later it became a term for
one of the styles that developed when Anglo-American record labels began
operating in the area shortly after the race series turned profitable. Peña's
theory of conjunto explains its emerging generic identity as a reflection of
general social processes of urbanization, Americanization, and class differentiation among Tejanos in the 1940s and 1950s (Peña 1985). The music's
associations with rural and working-class Tejano consciousness tightened
its generic boundaries vis-à-vis the more middle-class and Anglo-American-
oriented culture of *orquesta* music. Peña's study is a classic genre study in
that it adopts a narrative of rise and fall, focusing on the rise. We can also
adopt decentered models to look beyond this linear narrative and understand
the in-between condition of conjunto.

Flaco Jiménez is one of several artists whose musical careers can lead
us in the direction of more sophisticated explanations. He was just getting
started when, according to Peña, conjunto "had developed as far as it was
possible" (Peña 1985, 101).[27] Jiménez is firmly rooted in the conjunto tradition, which he learned from his father, one of the pioneers of the style,
but his music does not quite fit the description of conjunto as rural and
traditional. He was born and grew up in San Antonio, and his appreciation
of a wide variety of the popular musics that were available to him can be
heard in his playing. Early influences include Hank Williams, Clifton Che-
nier, Elvis Presley, and B. B. King.[28] Jiménez has worked as a professional
full-time musician for decades and has become known in wider circles since
the mid 1970s through collaborations with numerous rock, pop, and country
stars, and later as a member of the Texas Tornadoes and Los Super Seven.[29]
Throughout his solo career he has retained close ties to classical conjunto,
but with modernist sensibilities that have not yet been accounted for.

The Del Bravo label, which produced this recording of "Indita mia," was
a small company in San Antonio run by Salome Gutierrez. Footage from
his studio in the documentary *Chulas fronteras* (Blank 1975) shows that it
was an old shack or garage equipped with relatively inexpensive technology. Gutierrez's son told me in 2005 that most sessions were conducted on

Sundays and produced quickly so that the record could be on the radio the following day. He also told me that his father sings the second voice on this recording, and ad hoc decisions about personnel and other matters were probably common under such time constraints (Gutierrez, e-mail to author, 11 May 2005). All this is typical of the Tejano indie labels that emerged in San Antonio after the major Anglo labels lost interest in Tejano music in the mid 1940s and moved in on the national market in Mexico. Low-budget productions did not allow for much more than simple live studio recordings, and the music was distributed within a regional network without sophisticated marketing. In small-scale local networks, categorization is not as vital to distribution as in mass-culture contexts (cf. chapter 5). Artists also did not have to conform to mainstream stereotypes and could sing in their own language. It was common for conjunto recordings to list only the song title and the soloist or band name; the recording date and the names of musicians and producers remained unidentified. This is not surprising: the music mainly functioned as accompaniment to dancing, drinking, entertainment, and not as the object of art criticism.

Jiménez's rendition of "Indita mia" is in some ways typical of the classic late 1950s conjunto style, when many instrumental genres, including polka, more or less disappeared from the repertoire and were replaced by the sung *canción ranchera* or *corrido*, which musicians have described as "nothing more than a piece in tempo di polka with lyrics added" (Peña 1985, 74). The fast two-beat rhythm and driving accordion accompaniment are fundamental polka features, but the rhythmic feeling is a bit more complex, with snappy staccato playing and offbeat accents. Also typical is the classic Mexican duet singing in parallel thirds and the lyric about a man's unrequited love from his "little Indian girl" (the song title). The form is basically four stanzas with an accordion solo in the middle.

0:16 min.	Stanza 1	44 bars
0:59 min.	Stanza 2	40 bars
1:37 min.	Accordion solo	24 bars
2:01 min.	Stanza 3	45 bars
2:45 min.	Stanza 4	48 bars
3:31 min.	Ending	4 bars

The four lines of each stanza are simple melodic phrases, and they are sung relatively legato and without any change in dynamics. This creates a regular melodic flow with a slow pace because of the long pauses between the phrases. Although each phrase is three bars, the pauses are usually around

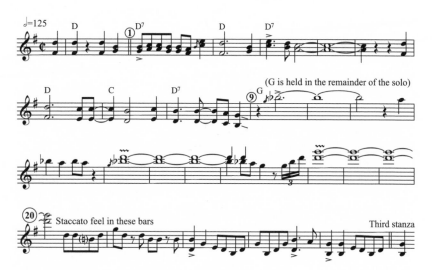

Musical Example 5 Flaco Jiménez, "Indita mia" (1976), 1:37–2:01 min., accordion solo.

eight bars. In the pauses, Jiménez plays polka riffs and runs to keep the energy going and create variation. As the song progresses, his playing becomes more adventurous and more central to the musical whole. This development accelerates in the middle section of the accordion solo when Jiménez suddenly departs from the steady conjunto style with a modernist jazz impulse. The shift occurs in the ninth bar, where Jiménez makes a big leap to a high note (bb"). Harmonically, the high note can be interpreted as a minor third or a sharp ninth, and it stands out as an unresolved dissonance for a few bars. It is unprepared and provides the effect of rhythmic and melodic contrast. The passage is informed by a jazz aesthetic and somewhat beyond the blues, although there are blues elements. (In the blues, the minor third would normally have been balanced by appearing in a straightforward pentatonic context and perhaps by a turn to the neighboring major third [b"].)

While Jiménez sustains the tension in the long notes, the bassist maintains his simple pattern of marking the downbeats. The drummer, however, departs from his complementary upbeat pattern and responds with relatively complicated improvised fills. Jiménez starts a smooth transition back to the conjunto-polka style in bar 20 and prepares for the third stanza with some of his typical passage work. These genre shifts in and after the middle section have some of the playfulness and sophistication that characterize his style. One easily recognizes these melodic formulas and rhetorical devices from listening to his many recordings.

Musical Example 6 Flaco Jiménez, "Indita mia" (1976), second phrase of fourth stanza and accordion fill, 2:59–3:12 min. The lyric "y siempre hablado con la verdad" means "and since there is no reason."

Jiménez's use of a single sharp and unmediated dissonance in bars 9–11 should be noted as a typical rhetorical device. He sometimes does similar things using a dissonant interval such as a tritone, which only intensifies the particular directness and wit of this device. His use of dissonances, moreover, extends into various forms of chromaticism. His fast chromatic runs are sometimes quickly ascending or descending, sometimes accumulating tension by remaining in a fixed position. An example of the latter occurs in the relatively long improvised space after the second phrase of the last stanza on this recording (see example 6).

This example of what we might call close chromaticism, because of the narrow pitch range, is preceded by chromaticism with larger intervals in the fill following the first phrase of this stanza. Again, Jiménez holds the tension rather than resolving it immediately. By repeating the chromatic motif in the same position he halts melodic movement and foregrounds structural and improvisatory play. The passage ends in a familiar place, as he smoothly moves into a polka turnaround and reestablishes stability. The whole passage between the second and third phrases is fifteen bars long, and the spaces between the phrases are generally longer in the last two stanzas, where Jiménez stretches out. As before, the bassist maintains his pattern, while the drummer experiments with jazzy fills.

It is clear that Jiménez has not only borrowed melodic ideas from jazz but also internalized some of its improvisatory procedures. The broader context of this is that throughout the 1960s and 1970s Jiménez matured and developed a greater sense of individuality as an instrumentalist (his singing did not change very much). Conjunto is to a large extent based on the accordion playing and has been a space for male instrumental virtuosity. It is as much an instrumental practice as a category, and we should therefore look at the agency and subjectivity of the performer. The work of other post-1955 accordionists shows that it is common for aesthetic explorations to grow out of the professional routine with a more functional mode of playing. Steve Jordan is famous for his rock-influenced solos, but he and several other accordionists also have a jazz-influenced sophistication. Jiménez has noted how the veteran accordionist Valerio Longoria introduced jazz harmony in conjunto and that the influence of jazz has grown over the years. "Now everybody jazzes up the accordion," he said in 2000 (PBS oral history interview [see note 28]).

I conclude that conjunto practice has changed after its initial codification in the 1950s, and that some of its key figures continue to move between larger generic spaces rather than within a strictly self-sufficient Tejano space. The classic conjunto style keeps informing the tradition, but contemporary conjunto is more than an echo or reiteration of its past. Traditions continue to generate new identities and meanings, even if the essentializing and centering forces of their canons try to make them stop and persuade us that this has happened. This case study of Jiménez also shows that the relation between ethnic and mainstream American musics is not always one between folk and popular music. He has a stronger connection to art jazz than to rock or pop, and he works in a regional culture where the folk/pop distinction has a different history.

꙳

Music between genres and cultures challenges conventional thinking about genre. It questions the ways categories organize and control social space, and it tells us that there are parts of reality that can better be reached via poetic metaphor than via cool reason and systematic control. This is not a meaningless paradox. Rather, it reflects the complexity of culture and points to one of the mechanisms through which categories are defined: Notions of difference and otherness intensify boundaries, as we have seen in many cases, from Cecil Sharp's purism to the specialization of insiders of contemporary genre scenes who prefer artists who master the genre rather than the mix of more pop-oriented mainstream artists.

This chapter has explored strategies for moving in and out of genre-centered discourse. One might read the entire book as a series of case studies employing different strategies for understanding genre across discursive boundaries. Looking at different subject positions and experiencing their conditions by moving physically in the field is an important strategy for recognizing diversity in spaces between centers and peripheries. This is not only an ethical ideal, but also a conceptual strategy. Studying music genres and their social ramifications helps us understand other aspects of social life because music has a constitutive role in our cultural and historical imagination.

My case studies in this chapter illustrate that music at the borders risks being forgotten if it does not have a powerful genre discourse. One could argue that the 1934 *juré* recording is "saved" by the Lomax canon and that the 1976 conjunto recording now has better chances for survival because of the growing fame of the soloist. It is worth noticing, however, that generic categories were part of the nuts and bolts of music making and perception even in these "small" traditions that lack a strong genre discourse. It was not difficult to identify generic codes and discover the impact of large genre traditions. This leads to the more general point that there are genres of music and music between genres, but not music without genre. I have noted that some reactions against categorization have led to rather uncritical celebrations of hybridity, but if we move away from genre discourse and do not return, if we ignore genre, we also ignore a part of social reality. I hope to have shown in this book that there is not just one truth about genre. This is one of the reasons why we need multiple critical models, plural narratives, and fieldwork across the boundaries of musical life in the modern world.

The Jeff Parker Discography

Much of Parker's recorded work is difficult to track down because its distribution is scattered across small, specialized networks. His work in different contexts has different and relatively separate audiences, and few libraries and record stores have as many as half of his recordings. It is telling that it would have been difficult to compile the following discography without Parker's help. The following discography is intended to be complete and to give a sense of Parker's broad range of recording activities with artists and labels associated with different categories. In this sense, I present the discography as an appendix to chapters 5 and 6 and as a reference for further studies.

Of the sixty-eight titles I located as of February 2006, fewer than ten are on major labels or subsidiaries thereof. These labels include Blue Note, EMI, JVC Victor, MCA, Nonesuch, and Warner. About half the titles are on independent labels in or near Chicago, and about half of those are on labels specializing in jazz (Atavistic, Delmark, 8th Harmonic Breakdown, 482 Music, Okka Disk) and the other half on labels primarily identified with rock, hip-hop, or electronica (Chocolate Industries, Drag City, Hefty, Overcoat, Perishable, Super Bro, Thrill Jockey, Truckstop, Wax Trax). More than ten titles are on small jazz labels based far from Chicago: Aesthetics (Portland, Oregon), Cryptogramophone (Los Angeles), HatHut, including hatART (Switzerland), and Silkheart (Sweden). Asian Improv is a San Francisco label dedicated to Asian American music. Lucky Kitchen is a Barcelona label focusing on experimental music. Merge, Wishing Tree, and Duophonic are rock-oriented labels based in Durham, North Carolina; Warren, Rhode Island; and London, respectively.

Abrams, Josh. 2003. *Cipher*. Delmark.

Aesop Quartet. 2000. *Fables for a New Millennium*. 8th Harmonic Breakdown.

Akito. 2000. *Hey Mister Girl*. EMI/Toshiba Japan.

Aluminum Group. 2000. *Pelo*. Hefty.

Aluminum Group. 2002. *Happyness*. Wishing Tree.

Anderson, Fred. 2000. *Live at the Velvet Lounge, Vol. 2*. Asian Improv.

Anderson, Fred. 2003. *Back at the Velvet Lounge*. Delmark.

Azita. 2003. *Enantiodromia*. Drag City.

Azita. 2004. *Life on the Fly*. Drag City.

Bauder, Matt, Jeff Parker, and Jason Ajemian. 2003. "Incidentally," *Document Chicago*. 482 Music.

Blur. 1998. *Bustin' and Dronin'* (John McEntire mix). MCA.

Boxhead Ensemble. 2001. *Two Brothers*. Atavistic.

Brian Blade Fellowship. 1998. *Brian Blade Fellowship*. Blue Note.

Buck 65. 2004. "Blanc-bec." On *Secret House against the World*. Warner Music Australia.

Cardew, Cornelius. 2004. *Material*. hatART.

Chicago Underground Orchestra. 1996. *Playground*. Delmark.

Chicago Underground Quartet. 1998. *12 Degrees of Freedom*. Thrill Jockey.

———. 1999. *Possible Cube*. Delmark.

———. 2001. *Chicago Underground Quartet*. Thrill Jockey.

Chicago Underground Trio. 2000. *Flamethrower*. Delmark Records.

Chocolat & Akito. 2005. *S/T*. JVC Victor Japan.

Diverse. 2003. *One A.M.* Chocolate Industries.

Eisenstadt, Harris. 2005. *The Soul and Gone*. 482 Music.

Ernest Dawkins's New Horizons Ensemble. 1992. *Southside Street Songs*. Silkheart.

———. 1994. *Chicago Now, Vols. I and II*. Silkheart.

———. 1997. *Mother's Blue Velvet Shoes*. Dawk.

———. 2000. *Jo'Burg Jump*. Delmark.

Eternals, The. 2001. *S/T*. Aesthetics.

Givens, Daniel. 2000. *Age*. Aesthetics.

———. 2002. *The Idea of Space*. Aesthetics.

———. 2003. *Freedom's Myth*. Aesthetics.

Great 3. 2002. *When You Were a Beauty*. Toshiba/EMI/Bodicious Japan.

———. 2003. *Climax*. Toshiba/EMI/Bodicious Japan.

Gregorio, Guillermo. 2002. *Faktura*. HatHut.

Him. 1999. *Sworn Eyes*. Perishable.

Jeb Bishop Trio/Quartet. 2000. *Afternoons*. Okka Disk.

Joshua Redman Elastic Band. 2005. *Momentum*. Nonesuch.

Isotope 217. 1998. *The Unstable Molecule*. Thrill Jockey.

———. 1999. *Hodah*. Aesthetics.

———. 1999. *utonian_automatic*. Thrill Jockey.

———. 2000. *Who Stole the I Walkman*. Thrill Jockey.

Parker, Jeff. 2003. *Like-Coping*. Delmark.

———. 2003. "Holiday for a Despot," *Chicago's Avant Today* (anthology). Delmark.

———. 2004. *The Relatives*. Thrill Jockey.

Parker, Jeff, Kevin Drumm, and Michael Zerang. 2003. *out trios volume two*. Atavistic.

Parker, Jeff, and Yasuhiro Ohtani. 2002. *Envy*. Asian Improv.

Peabody & Sherman. 2004. *Hotboxing Nicorette*. Super Bro.

Scott Amendola Band. 2005. *Believe*. Cryptogramophone.

Scott Fields Ensemble. 1999. *Denouenent*. Geode.

Smog. 2000. *Dongs of Sevotion*. Drag City.

Tchicai, John, and Yusef Komuunyaka. 1998. *Lovesongs From the Madhouse*. 8th Harmonic Breakdown.

Ted Sirota's Rebel Souls. 1996. *Rebel Roots*. Naim.

———. 1998. *Propaganda*. Naim.

———. 2001. *Vs. the Forces of Evil*. Naim.

———. 2004. *Breeding Resistance*. Delmark.

Toe. 2000. *Variant*. Truckstop.

Toe 2000. 1998. *S/T*. Truckstop.

Tortoise. 1994. *Gamera b/w Cliff Dweller Society*. Duophonic.

———. 1998. *TNT*. Thrill Jockey.

———. 2000. *Standards*. Thrill Jockey.

———. 2004. *It's All Around You*. Thrill Jockey.

Tortoise and Bonnie "Prince" Billy. 2006. *The Brave and the Bold*. Overcoat.

Tortoise and Jeff Parker. 1996. *OFFBEAT, A Red Hot Sampler*. Wax Trax.

Tricolor. 1998. *Mirth + Feckless*. Atavistic.

———. 2000. *NonParticipant + Milk*. Atavistic.

Urban Renewal Program. 2002. Chocolate Industries.

Vega Trio. 2002. *Live at 7 Lézards*. Merge.

Who Cares How Long You Sink. 2004. *Who Cares How Long You Sink*. Lucky Kitchen.

NOTES

CHAPTER ONE

1. I am referring to Pink Floyd's 1990 show in Berlin at the occasion of the fall of the Wall, Elton John's performance of "Candle in the Wind" at Diana's funeral in 1997, and the Live Aid concerts ahead of the G8 summit in July 2005. Music at Soccer World Cups is discussed in chapter 7.

2. On the legitimization of popular culture in academia, see Mukerji and Schudson 1991, 3. The canonization of popular music studies can be registered in journals and books on the subject. Among the main journals are *Popular Music, Popular Music and Society, Chapter & Verse,* and *Journal of Popular Music Studies.* A list of popular music books with a foundational role or ethos should include Brackett 1995; Frith 1996; Gendron 2002; Middleton 1990; Middleton 2000; Moore 1993/2001; and Toynbee 2000.

3. Ryall has made a similar claim (1998, esp. 337). I say more about different types of categories later in this chapter. The term generic refers to general concepts, to kinds, types, or classes (*Webster's New Universal Unabridged Dictionary,* rev. and updated, deluxe ed. [New York: Barnes and Noble Books, 1996], s.v. "generic"; Prechtl and Burkard 1996, 184).

4. Notions of transgression and hybridity took on positive values in "postmodern classics" by such writers as Lyotard (1979) and Clifford (1986). Some of this was echoed in Western art musicology, with Kramer, for instance, who claimed to represent a "postmodern musicology" that works from an "ethos" rather than a "system" (1995, 5).

5. I am thinking of Diderot's *Encyclopédie* and Kant's and Hegel's multivolume treatises. For a further discussion of cultural representation and categorization in this era, see Foucault 1966. Musicological pioneers such as Guido Adler were influenced by Darwinian evolutionism. In the 1960s, Walter Wiora reacted against evolutionism, and Carl Dahlhaus drew attention to the historicity of generic systems. For further details on German musicology, see Danuser 1995, 1055–59. Evolutionism was also under attack in the early years of modern American ethnomusicology (cf. Bohlman 1992, 124). It should be mentioned that musical scholarship is still deeply structured

by genre boundaries. The entries on genre in *Musik in Geschichte und Gegenwart* (*MGG*) (Danuser 1995) and *The New Grove Dictionary of Music and Musicians* (Samson 2001) do not deal with either popular or non-Western music.

6. Toynbee's discussion is hardly groundbreaking, and his use of the term genre culture is idiosyncratic. His list of genre cultures includes "race music," which is better understood as a marketing category; "crossover," which is better understood as a market mechanism; and "mainstream," which is better understood as a contrast to genre cultures, as argued above. None of those categories can be meaningfully described as a genre culture.

7. Todorov has offered a critique of the notion of genres as classes of texts and called attention to practice (1976, 165 and 169).

8. Some useful reference works are Frith et al. 2001; Shuker 1998; White 1998; Wicke et al. 1997; *All Music Guide*; and *Grove Music Online*.

9. Ambitious attempts at mapping large systems occurred in early musicology (see note 5 above) and in the formative years of genre research in film studies (Ryall 1998, 328–29, 331).

10. See note 8 for popular and academic reference works. The Recording Industry Association of America (RIAA) has conducted surveys based on categories used by the industry. DeVeaux has studied data obtained from a 1992 questionnaire survey of "participation in the arts" for the National Endowment for the Arts (DeVeaux 1995, 58–64). Item 37a in the questionnaire listed twenty different "types of music," and respondents were asked, "Which of these types of music do you like to listen to?" The ten most popular were country/western, rock, blues/R & B, big band, jazz, classical/chamber, bluegrass, show tunes/operettas, soul, and folk (DeVeaux 1995, 36 and 62). The choice of terms was not particularly systematic, and I wonder how people would have responded had they been asked to use their own terms.

11. By Muzak I mean music produced for background listening in elevators, shopping malls, and pornographic film, for instance. Music produced for this purpose is often based on simple and standardized schemes and has a smooth, subdued character in order not to disturb or distract listeners from the main action. The boundaries of Muzak have expanded considerably, though (Owen 2006).

12. There is some confusion among scholars about the distinction between genre and style. See, for instance, Moore 1993/2001, 1–3; Shuker 1998, 145, 158, 237 et passim. Shuker dodges the question by writing that "punk rock" is a musical "style/genre" (1998, 237). The overlap between genre and style is demonstrated in the empirical analyses by Fabbri (1999, 10).

13. On contemporary practice in the Muzak industry, see Owen 2006.

14. Middleton has noted that structuralist listening has imprisoned the body (2000, 24).

15. I say "about" because the number has continually decreased over the past fifteen years or so. Currently, there are EMI (includes Virgin), Sony/BMG (includes CBS, Columbia, RCA, and Arista), Warner Music Group, and Universal Music Group (includes PolyGram, Geffen, MCA, Motown, and Verve). Cf. Negus 1999, 35–45.

16. Based on record company estimates, the International Federation of the Phonographic Industry estimated in October 2005 that sales of digital music files had tripled since 2004 and that this was one of the reasons for the decline in sales of "CDs and other physical formats" ("Digital Music Market More than Triples" 2005.).

17. MySpace.com, http://groups.myspace.com/index.cfm?fuseaction=groups.List Groups&categoryID=21&Mytoken=D748B376-FB11-B635-8CB2FFDE03B981D45859337 (accessed 28 August 2006). Yahoo!, http://dir.groups.yahoo.com/dir/ (accessed 28 August 2006).

CHAPTER TWO

1. The modern invention of folk music in the late eighteenth and early nineteenth centuries reflected tensions within modernity. To people who were experiencing industrialization and urbanization, folk music represented idealized images of community, tradition, and nature in a simple, rural world. From early on, folk music discourses were marked by nostalgia and enjoyed a close relationship with nationalism and philosophies of nature and civilization. For an analysis of theories of folk music and its place in modernity, see Bohlman 1988.

2. An influential approach was pioneered by Tagg, who stated that popular music is "all music which is neither folk or art music" and outlined a combinational definition (1979, chapter 2). There was much discussion of definitions of popular music in the early years of IASPM, as reflected by its annual publication *Popular Music Perspectives.* Relevant articles include Charles Hamm's historical study in the first volume and the more theoretical articles by Chris Cutler, Umberto Fiori, and John Shepherd in the second. The articles indicate that there was a broad impulse toward recognizing popular music as a complex category without a clear definition, but they also included defining gestures and crude discriminatory generalizations. Middleton, Frith, and others have since refined the discussion, but the field has not settled on a single definition or theory as the standard. For references and more context, see chapter 1, which draws on a number of seminal works in popular music studies.

3. The first part of Foster's life was spent in what has been called the White Cottage, which seems to have been substantial enough to require a servant, and he spent most of his life in the urban areas of Pittsburgh, Cincinnati, and New York City. Mariana Whitmer, e-mail to author, 17 January 2004; Kathy Haines, e-mail to author, 17 January 2004. The song has been recorded many times since. For instance, it appears on Bob Dylan's *Good as I Been to You* (Sony, 1992) and Emmylou Harris's *At the Ryman* (Warner Bros., 1992). Harris left out the word cabin, though.

4. The Carter Family, "Little Log Cabin by the Sea" (Victor, 1927); Hank Williams, "A Mansion on the Hill" (MGM, 1947); Dolly Parton: "My Tennessee Mountain Home," "Wrong Direction Home," and other songs on *My Tennessee Mountain Home* (RCA, 1974).

5. Everett's urban attitude is reflected in the early scene (selection 4 on the DVD) where he wants to buy hair pomade in a very small grocery. He is the only customer

in the store. The clerk says that he only has one brand and that it will take two weeks to get the brand Everett wants. Everett comments on the "geographical oddity" of the place and concludes: "This is two weeks from everywhere. Forget it."

6. Chris Thomas King (b. 1964) is a blues guitarist and singer. It is generally believed that there are only two photographs of Robert Johnson in existence. Both are printed in Santelli, Warren, and Brown 2001, 47. Cf. Wyman and Havers 2001, 216. The character Tommy Johnson resembles Robert Johnson in those photos in age, looks, clothes (suit and hat), way of holding the guitar, and calm facial expression. A short biography and photo of the historical Tommy Johnson can be found in National Park Service 2001.

7. The Dust Bowl era was a period of severe dust storms on the Great Plains in the Southwest in the 1930s. The storms resulted from a combination of drought, overfarming, and poor soil conservation practices, and they led to massive migration.

8. James Carter and the Prisoners, "Po' Lazarus"; Ed Lewis and the Prisoners, "Tom Devil." Both of these recordings are from 1959 and 1960 and are available on *The Alan Lomax Collection: Southern Journey, vol. 5* (Rounder, 1997). Harry McClintock (1882–1957), "Big Rock Candy Mountain" (Victor, 1928); Stanley Brothers, "Angel Band" (Mercury, 1955).

9. Joe Hickerson, backstage conversation with author at the University of Chicago Folk Festival, 8 February 2003.

10. "Best-Selling Albums of 2002" 2003. Cf. Recording Industry Association of America, "Gold and Platinum Searchable Database," http://www.riaa.com/gp/database/default.asp (accessed 28 August 2006).

11. Some of the CDs related to the film include Ralph Stanley and the Clinch Mountain Boys, *Man of Constant Sorrow* (Rebel, January 2001); *Songcatcher: Music from and Inspired by the Motion Picture* (Vanguard, May 2001); *Down from the Mountain: Live Concert Performances by the Artists and Musicians of O Brother, Where Art Thou?* (Rounder, July 2001); *O Sister: The Women's Bluegrass Collection* (Rounder, October 2001); *Blue Trail of Sorrow* (Rounder, October 2001); *Lonesome Valley* (Manteca, March 2002); *Bona Fide Bluegrass and Mountain Music* (RCA/BMG, April 2002); *Man of Constant Sorrow: And Other Timeless Mountain Ballads* (Yazoo, May 2002); *More Bona Fide Bluegrass & Mountain Music* (RCA/BMG, October 2002); *Roots and Branches* (Capitol, October 2002); *O Brothers! Family Harmony and Old-Time Music* (Living Era/EMI, January 2003).

12. A new edition of a dictionary of blues and folk music was subtitled *The Premier Encyclopedia of American Roots Music* (Stambler and Stambler 2001). Other encyclopedias and dictionaries have been targeted to the roots market. In 2003, the main page of the All Music Guide Web site presented five "music styles:" "rock & roll," "blues," "country," "jazz," "roots," and "more." "Roots" included "gospel," "Cajun," "folk," "bluegrass," "world," "new age," and "easy listening." "All Music Guide: Styles," http://www.allmusic.com/mus_Styles.html (accessed 2 August

2003). Rounder Records marked its thirtieth anniversary in 2001 by compiling a four-CD box set of recordings from the vaults under the title *Roots Music: An American Journey*. The Rough Guides label issued the CD anthology *The Rough Guide to USA Roots Music* in 2003, following its anthologies of "English roots music" (1998) and "world roots music" (2000).

13. The NEA grant was for $225,000. National Endowment for the Arts, http://www.nea.gov/learn/oogrants/ARTVgrants.html/ (accessed 28 July 2003). For more information on the production and funding of the Web site of the PBS series, see Public Broadcasting Service 2001a and the preface in Santelli, Warren, and Brown 2001, esp. 10. *O Brother* premiered in June 2000, and the soundtrack was released in December of the same year.

14. My warning here is a minor critical response to Feld's impressive Danziger lecture at the University of Chicago on 20 April 2004 titled "Nostalgia and Modernity, or, *The Odyssey* from Greece to Appalachia via New Guinea and Europe." I think Feld's focus on 9/11 and his animosity toward conservatism in southern country music created a somewhat reductive explanatory framework in his analysis of the social contexts of *O Brother*.

15. Three of the twenty-one board members are musicologists (Public Broadcasting Service 2001b).

16. The listings provided the most rudimentary information on who, where, and when a show would take place. Mentioned in descending order by the number of events, the categories were: "DJ/electronic music," "rock/hip hop," "jazz/blues," "folk/country/Irish," "Latin/salsa," "lounge/cabaret," and "open mike" (*SF Weekly* 2003a). The same categories were used in the Internet edition of the paper, with an additional category for regular events (*SF Weekly* 2003b).

17. The concert series was held in the Music Store, 66 West Portal Avenue, and ran at least throughout most of 2003. At the show I attended, an amateur old-time country music band played for tips and sold a few of their CDs. The owner had organized the series out of his passion for country music, and the concerts attracted more customers to the store. There was an audience of about fifteen to twenty-five people.

18. The Crooked Jades, http://www.crookedjades.com/ (accessed 28 August 2006).

19. The San Francisco Bluegrass and Old-Time Festival, http://www.sfbluegrass.org/specialevents/downfromthemtn.html (accessed 9 August 2003). *Down from the Mountain* is a documentary of a concert at the Ryman Auditorium in Nashville featuring artists that appear on the *O Brother* soundtrack.

20. The organization's name is the Americana Music Association.

21. Two popular music textbooks give a sense that roots music is virtually ignored in the academic canon: Frith, Straw, and Street 2001; and Starr and Waterman 2003. The former is not a history book, but it certainly outlines a canon.

22. DeVeaux (1991) has studied this narrative, which still dominates jazz history textbooks in one form or another.

DOUBLE SESSION ONE

1. This informant shall remain anonymous, but it is not difficult to find similar views in print. See, e.g., Malone 2002a, 247. See also Guralnick 1994, 311f. and 337f.; Stearns and Stearns 1979, 1–2.

2. This can be seen in rock magazines and books. One example is Cohn's *Rock from the Beginning* (1969), which outlines a chronology of artists and styles. Another is Marcus's *Mystery Train* (first published in 1975), in which Elvis is a central case study. Marcus concludes that along with Robert Johnson, who belongs to the pre-rock era, Elvis is "the grandest figure in the story I have tried to tell" (Marcus 1990, 175). To Robert Palmer, writing for the *Rolling Stone History of Rock and Roll* in 1976, the rock era really began in 1956 when Elvis, Chuck Berry, Fats Domino, and Little Richard crossed over to the pop charts (Palmer 1976, 21).

3. For a brief introduction to the concept of modernization, see Apthorpe 1996; Spencer 1996. For a critical response and alternative theorizations, see Appadurai 1996, esp. 2, 9, and 202 n. 3.

4. Sloan has been a deejay and owner of three major commercial radio stations in the Southwest since the mid-1950s. He has also worked with the Country Music Association.

5. Several histories of popular music view rock and roll as the beginning of a major era. Cf. Garofalo 2002, 4–8, 123–25; Middleton 2004).

6. The five music categories mentioned above are taken from a marketing survey indicating that popular music in these areas constitute the main markets for music in America (RIAA 2003).

CHAPTER THREE

1. The TV series *The Beverly Hillbillies* (1962–71) and *Hee Haw* (1969–93) were notorious examples of hillbilly stereotypes in the national media. A recent example of resistance to the hillbilly stigma is Gretchen Wilson's "Redneck Woman" on the album *Here for the Party* (Sony, 2004), in which the singer expresses pride in her rural background. The dialectic nature of this history is recognized by Malone, for example in his discussion of the role of northerners in the creation of nostalgic images of the South (Malone 2002b, chapter 3).

2. The Mullican song is "What Have I Done That Made You Go Away?" (King, 1946). As in many other cases, one cannot be completely sure if the similarities between two songs originate in the use of common generic models or in the particular form of imitation associated with the concept of the cover. Another boogie-based song by a country artist is Tennessee Ernie Ford's "Shotgun Boogie" (Capitol, 1950).

3. The poster for this show (6 February 1955) was included in the main exhibit at the Country Music Hall of Fame in 2004. The other artists were Faron Young, Ferlin Husky, the Wilburn Brothers, and Martha Carson. According to Guralnick (1976,

35), Elvis was listed as the eighth most promising new hillbilly artist in *Billboard*'s annual poll at the end of 1954. See also Marcus 1990, 128–33.

4. These observations are based on interviews with historian John Rumble and other experts as well as Harold Bradley who recalled hearing the complaints. I conducted these interviews in Nashville in November 2004.

5. Peterson says that the rockabillies "absented themselves or were temporarily banished from country" (1997, 224). See also Guralnick's account of Elvis's first appearance on the Opry in September 1954 and the circumstances that preceded it (1994, 121–30).

6. Robert Oermann has witnessed this in his many encounters with country artists over the years. Oermann, conversation with author, 12 November 2004.

7. Ackerman mentions that Nashville music executives once asked him to take Elvis off the country charts in *Billboard*, and that one of them added: "He sings nigger music!" (Ackerman 1958, 37).

8. The ad for "Gone" was published in *The Country Music Reporter*, 16 February 1957, 3.

9. The words whiny, sour, smooth, and lush were all common. I have found it in magazines, and several of my informants have told me about them. One of them is radio deejay Jim Sloan who worked in New Mexico in the 1950s (Jim Sloan, conversation with author, 4 November 2004).

10. Harold Bradley says that everyone knew that Cline and Owen Bradley often argued on the sessions, but that her skepticism faded when the records became very popular. Bradley, conversation with author, 12 November 2004.

11. There are no comprehensive empirical studies and no in-depth ethnographies of the music's circulation in social life. Retrospective accounts of and by famous artists can be found in biographies and autobiographies. Audience reactions have been described in historical studies, but only briefly and in general terms, without much attention to particular individuals and collectivities. Jensen 1998; Malone 2002a, chapter 8.

12. Rosenberg (1985) argues that bluegrass became a genre in itself, but it has continued to circulate within the social networks of country music, both in religious contexts and in secular contexts, as in the case of *O Brother, Where Art Thou?* (cf. chapter 2).

13. The full text is: "I shall sing no song that is not a country song. / I shall make no record that is not a country record. / I refuse to be known as anything but a country singer. / I am proud to be associated with country music. / Country music and country music fans made me what I am today. / And I shall not forget it."

14. According to a deejay with inside knowledge of the industry, the target audience is women between eighteen and forty-five (Patrick, conversation with author, 6 May 2004).

15. Campbell is the owner of the Kentucky Opry.

CHAPTER FOUR

1. Washington's legacy in jazz has been discussed by DeVeaux (1997, chapter 1).

2. The Woodstock festival in 1969 was a culminating point of the mass success of the folk revival. In the early 1970s, artists such as Joan Baez and Donovan, who did not adapt to rock music or contemporary pop, began to sound old-fashioned to many rock fans.

3. Lake and others have said that Lennon made this statement in the late 1960, but I have not been able to identify a specific time and date. In his lengthy biography, Ray Coleman references various events in the late 1950s and 1960s suggesting that Lennon hated jazz from early on (Coleman 1986, 59, 69, 182–83). Coleman acknowledges that his perspective is informed by that fact that he was an assistant editor of *Melody Maker* in this period when it shifted focus from jazz to rock. One can also get a sense of how some rock musicians distanced themselves from jazz by watching the footage from the 1965 Dylan tour featured in the documentary *Dont Look Back* (Pennebaker 1967). In one scene, Dylan and his companions are at a reception and make fun of jazz and bodily gestures associated with jazz while jazz is being performed in the next room. It strikes me that this is an attitude of being anti-bourgeois, young, rude, and provocative. They are clearly mocking the music associated with an older age group.

4. Cf. Gendron 2002, chapter 8.

5. Rivelli wrote: "Let's forget categories as much as we can, and remember that music first of all is that great transcendent that has been blowing minds, salving souls, and telling us where we've been at for all of human history. To paraphrase Bob Dylan, 'It's all music, man!'" (1967, 17). Rivelli, letter to author, 8 February 2005.

6. This is not hard to see, and if one asks those who defended fusion throughout the 1970s, the response is quick and certain (Neil Tesser, conversation with author, Chicago, 2 May 2004). Kofsky did not hesitate to report on negative attitudes. He wrote that the jazz establishment found rock vulgar and considered the word teenager a pejorative (Kofsky 1967, 24).

7. The Tenth Monterey Jazz Festival ran from 15 to 17 September.

8. These circles include Larry Coryell, the Free Spirits, and Michael and Randy Brecker, who played in both Manieri's White Elephant and in Blood, Sweat, and Tears. Cf. Nicholson 1998, chapters 3–4.

9. The ad can be found in various issues, including *Jazz and Pop* 9, no. 1 (January 1970): 3.

10. Wilson was a core jazz writer, and Rivelli felt that the skepticism in his reports from the festival was unjust (Rivelli 1969).

11. Szwed is a particularly valuable commentator on Davis's life and career during these years because he is an astute historical witness. He also wrote for *Jazz and Pop*, primarily about rock.

12. This all-lowercase style was also used by E. E. Cummings, for instance, but it is safe to say that the audience for this album would associate it with beat writers and underground publications more generally.

13. A more detailed account of Davis's life and career in these years is provided in Szwed 2002, chapters 7–9.

14. For a further discussion of identity issues and Davis's fusion, see Tomlinson 1997.

CHAPTER FIVE

1. Wilkerson's *Harold in Chicago* was performed in the HotHouse on 12 December 2003. Dawkins's *Misconception of a Delusion and Shades of a Charade* was performed at the Chicago Jazz Fair in the Cultural Center on 22 January 2004.

2. Another case is Ted Sirota's album *Breeding Resistance* (Delmark, 2004). Delmark allowed him to include the following statements in his liner notes: "This is a time when young Black & Latino men are criminalized and warehoused in state of the art penitentiaries. . . . This is a time when we are persuaded to mistrust entire religions and nations of people and dismiss them as 'terrorists' and 'evil-doers.'" Few critics discussed these statements, and one club owner forbade any mention of it at the release party in his club. Ted Sirota, e-mail to author, 5 March 2004.

3. Thrill Jockey, Atavistic, 482 Music, Delmark, and other labels market their products through their Web sites as well as through Internet vendors such as Amazon.com and Barnes&Noble.com. The labels also have distributors in other countries, primarily Western countries. In Europe, Delmark Records, for instance, is distributed in England, France, Germany, Italy, the Netherlands, Portugal, Slovenia, Sweden, and Switzerland (Mike Siniscalchi, e-mail to author, 25 February 2004). There are no scholarly publications on jazz in Chicago after 1990. The monographs by Radano (1993) and Lewis (in press) are not about the general scene, and Lewis does not focus on the present. Mandel has a couple of pages on musicians of the Association for the Advancement of Creative Musicians (AACM) and on clubs in *Future Jazz* (1999), and Hughes has two chapters on jazz in her impressionistic and romanticizing book on popular music in Chicago (2004).

4. The only guide to the scene is Hughes 2004, described in note 3 above. A sample of general guide books should include Berkmoes 2001, Terry 2004, and *Time Out: Chicago* 2002.

5. I received promotional material from the publisher on 4 January 2002 as a reviewer of this work, but the expansion is also noted in the first paragraph of the preface in the first volume. Many of the new biographies are of minor figures.

6. I am referring here to WBEZ Chesterton, which positions itself as a talk-oriented station during the day. WNIU in northern Illinois is a full-time jazz station, but it does not cover a lot of local jazz either.

7. Groll described himself as "assistant jazz format chief" at WHKP.

8. See, e.g., Margasak's notes on Chicago in Taylor 2002, 22, 33, 56, and passim.

9. The *New York Times* and the *Los Angeles Times* each have a full-time jazz writer.

10. See, e.g., Howard Reich, "Jeff Parker's Succinct Style of Play Begin to Pay off," *Chicago Tribune*, 13 September 1995; Reich, "No Slim Pickin' in Chicago: City's Jazz Guitar Scene Reaching New Heights," *Chicago Tribune*, 10 December 1995.

11. This was the theme of the week on the daily program *Eight Forty-Eight*. The shows were broadcast from 26 January to 1 February 2004.

12. Another significant statement was made by the actor and filmmaker John Farrell, who performed at the Improv Olympic for years but moved in his late twenties: "People in L.A. and New York aren't auditioning for, you know, baloney commercials. They're making a living on TV shows and in movies. Chicago is sort of a thankless place." Chicago Public Radio, 1 February 2004.

13. Koransky has played some jazz: "I grew up playing trumpet, and I actually played classical trumpet. I was in the Skokie Symphony here. I played jazz. I played some funk."

14. This is most evident when Koransky talks about some of the young experimental musicians: "If I hear someone who can't swing and doesn't have a command of the instrument, and I do hear that a lot unfortunately—the young musicians who are trying to create new jazz or free jazz—and then I look at someone like Ken Vandermark and say 'that guy can play his ass off, he can play anything because he's grounded in the tradition,' you know." Koransky, conversation with author, Elmhurst, Illinois, 5 December 2003.

15. See also Richards's statements in Greg Kot, "Music that Works: In Chicago, the Record Business Is Not So Much a Money-Making Venture as a Creative Free-for-All," *Chicago Tribune*, 7 September 1997. See also Kot, "Unlikely Mates Celebrate Indie Label's Success," *Chicago Tribune*, 9 September 2002.

16. The project description Parker refers to is no longer available on the Internet.

17. In September 2005 I was unable to find decent research on the etymology of "scene" in jazz, so I contacted a few jazz experts who have been insiders of the New York scene for several decades. Dan Morgenstern, Ira Gitler, and George Avakian all agreed that the term has existed since the 1950s. Gitler referred to the famous 1949 recording "The Jazz Scene," produced by Norman Granz, as an early example. Avakian was convinced that the term had been used in the 1930s and maybe the 1920s but did not provide any details to substantiate his belief.

18. At the height of the decline, 1967–82, about 60 percent of all manufacturing jobs were lost, and 43 percent of the white population left the city between 1970 and 1990; the majority relocated to the suburbs (Abu-Lughod 1999, 331).

19. There are weekly jam sessions at the New Apartment Lounge, the Woodlawn Tap, and a few other places, and monthly jam sessions at the Quadrangle Clubs and the Ramada Inn in Hyde Park, for instance. The Velvet relocated in 2006 after a long fund-raising drive. The precarious situation is indicated by the fact that the club was

"rescued" when a wealthy man donated a large sum in the final stages of the fund-raising drive.

20. Fred Anderson, a legendary local sax player and owner of the Velvet Lounge, says he is far from able to hire the stars that play in the Jazz Showcase. Anderson, conversation with author, Chicago, 26 November 2003.

21. Muhal Richard Abrams has performed at the Jazz Showcase, and there is a video of a 1981 concert with the Art Ensemble in this club, but these are rare exceptions.

22. Sassen 2001. U.S. Bureau of Census 1998, 72.

23. U.S. Bureau of the Census, http://factfinder.census.gov/ (accessed 28 August 2006).

24. Local smooth jazz artists include Mike Logan and Ramsey Lewis, who is also hosting a show on "WNUA 95.5 FM—Smooth Jazz." This station organizes live shows at the Navy Pier and in Grant Park. This music can also be found at clubs like Isaac Hayes and Pops for Champagne. Its discursive location as a genre is unclear, but musically it draws a lot on jazz and contemporary R & B. Trad jazz can be heard at clubs like Joe's Be-Bop Café and Al Capone's Hideaway where Parker never comes. Parker and his peers have made several records for Delmark and have a distant relation with the label's "traditional jazz" series. Parker also has a peripheral relation to the jazz-influenced music in the musician community of experimental electronic music. Most of them are semi-professionals without a solid training in jazz and that alone makes them somewhat marginal to the jazz scene. They occasionally present music in private homes and some have performed at Deadtech, Myopic Books, the Empty Bottle, and the Candlestick Maker. One of the grassroots, Greg Davis, organized a second annual experimental music workshop in his apartment in March 2004. This music gets some airplay on WLUW.

25. Anderson and Bowden are among the AACM musicians who have come to Freeman to learn the craft of swing and bebop (Mwata Bowden, conversation with author, Chicago, 26 February 2004). Freeman also influenced musicians on the 1980s' avant-garde scene in Manhattan, including Greg Osby and Steve Coleman (Mandel 1999, 148–49). Some of these musicians supposedly still listen to Freeman (Koransky, conversation with author, 5 December 2003).

26. Walton showed me the documentary.

27. This is a common complaint in many parts of Chicago, and a typical version is given by Franz (2000) who lived in Wicker Park from 1991 to 1997. A couple of members of Tortoise moved west in 2003.

28. Chad Taylor and Jeff Parker have always collaborated with white musicians. They have played in the Chicago Underground Quartet, and Parker plays in Ted Sirota's Soul Rebels and Josh Abrams quartet, for instance. Avreeayl Ra is a member of the AACM but has collaborated with whites associated with the indie community in the band Active Ingredients. Vandermark has played with a couple of black musicians, including the drummer Robert Barry. White musicians have also played in predominantly black clubs and bands. Josh Abrams played for three years in the house

band at the Velvet Lounge and still plays with Nicole Mitchell and David Boykin, for instance.

29. There are only a few more musicians in this community than the ones I have just mentioned. Chad Taylor came to Chicago in 1988, moved to New York in 1992, returned in 1999, and then moved back to New York in 2001, but he has worked regularly with people in Chicago since he first came to the city and is strongly identified with Chicago. Chris Lopes moved to Providence, Rhode Island around 2000. Sara Smith moved to Tucson, Arizona and no longer plays. Whitehead 2003; Jeff Parker, conversation with author, 3 April 2004.

30. Shelton moved to San Francisco in 2005. This circle also includes Frank Rosaly, Nick Broste, and Keefe Jackson. Members of the Vandermark circle formed the cooperative Umbrella Music in response to the closing of important venues for their music (Peter Margasak, "The Jazz Posse," *Chicago Reader*, 7 April 2006).

31. Corbett co-organized the series with Vandermark. He once hosted a show at WHPK and still produces records. In one interview Corbett refused to identify with the concept of jazz but indirectly declares himself a fan of 1960s avant-garde jazz: when asked about his five favorite recordings, he mentioned Albert Aylor, Cecil Taylor, Derek Bailey, Peter Brötzmann, and Alexander Schlippenbach. Fred Jung, "A Fireside Chat with John Corbett," http://www.jazzweekly.com (accessed 28 August 2006). Cf. Corbett 1994.

32. I am inspired here by Turino's notion of "cosmopolitan loops" in his study of Zimbabwean music (2000, 141).

33. As of the time of writing, the Empty Bottle and the *Wire* had been organizing their Adventures in Modern Music festival for four consecutive years (24–28 September 2003; 22–26 September 2004; 21–25 September 2005; and 20–24 September 2006).

34. I have discussed the magazine primarily with musicians in Chicago, but also with German colleagues and with my friend Tobias Kirstein in Copenhagen (17 December 2003), who has been part of a group of core readers for more than ten years. Kirstein makes experimental music and gave a rich account of the magazine's development and responses in different reader communities.

CHAPTER SIX

1. Shumavon came to Chicago in 1991. He was a graduate student at the University of Chicago, a deejay at WHPK, and executive director at Doc Films. He met Parker while he was playing in the New Horizons and hung out in the rock community in and around the Idful Music studio, which closed around 2000. Shumavon moved to the Bay Area in 2000.

2. Parker guided me to Dirac's playing on the Mat Maneri Quintet's *Acceptance* (Hatology, 1998).

3. The crossover to the rock audience has also been pointed out to me by Marina Peterson, who at the time was a graduate student at the University of Chicago and a cellist who performed contemporary classical music in particular.

4. Several people reported this to me. Cf. Keenan 2001b, 32.

5. The reporter was Aaron Cohen, with whom I was in touch at the time, and he kindly sent me a transcript of all the interviews that were conducted in March 2004.

6. Cf. *The Rough Guide to Bhangra* (World Music Network, 2000); Moby, *Play* (Mute Records, 1999).

7. Van Halen, "You Really Got Me," *Van Halen* (Warner Bros., 1978); the Fugees, "Killing Me Softly," *The Score* (Sony, 1996); Cassandra Wilson, "The Weight," *Belly of the Sun* (Blue Note, 2002).

8. Another good example of this is his solo on "Saro-Wiwa" on Sirota's *Breeding Resistance* (Delmark, 2004).

CHAPTER SEVEN

1. For a more detailed discussion, see Crawford 2001, chapter 19.

2. *The Land Where the Blues Began* (Lomax 1993) gives a sense of how central these African American traditions were to Alan. He also reflects on his own experience of race and racism.

3. The public spectacle of the minstrel show marks the beginning of the mass popularity of black expressive culture among whites (Lott 1993). On the foundational role of blacks, see Ellison (1986) and Morrison (1992).

4. Lowe's statement is quoted in Wong 2004, 13.

5. Gronow's role as editor is not stated in the book.

6. The phrase "American Roots Music Originals!" appeared in the promotional description of the CD on Rounder's Web site. http://www.rounder.com/index .php?id=album.php&catalog_id=6504 (accessed 28 August 2006).

7. A comprehensive documentation of the broad tendencies observed in this paragraph is beyond the scope of this book, and although I can provide a few citations, much of it is informed by undocumented discussions in classrooms and corridors and at conferences and faculty meetings. For Wong's critique, see Wong 2004, 12–13. Two good examples of "American popular music" textbooks are Werner's (1999), which does not have an academic focus but is used as a textbook, and the one that Starr and Waterman (2003) did with Oxford University Press. Both books discuss race largely in terms of black and white. In Britain, Hesmondhalgh and Negus have already done a lot to broaden the cultural range of popular music studies (Negus 1999; Born 2000; Hesmondhalgh and Negus 2002).

8. I would like to list as sources for further critical study Kramer's (2003) concept of "cultural musicology" and Abbate's (2004) theorization of performativity.

9. . Malone wrote the first edition alone.

10. One example is rock and roll (Malone and Stricklin 2003, 109 and 116). Malone has also been skeptical of the mainstream orientation of the Nashville Sound and new country (cf. my discussion of country music in chapter 3).

11. A case in point is his approach to the history of the blues (Malone and Strick-lin 2003, 41–51).

12. For a chronology of Martin's career see Rock on the Net.com, http://www .rockonthenet.com/artists-m/rickymartin_main.htm (accessed 28 August 2006).

13. The verse has an A (4 + 4) and B (4 + 4 + 2) section. The 8-bar refrain also has a 4 + 4 bar structure.

14. There was also a sponsorship issue because Martin was backed by Pepsi and Coca-Cola was a major sponsor of the World Cup.

15. One of many Web sites listing these figures on the broadcast is La Mu-sica.com. http://www.lamusica.com/RickMartin.shtml (accessed 28 August 2006).

16. *Music of the World Cup: Allez! Ola! Olé!* (Columbia/Sony, 1998). *Fever Pitch: The Official Music of the 2002 FIFA World Cup* (Epic/Sony, 2002).

17. Martin's performance created an immediate media flash and its effect was witnessed by journalists and fans on numerous Web sites. Apparently, one of the immediate responses was Madonna's proposal to record with him. Cf. Bergquist 1999, 27–31.

18. Rosa wrote: "This is a very partisan act. This is a President who would have people in his cabinet who would obstruct the exercise of civil rights, human rights, consumer rights, the rights to choose, the right to be free of gun violence and the right to a clean environment. This is a betrayal of everything that every Puerto Rican should stand for" ("Ricky Martin's Songwriter/Producer" 2001). See also Josh Kun, "The Many Voices of Robi Rosa," *New York Times*, 4 April 2004. For national news coverage, see Habell-Pallán and Romero 2002, 16–17, nn. 6–8.

19. Though there is no universal definition, Creoles are commonly identified as African French people in and around the Caribbean, whereas Cajun has been reserved for the whites of French descent who came to Louisiana via Nova Scotia (cf. Spitzer 2003, 58–65).

20. He goes on to describe the music, but this description fits the other *juré* recording, "S'en aller chez moreau."

21. New Orleans Jazz and Heritage Festival, 2005, http://www.nojazzfest.com/ special/faq_002.html (accessed 8 July 2005); Festival International de Louisiane, 2003, http://www.festivalinternational.com.site1.php (accessed 8 July 2005).

22. An example of this sort of populist anthropology is the coffee table book *Zydeco Shoes* which includes a CD (Hayes 2004). The book juxtaposes paintings, food recipes, and music, and one of the tropes that tie all this together is the notion of having a good time. There is a full-page statement of the cliché "Laissez bon temps roulez!" even before the foreword.

23. The cover of the zydeco compilation issued in 2000 said "file under Zydeco/World/Putumayo" (*Zydeco* [Putumayo World Music, 2000]).

24. Simon's confusing use of the term Cajun is less important here.

25. For further discussion of this album, see Erlmann 1999, esp. chapter 10; Feld 1994c; and Meintjes 1990.

26. The Latino population constitutes 32 percent in Texas, 41.1 percent in New Mexico, 25.3 percent in Arizona, and 32.4 percent in California. U.S. Bureau of Census 2000, 25 January 2002, http://factfinder.census.gov (accessed 28 August 2006).

27. It should be noted that Peña has not fundamentally changed his narrative of conjunto in more recent publications (cf. Peña 1996, chapter 3, esp. 105f.).

28. He has talked about influences in several interviews. A good interview is the one that was done in the PBS oral history series as part of the American Roots Music project, http://www.pbs.org/americanrootsmusic/pbs_arm_oralh_flacojimenez.html (accessed 28 August 2006). The name of the interviewer is listed; according to the "behind the scenes" information, on the Web site, the interview was conducted in July 2000.

29. A long list of names on stars that Jiménez has played with is found at "The Official Web site of Flaco Jiménez," http://www.flacojimenezmusic.com/biography.asp (accessed 28 August 2006).

REFERENCES

Abbate, Carolyn. 2004. "Music—Drastic or Gnostic?" *Critical Inquiry* 30, no. 3 (Spring): 505–36.

Abu-Lughod, Janet L. 1999. *New York, Chicago, Los Angeles: America's Global Cities*. Minneapolis: University of Minnesota Press.

Ackerman, Paul. 1958. "What Has Happened to Popular Music?" *High Fidelity* (June): 34–37, 107–9.

The Alan Lomax Collection: Southern Journey, Vol. 5: Bad Man Ballads: Songs of Outlaws and Desperados. 1997. Rounder.

Albertson, Chris. 1971. "The Unmasking of Miles Davis." *Saturday Review*, 27 November, 67–69 and 87. Reprinted in *A Miles Davis Reader*, edited by Bill Kichner. Washington, D.C.: Smithsonian Institution Press, 1997. 190–97.

All Music Guide. N.d. All Media Guide. http://www.allmusic.com (accessed 23 August 2006).

Appadurai, Arjun. 1996. *Modernity at Large: Cultural Dimensions of Globalization*. Minneapolis: University of Minnesota Press.

Apthorpe, Raymond. 1996. "Modernization." In *The Social Science Encyclopedia*, 2nd ed., edited by Adam Kuper and Jessica Kuper. London and New York: Routledge. 547–48.

Bangs, Lester. 1969. Review of Miles Davis, *In a Silent Way*. *Rolling Stone* 46, 15 November, 33.

Barone, Nick. 1964a. Letter to the editor. *Music City News* 2, no. 16 (September): 2.

———. 1964b. Letter to the editor. *Music City News* 2, no. 6 (December): 2.

———. 1965. Letter to the editor. *Music City News* 2, no. 9 (March): 2.

Bergquist, Kathie. 1999. *Ricky Martin: The Unofficial Book*. London: Virgin Books.

Berkmoes, Ryan Ver. 2001. *Lonely Planet Chicago*. Melbourne: Lonely Planet.

Berry, Jason 2001. "Native Sounds: Indigenous Music Recordings of Label Putumayo World Music and Partnership with Louisiana Office of Tourism." *New Orleans Magazine* 35, no. 8 (May): 34.

"Best-Selling Albums of 2002." 2003. *Billboard*, 18 January, 54.

Bhawnani, Namrata 1998. "I'm the King of the World." *Rediff on the Net*, 20 June. http://www.rediff.com/style/1998/jun/20ricky.htm (accessed 23 August 2006).

Blank, Les, dir. 1976. *Chulas Fronteras* [Beautiful Borders]. Documentary. DVD edition 2003. El Cerrito, Calif.: Arhoolie Records.

Bohlman, Philip V. 1988. *The Study of Folk Music in the Modern World*. Foreword by Alan Dundes. Bloomington: Indiana University Press.

——. 1992. "Ethnomusicology's Challenge to the Canon; The Canon's Challenge to Ethnomusicology." In *Disciplining Music: Musicology and Its Canons*, edited by Katherine Bergeron and Philip V. Bohlman. Chicago and London: University of Chicago Press. 116–36.

Born, Georgina. 2000. Introduction to *Western Music and Its Others: Difference, Representation, and Appropriation in Music*, edited by Georgina Born and David Hesmondhalgh. Berkeley and Los Angeles: University of California Press. 31–47.

Borthwick, Stuart, and Ron Moy. 2004. *Popular Music Genres*. London and New York: Routledge.

Bourdieu, Pierre. 1977. *Outline of a Theory of Practice*. Cambridge and New York: Cambridge University Press.

Brackett, David. 1995. *Interpreting Popular Music*. Cambridge: Cambridge University Press.

——. 2002. "(In Search of) Musical Meaning: Genres, Categories and Crossover." In *Popular Music Studies*, edited by David Hesmondhalgh and Keith Negus. London: Arnold. 65–83.

Brewster, Bill, and Frank Broughton. 2000. *Last Night a DJ Saved My Life: The History of the Disc Jockey*. New York: Grove Press.

Burton, Gary. 1967. "A Day in the Country." *Jazz* 6, no. 4 (April): 10–12.

Christman, Ed. 2003. "UMVD Expands Market-Share Dominance." *Billboard*, 18 January, 1, 53.

Ciccone, Richard F. 1999. *Chicago and the American Century: The Hundred Most Significant Chicagoans of the Twentieth Century*. Chicago: Contemporary Books.

Clifford, James. 1986. "Introduction: Partial Truths." In *Writing Culture: The Poetics and Politics of Ethnography*, edited by James Clifford and George E. Marcus. Berkeley and Los Angeles: University of California Press. 1–26.

Coen, Ethan, and Joel Coen, dirs. 2000. *O Brother, Where Art Thou?* Touchstone Home Video Edition on DVD. Burbank, Calif.: Buena Vista Home Entertainment (distributor for Universal).

Cohn, Nik. 1969. *Rock from the Beginning*. New York: Pocket Books.

Coleman, Ray. 1986. *Lennon*. New York: McGraw-Hill.

"Columbia Modernizes CW." 1956. *Country Music Reporter* 1, no. 8 (22 December): 1, 4.

Corbett, John. 1994. *Extended Play: Sounding Off from John Cage to Dr. Funkenstein*. Durham, N.C.: Duke University Press.

Crawford, Richard. 1993/2000. *The American Musical Landscape: The Business of Musicianship from Billings to Gershwin*. Updated ed. Berkeley and Los Angeles: University of California Press.

———. 2001. *America's Musical Life: A History*. New York: W. W. Norton.

Danuser, Hermann. 1995. "Gattung." In *Die Musik in Geschichte und Gegenwart*, Sachteil 3, zweite neubearbeitete Ausgabe, edited by Ludwig Finscher. Kassel: Bärenreiter. 1042–69.

Darwin, Charles. 1859/1958. *The Origin of Species*. Introduction by Julian Huxley. New York: New American Library.

Dávila, Arlene. 2002. "Talking Back: Spanish Media and U.S. Latinidad." In *Latino/a Popular Culture*, edited by Michelle Habell-Pallán and Mary Romero. New York: New York University Press. 25–37.

Davis, Miles, with Quincy Troupe. 1989. *Miles: The Autobiography*. New York: Simon & Schuster.

DeVeaux, Scott. 1991. "Constructing the Jazz Tradition: Jazz Historiography." *Black American Literature Forum* 25, no. 3 (Fall 1991): 525–60.

———. 1995. *Jazz in America: Who's Listening?* Carson, Calif.: Seven Locks Press.

———. 1997. *The Birth of Bebop: A Social and Musical History*. Berkeley and Los Angeles: University of California Press.

"Digital Music Market More than Triples." 2005. Associated Press, 3 October. Cited in *Yahoo! News*. http://news.yahoo.com/s/ap/20051003/ap_on_en_mu/britain _music_market (4 October 2005).

Dornfeld, Barry. 2002. "Putting American Public Television Documentary in Its Places." In *Media Worlds: Anthropology on New Terrain*, edited by Faye Ginsburg, Lila Abu-Lughod, and Brian Larkin. Berkeley: University of California Press. 247–63.

Drouot, Alain. 2001. "Interview with Mwata Bowden." http://www.jazzinchicago .org/Internal/Articles/tabid/43/articleType/ArticleView/articleId/2/ AconversationwithMwataBowden.aspx (accessed 25 August 2006).

Ellison, Ralph. 1986. "What America Would Be Like without Blacks." In *Going to the Territory*. New York: Vintage International. 104–12.

Emmeche, Claus. 1995. "Darwin." In *Naar mennesket undrer sig* [When Man Wonders], edited by Birgitte Rahbek. Viby Jylland, Denmark: Centrum. 299–312.

Erlmann, Veit. 1999. *Music, Modernity, and the Global Imagination*. Oxford and New York: Oxford University Press.

Ethnic Recordings in America: A Neglected Heritage. 1982. Washington, D.C.: American Folklife Center, Library of Congress.

Fabbri, Franco. 1982. "A Theory of Popular Music Genres: Two Applications." In *Popular Music Perspectives*, edited by David Horn and Philip Tagg. Göteborg and Exeter: A. Wheaton. 52–81.

———. 1999. "Browsing Music Spaces: Categories and the Musical Mind." http:// www.tagg.org/xpdfs/ffabbri990717.pdf (accessed 23 August 2006).

Farley, Christopher John. 2001. "Back to Country's Roots." *Time*, 11 June. http://
www.time.com/time/sampler/article/0,8599,166247,00.html (accessed
23 August 2006).

Feather, Leonard. 1975. "Hancock, Jones: Is Rock the Right Direction?" *Melody
Maker*, 4 January, 29.

Feld, Steven. 1994a. "Aesthetics as Iconicity of Style (Uptown Title); Or,
(Downtown Title) 'Lift-Up-Over Sounding': Getting into the Kaluli Groove." In
Music Grooves: Essays and Dialogues, edited by Steven Feld and Charles Keil.
Chicago: University of Chicago Press. 109–50.

———. 1994b. "From Schizophonia to Schismogenesis: On the Discourses and
Commodification Practices of 'World Music' and 'World Beat.'" In *Music
Grooves: Essays and Dialogues*, edited by Charles Keil and Steven Feld.
Chicago: University of Chicago Press. 257–89.

———. 1994c. "Notes on 'World Beat.'" In *Music Grooves: Essays and Dialogues*,
edited by Steven Feld and Charles Keil. Chicago: University of Chicago Press.
238–46.

Filene, Benjamin. 2000. *Romancing the Folk: Public Memory and American Roots
Music*. Chapel Hill: University of North Carolina Press.

Fornäs, Johan. 1995. "The Future of Rock: Discourses that Struggle to Define a
Genre." *Popular Music* 14, no. 1: 111–25.

Foucault, Michel. 1966. *Les mots et les choses: Une archéologie des sciences
humaines*. Paris: Gallimard.

Fox, Aaron A. 2004. *Real Country: Music and Language in Working-Class Culture*.
Durham, N.C.: Duke University Press.

Franz, Bill 2000. *Alternative Chicago: Unique Destinations beyond the Magnificent
Mile*. Nashville: Cumberland House.

Friedman, Michael. 1998. "Patricia Barber on 'Modern Cool.'" *All About Jazz*
(November). http://www.allaboutjazz.com/iviews/pbarber.htm (accessed 30
August 2006).

Frith, Simon. 1996. *Performing Rites: On the Value of Popular Music*. Cambridge,
Massachusetts: Harvard University Press.

———, ed. 2004. *Popular Music: Critical Concepts in Media and Cultural Studies*.
4 vols. London and New York: Routledge.

Frith, Simon, Will Straw, and John Street, eds. 2001. *The Cambridge Companion to
Pop and Rock*. Cambridge: Cambridge University Press.

Gabbard, Krin. 1996. *Jammin' at the Margins: Jazz and the American Cinema*.
Chicago: University of Chicago Press.

Garofalo, Reebee. 1993. "Black Popular Music: Crossing Over or Going Under?" In
Rock and Popular Music: Politics, Policies, Institutions, edited by Tony
Bennett, Simon Frith, Lawrence Grossberg, John Shepherd, and Graeme Turner.
London: Routledge. 231–47.

———. 1997/2002. *Rockin' Out: Popular Music in the USA*. 2nd ed. Upper Saddle
River, N.J.: Prentice Hall.

Garrity, Brian. 2006. "MTV Gets the Urge." *Billboard*, 27 May, 12.

Gendron, Bernard. 2002. *Between Montmartre and the Mudd Club: Popular Music and the Avant-Garde*. Chicago: University of Chicago Press.

"Genre." 2006. *Oxford English Dictionary*. Online ed. Oxford University Press. http://www.oed.com (accessed 5 April 2006).

Gillett, Charlie 1970/1983. *The Sound of the City: The Rise of Rock and Roll*. Rev. and expanded ed. New York: Pantheon Books.

Gleason, Ralph, ed. 1958. *Jam Session: An Anthology of Jazz*. New York: G. P. Putnam's Sons.

———. 1967a. "Like a Rolling Stone." *Jazz and Pop* 6, no. 11 (November): 12.

———. 1967b. "Monterey Jazz Festival." *Jazz and Pop* 6, no. 11 (November): 16–19.

———. 1969/1999. Liner notes to Miles Davis, *Bitches Brew*. CD. New York: Columbia.

Goldman, Albert. 1971a. "The Apple at Its Core." In *Freakshow: Misadventures in the Counterculture, 1959–1971*. New York: Cooper Square Press. 265–70.

———. 1971b. "Jazz: The Art That Came in from the Cold." In *Freakshow: Misadventures in the Counterculture 1959–1971*. New York: Cooper Square Press. 300–325.

Goldsmith, Peter D. 1998. *Making People's Music: Moe Asch and Folkways Records*. Washington, D.C.: Smithsonian Institution Press.

Graham, Bill. 1971. "A Letter from Bill Graham." *Village Voice*, 6 May, 45.

Grazian, David 2003. *Blue Chicago: The Search for Authenticity in Urban Blues Clubs*. Chicago: University of Chicago Press.

Grove Music Online. N.d. Oxford University Press. http://www.grovemusic.com (accessed 18 August 2005).

Guralnick, Peter. 1971/1999. *Feel like Going Home: Portraits in Blues and Rock 'n' Roll*. Boston: Back Bay Books.

Guralnick, Peter. 1976. "Elvis Presley." In *The Rolling Stone Illustrated History of Rock and Roll*, edited by Jim Miller, 30–41. New York: Random House.

———. 1994. *Last Train to Memphis: The Rise of Elvis Presley*. Boston: Back Bay Books.

Habell-Pallán, Michelle, and Mary Romero. 2002. *Latino/a Popular Culture*. New York: New York University Press.

Haley, Alex. 1976. *Roots*. Garden City, N.Y.: Doubleday.

Hall, Perry. 1997. "African-American Music: Dynamics of Appropriation and Innovation." In *Borrowed Power: Essays on Cultural Appropriation*, edited by Bruce Ziff and Pratima V. Rao. New Brunswick, N.J.: Rutgers University Press. 31–51.

Hamm, Charles. 2000. "Genre, Performance, and Ideology in the Early Songs of Irving Berlin." In *Reading Pop: Approaches to Textual Analysis in Popular Music*, edited by Richard Middleton. Oxford and New York: Oxford University Press. 297–306.

Hayes, Alexandra. 2004. *Zydeco Shoes: A Sensory Tour of Cajun Culture*. Gretna, La.: Pelican.

Hentoff, Nat. 1956. "Musicians Argue Values of Rock and Roll." *Down Beat* 23, no. 11, (30 May): 12.

———. 1961/1975. *The Jazz Life*. New York: Da Capo Press.

Hesmondhalgh, David. 2005. "Subcultures, Scenes or Tribes? None of the Above." *Journal of Youth Studies* 8, no. 1 (March): 21–40.

Hesmondhalgh, David, and Keith Negus, eds. 2002. *Popular Music Studies*. London: Arnold.

Himes, Geoffrey. 2003. "The Speaking Quietude: Less Becomes More within the Delicate Grooves of the Be Good Tanyas' Music." *No Depression* 44 (March–April): 66–75.

Hobsbawm, Eric. 1998. "Jazz since 1960." In *Uncommon People: Resistance, Rebellion and Jazz*. London: Weidenfeld & Nicholson. 281–92.

Hodeir, André. 1954. *Hommes et problèmes du jazz*. Paris: Au Portlan chez Flammarion.

———. 1956. *Jazz: Its Evolution and Essence*. Translated by David Noakes. New York: Grove Press.

Holt, Fabian. 2006. "Across the Atlantic: Acculturation and Hybridization in Jazz and the African Diaspora." In *Jazzforschung/Jazz Research* 38: 11–23.

———. In press. "World Music." *Encyclopedia of the Modern World*. Oxford and New York: Oxford University Press.

Hubbard, Bruce. 1964. Letter to the editor. *Music City News* 2, no. 16 (September): 2.

Hughes, Claire. 2004. *Walking up in Chicago: A Musical Tour of the Windy City*. London: Sanctuary.

"An Interview with George Wein." 1969. *Jazz and Pop* 8, no. 4–5 (April–May): 44–47.

Ivey, Bill. 1998. "The Nashville Sound." In *The Encyclopedia of Country Music*, edited by Paul Kingsbury. New York: Oxford University Press. 371–72.

Jensen, Joli. 1998. *The Nashville Sound: Authenticity, Commercialization, and Country Music*. Nashville, Tenn.: Country Music Foundation Press and Vanderbilt University Press.

Johnson, Mark. 1987. *The Body in the Mind: The Bodily Basis of Meaning, Imagination, and Reason*. Chicago: University of Chicago Press.

Jung, Fred. 2002. "A Fireside Chat with Jeff Parker." http://www.jazzweekly.com/interviews/jparker.htm (accessed 25 August 2006).

Kampmann, Wolf. 2000. Liner notes to *Chicago 2018...It's Gonna Change*. CD. Clearspot.

Keenan, David. 2000. "The Chicago Underground: Goodfellas." *Wire* 201 (November): 34–41.

———. 2001a. "Jim O'Rourke: The Man Who Fell to Earth." *Wire* 213 (November): 34–41.

———. 2001b. "Tortoise: Standard Bearers." *Wire* 204 (February): 26–33.

Keepnews, Peter. 1979. "Why Big Record Companies Let Jazz Down." *Jazz Magazine* 4, no. 1 (Winter): 60–64.

Keil, Charles. 1966/1991. *Urban Blues*. Chicago: University of Chicago Press.

Kernfeld, Barry, ed. 2002a. *The New Grove Dictionary of Jazz*. 3 vols. 2nd ed. London: Macmillan.

——. 2002b. "Soul Jazz." In *The New Grove Dictionary of Jazz*, vol. 3, edited by Barry Kernfeld, 2nd ed. London: Macmillan. 635–36.

Kingsbury, Paul, ed. 1998. *The Encyclopedia of Country Music*. New York: Oxford University Press.

Kofsky, Frank 1967. "The Scene." *Jazz and Pop* 6, no. 8 (August): 24–27.

Kramer, Lawrence. 1995. *Classical Music and Postmodern Knowledge*. Berkeley and Los Angeles: University of California Press.

——. 2003. "Subjectivity Rampant! Music, Hermeneutics, and History." In *The Cultural Study of Music*, edited by Martin Clayton, Trevor Herbert, and Richard Middleton. New York: Routledge. 124–35.

Lake, Steve. 1974. "Wah-Wah Jazz and All That Rock!" *Melody Maker*, 17 August, 28–29.

Lawrence, Tim. 2003. *Love Saves the Day: A History of American Dance Music Culture, 1970–1979*. Durham, N.C.: Duke University Press.

Lewis, George. In press. *Power Stronger than Itself: The Association for the Advancement of Creative Musicians*. Chicago: University of Chicago Press.

Lomax, Alan. 1993. *The Land Where the Blues Began*. London: Methuen.

——. 1999. Liner notes to Alan Lomax and John A. Lomax, *The Classic Louisiana Recordings: Cajun & Creole Music II, 1934/1937*. Rounder CD

Lomax, John. 1935. "Archive of American Folk Songs: A History, 1926–1939." Chap. 8. Compiled from the Annual Reports of the Librarian of Congress. Library of Congress Project, unpublished.

Lomax, John, and Alan Lomax. 1910/1938. *Cowboy Songs and Other Frontier Ballads*. Rev., enlarged, and reset. New York: Macmillan.

——. 1934. *American Ballads and Folk Songs*. New York: Macmillan.

——. 1947/1975. *Folk Song U.S.A.* New York and Scarborough, Ontario: Plume.

——. 1941/2000. *Our Singing Country: Folk Songs and Ballads*. Mineola, N.Y.: Dover.

Lyotard, Jean-François. 1979. *La condition postmoderne: Rapport sur le savoir*. Paris: Editions de minuit.

Malone, Bill C. 1982. "Honky Tonk: The Music of the Southern Working Class." In *Folk Music and Modern Sound*, edited by William Ferris and Mary L. Hart. Jackson: University Press of Mississippi. 119–28.

——. 1968/2002a. *Country Music, U.S.A.* 2nd rev. ed. Austin: University of Texas Press.

——. 2002b. *Don't Get above Your Raisin': Country Music and the Southern Working Class*. Urbana: University of Illinois Press.

——. 2003. Foreword to Malone and Stricklin, *Southern Music/American Music,*. ix–xi.

Malone, Bill C., and David Stricklin. 1979/2003. *Southern Music/American Music*. Rev. and expanded ed. Lexington: University Press of Kentucky.

Mandel, Howard. 1999. *Future Jazz*. Oxford and New York: Oxford University Press.

Malthus, Thomas R. 1798/1989. *An Essay on the Principle of Population or a View of Its Past and Present Effects on Human Happiness*, edited by Patricia James. Cambridge: Cambridge University Press.

Marcus, Greil. 1975/1990. *Mystery Train: Images of American in Rock 'n' Roll Music*. New York: Plume.

Marshall, Rob, dir. 2002. *Chicago*. New York: Miramax.

Martin, Ricky 1999. *The Ricky Martin Video Collection*. DVD. New York: Sony.

Meintjes, Louise. 1990. "Paul Simon's *Graceland*, South Africa, and the Mediation of Musical Meaning." *Ethnomusicology* 34 (Winter): 37–73.

Middleton, Richard. 1990. *Studying Popular Music*. Milton Keynes: Open University Press.

———. 2004. "Popular Music I: Popular Music in the West: 1. Definitions." *Grove Music Online*. http://www.grovemusic.com (accessed 15 October 2004).

———, ed. 2000. *Reading Pop: Approaches to Textual Analysis in Popular Music*. Oxford and New York: Oxford University Press.

Minton, John. 1996. "Houston Creoles and Zydeco: The Emergence of an African American Urban Popular Style." *American Music* 41, no. 3: 480–526.

Moore, Alan F. 1993/2001. *Rock, the Primary Text: Developing a Musicology of Rock*. Aldershot: Ashgate.

Morgenstern, Dan. 1967. "A Message to Our Readers." *Down Beat*, 29 June, 13.

Morrison, Toni. 1992. *Playing in the Dark: Whiteness and the Literary Imagination*. New York: Vintage Books.

Mukerji, Chandra, and Michael Schudson. 1991. "Introduction: Rethinking Popular Culture." In *Rethinking Popular Culture: Contemporary Perspectives in Cultural Studies*, edited by Chandra Mukerji and Michael Schudson. Berkeley and Los Angeles: University of California Press. 1–61.

"The Music Festival Homepage." 1996. http://www.geocities.com/~music-festival/ monterey.htm (accessed 28 August 2006).

National Park Service. 2001. "Trail of the Hellhound: Delta Blues in the Lower Mississippi Valley." http://www.cr.nps.gov/delta/blues/people/tommy_johnson .htm (accessed 28 August 2006).

Neale, Steve. 1995. "Questions of Genre." In *Film Genre Reader II*, edited by Barry Keith Grant. Austin: University of Texas Press. 159–83.

Negus, Keith. 1999. *Music Genres and Corporate Cultures*. London and New York: Routledge.

Nettl, Bruno. 1983. *The Study of Ethnomusicology: Twenty-nine Issues and Concepts*. Urbana: University of Illinois Press.

Nicholson, Stuart 1998. *Jazz-Rock: A History*. Edinburgh: Canongate Books.

Owen, David. 2006. "The Soundtrack of Your Life: Music in the Realm of Retail Theatre." *New Yorker*, 10 April. http://www.newyorker.com/fact/content/ articles/060410fa_fact (accessed 23 August 2006).

Owens, Buck. 1965. "Pledge to Country Music." *Music City News* 2, no. 9 (March): 5.

Palmer, Robert. 1976. "Rock Begins." In *The Rolling Stone Illustrated History of Rock & Roll*, edited by Jim Miller. New York: Random House. 10–25.

Peña, Manuel. 1985. *The Texas-Mexican Conjunto: History of a Working-Class Music*. Austin: University of Texas Press.

———. 1996. *Música Tejana: The Cultural Economy of Artistic Transformation*. College Station: Texas A & M University Press.

Pennebaker, D. A., dir. 1967/1999. *Dont Look Back*. Collector's Edition on DVD. New York: Docurama.

Peterson, Richard A. 1997. *Creating Country Music: Fabricating Authenticity*. Chicago: University of Chicago Press.

Pleasants, Henry 1955. "What Is This Thing Called Jazz?" In Gleason, *Jam Session*. 173–85.

"Pop Talk." 1967. *Jazz and Pop* 6, no. 9 (September): 20.

Porter, Lewis, and Michael Ullman, with Edward Hazell. 1993. *Jazz: From Its Origins to the Present*. Englewood Cliffs, N.J.: Prentice Hall.

Prechtl, Peter, and Franz-Peter Burkard, eds. 1996. *Metzler Philosophie Lexikon: Begriffe und Definitionen*. Stuttgart: Metzler.

Public Broadcasting Service. 2001a. *American Roots Music*. http://www.pbs.org/americanrootsmusic/ (accessed 28 July 2003).

Public Broadcasting Service. 2001b. "*American Roots Music*: Behind the Scenes: Board of Advisors." http://www.pbs.org/americanrootsmusic/pbs_arm_bts _board.html/ (accessed 3 August 2003).

Pugh, Ronnie 1996. *Ernest Tubb: The Texas Troubadour*. Durham, N.C.: Duke University Press.

———. 1997. "Country Music: An Etymological Journey." *Journal of Country Music* 19, no. 1: 32–38.

Radano, Ronald M. 1993. *New Musical Figurations: Anthony Braxton's Cultural Critique*. Chicago: University of Chicago Press.

Ramsey, Frederic, and Charles Edward Smith, eds., 1939. *Jazzmen*. New York: Harcourt.

Recording Industry Association of America. 2003. "2003 Consumer Profile." Survey conducted by Peter Hart Research. http://www.riaa.com/news/marketingdata/ pdf/2003consumerprofile.pdf (accessed 23 August 2006).

"Ricky Martin's Songwriter/Producer Reacts Angrily to Inaugural Performance of His Song." 2001. Press release newswire, 12 January. http://www.mcsweeneys .net/links/press01/cupofdubya.html/ (accessed 23 August 2006.

Ritter, Tex. "Tex Ritter Speaks out on Keeping Country Music Country." *Music City News* 2, no. 1 (July): 2.

Rivelli, Pauline. 1967. Editorial. *Jazz and Pop* 6, no. 8 (August): 5, 17.

———. 1969. "Newport Jazz Festival." *Jazz and Pop* 8, no. 9 (September): 31–33.

Rosenberg, Neil V. 1985. *Bluegrass: A History*. Urbana: University of Illinois Press.

Rumble, John 1998. "RCA Victor Records." In *The Encyclopedia of Country Music*, edited by Paul Kingsbury. New York: Oxford University Press. 431.

Ryall, Tom. 1998. "Genre and Hollywood." In *The Oxford Guide to Film Studies*, edited by John Hill and Pamela Church Gibson. Oxford and New York: Oxford University Press. 327–38.

Samson, Jim. 2001. "Genre." In *The New Grove Dictionary of Music and Musicians*, vol. 9, edited by Stanley Sadie. London and New York: Macmillan. 657–59.

Santelli, Robert, Holly George-Warren, and Jim Brown, eds. 2001. *American Roots Music*. Foreword by Bonnie Raitt. New York: Harry N. Abrams.

Sassen, Saskia. 2001. *The Global City: New York, London, Tokyo*. 2nd ed. Princeton, N.J.: Princeton University Press.

Scutt, Roger. 1964. "What's All This Jazz." *Music City News* 1, no. 10 (March): 2.

SF Weekly. 2003a. *SF Weekly* 22, no. 8, 26 March–1 April, 87–104.

SF Weekly. 2003b. *SF Weekly*, 7 August. http://www.sfweekly.com/issues/current/music_toc.html/ (accessed 28 August 2006).

Shuker, Roy. 1998. *Key Concepts in Popular Music*. London and New York: Routledge.

Simon, Paul. 1986. Liner notes to *Graceland*. Warner Bros.

Simonett, Helena. 2001. *Banda: Mexican Musical Life across Borders*. Middletown, Conn.: Wesleyan University Press.

Solie, Ruth A. 1980. "The Living Work: Organicism and Musical Analysis." *Nineteenth-Century Music* 4, no. 2 (Autumn): 147–56.

Spencer, Jonathan. 1996. "Modernism, Modernity, and Modernization." In *Encyclopedia of Social and Cultural Anthropology*, edited by Alan Barnard and Jonathan Spencer. London and New York: Routledge. 376–79.

Spitzer, Nicholas. 1998. *Zydeco and Mardi Gras: Creole Identity and Performance Genres in Rural French Louisiana*. Austin: University of Texas Press.

———. 2003. "*Monde Créole:* The Cultural World of French Louisiana Creoles and the Creolization of World Cultures." *Journal of American Folklore* 116, no. 459 (Winter): 57–72.

Stambler, Irvin, and Lyndon Stambler. 2001. *Folk and Blues: The Encyclopedia; The Premier Encyclopedia of American Roots Music*. New York: St. Martin's Press.

Starr, Larry, and Christopher Waterman. 2003. *American Popular Music: From Minstrelsy to MTV*. Oxford and New York: Oxford University Press.

Stearns, Marshall. 1956. *The Story of Jazz*. New York: Oxford University Press.

Stearns, Marshall, and Jean Stearns. 1968/1979. *Jazz Dance: The Story of American Vernacular Dance*. New York: Schirmer Books.

Stokes, Martin. 2004. "Music and the Global Order." *Annual Review of Anthropology* 33: 47–72.

Strongin, Dan. 1970. "Herbie Hancock." *Jazz and Pop* 9, no. 9 (October): 30–33.

Szwed, John. 2002. *So What: The Life of Miles Davis*. New York: Simon & Schuster.

Tagg, Philip. 1979. *Kojak: 50 Seconds of Television Music; Towards an Analysis of*

Affect in Popular Music. Gothenburg: Department of Musicology, University of Gothenburg.

Taylor, Yuval, ed. 2002. *The Future of Jazz.* Chicago: A Capella Books.

Terry, Cliff. 2004. *Chicago: Off the Beaten Path.* Guilford, Conn.: Globe Pequot Press.

Thurman, Chuck. 2001. "Paradise Regained." *Monterey County Weekly,* 14 June. http://www.montereycountyweekly.com/articles/6792 (accessed 28 August 2006).

Tichi, Cecilia. 1998. "Country Music, Seriously: An Interview with Bill C. Malone." In *Reading Country Music: Steel Guitars, Opry Stars, and Honky-Tonk Bars,* ed. Cecilia Tichi. Durham, N.C.: Duke University Press. 290–306.

Time Out: Chicago. 2002. London: Penguin Books.

Todorov, Tzvetan. 1976. "The Origin of Genres." *New Literary History* 8, no. 1 (Autumn): 159–70.

Tomlinson, Gary. 1997. "Miles Davis, Musical Dialogician." In *A Miles Davis Reader,* edited by Bill Kirchner. Washington, D.C.: Smithsonian Institution Press. 234–49.

Toynbee, Jason. 2000. *Making Popular Music: Musicians, Creativity and Institutions.* London: Arnold.

Turino, Thomas. 2000. *Nationalists, Cosmopolitans, and Popular Music in Zimbabwe.* Chicago: University of Chicago Press.

U. S. Bureau of the Census. 1998. *State and Metropolitan Area Data Book, 1997–98.* 5th ed. Washington, DC: The Bureau. http://www.census.gov/prod/3/98pubs/smadb-97.pdf (accessed 11 September 2006).

Van Maanen, John. 1988. *Tales of the Field: On Writing Ethnography.* Chicago: University of Chicago Press.

Walser, Robert. 1993. *Running with the Devil: Power, Gender, and Madness in Heavy Metal Music.* Hanover, N.H.: Wesleyan University Press.

Waterman, Christopher A. 1952. "African Influence on the Music of the Americas." In *Acculturation in the Americas: Proceedings and Selected Papers of the 29th International Congress of Americanists,* edited by Sol Tax. New York: Cooper Square. 207–18.

Waxer, Lise. 2002. "Situating Salsa: Latin Music at the Crossroads." In *Situating Salsa: Global Markets and Local Meaning in Latin Popular Music,* edited by Lise Waxer, 3–22. New York: Routledge.

Werner, Craig. 1999. *A Change Is Gonna Come: Music, Race, and the Soul of America.* New York: Plume.

White, Douglas. 1998. *Dictionary of Popular Music Styles of the World.* Lawndale, Calif.: Douglas White Music Research.

Whitehead, Kevin. 2003. Liner notes to Active Ingredients, *Titration.* Delmark.

Wicke, Peter, Kai-Erik Ziegenrücker, and Wieland Ziegenrücker, eds. 1997. *Handbuch der populären Musik.* 3. überarbeitete und erweiterte Auflage. Mainz: Atlantis-Musikbuch-Verlag.

Wilson, Teddy, with Arie Ligthart and Humphrey van Loo. 1996. *Teddy Wilson Talks Jazz*. London and New York: Cassell.

Wong, Deborah. 2004. *Speak It Louder: Asian Americans Making Music*. New York: Routledge.

Wyman, Bill, with Richard Havers. 2001. *Bill Wyman's Blues Odyssey*. London: Dorling Kindersley.

Foster, Stephen, 156. *See also* cabin myth
Frisell, Bill: country music influence, 89;
    roots-oriented jazz, 39, 49
Frith, Simon: concepts of genre world and
    genre culture, 19; genre theory, 6, 8
fusion. *See* genre: mixing and blending; jazz

genre: biological metaphors, 13–14; borders
    and boundaries, theorized, 20–29, 59–60,
    158–60 (*see also* in between, a poetics of
    music in between genres; mainstream vs.
    genre; modernization; reactions to rock
    and roll and rock music; reimagination);
    centered vs. decentered concepts of,
    159–60; codes, 22; collectivities, 21;
    conventions, 22–24; and cultural
    difference, chapter 7; and cultural history,
    11, 158; defining vs. understanding, 8–9;
    disruption, outreach, resistance (in
    process of genre transformation), 59–60;
    emergence, 20; in European American art
    music, 2, 15; a general framework of, 9,
    20–29; general introduction to, 1–4; genre
    culture, 6, 19–20; genre theory in popular
    music studies, 6–7; hybridity and
    hybridization, 12; limited scholarly
    interest in, 4–6; list of genre categories,
    15–16; mixing and blending, 4, 11, 14,
    109, 134, 136, 138–40, 164, 169–70, 175,
    179, 180 (*see also* jazz: jazz-rock fusion;
    modernization: jazz-rock fusion);
    modernity and late modernity, 5–6;
    modernization (*see* modernization); and
    musical signification, 5; music vs. film
    genres, 4–5; narratives of death and
    decline, 14 (*see also* country music; jazz);
    networks, 20–22; reimagination of,
    48–49; and standardization, 4; and
    subculture, 6, 116; transformation,
    53–60; transgression, 12, 96, 159; in
    urban space (*see* ethnography); values,
    23–24. *See also* centered vs. decentered
    concepts of genre; discourse; hybridity; in
    between, a poetics of music in between
    genres; industry, the corporate music
    industry; mainstream vs. genre;
    modernization; popularization; popular
    music; radio; scene; vernacular music
Gleason, Ralph: liner notes to *Bitches Brew*
    (1969), 95–96; report from Monterey
    festivals in 1967, 91; on rock and roll,
    83–84

globalization: and American roots music, 40;
    impact on contemporary music scenes in
    Chicago, 11, 118
Goldman, Albert, 86–87
Graceland (1986). *See* Simon, Paul
Grammer, Billy, 78
Grammy Awards 1999, Ricky Martin
    performance, 165–66
Grand Ole Opry, the, 63, 72; Elvis, 67
Green Mill, the (Chicago), 108, 120
Gronow, Pekka, 156
groove, genre, and culture, 137–40; Davis,
    Miles, 98; in Jeff Parker's musical
    practice, 140–46; in Ricky Martin's "The
    Cup of Life," 163–64; ring shout, 169
Guralnick, Peter, on rock and roll, 54
Guthrie, Woody, as roots music and
    Americana, 44, 47

Hamm, Charles, genre in popular music
    studies, 4
Harris, Emmylou: Americana, 46; in *O
    Brother*, 35; roots music, 39
heavy metal, 16
"Heartbreak Hotel" (1956, Elvis Presley), 64
Hentoff, Nat: on rock and roll, 82–83; on rock
    music, 85–87
Hesmondhalgh, David, 6, 7; critique of scene
    theory, 116–17
Hinton, Milt, reaction to rock and roll, 83
hip-hop, 16; and the corporate music industry,
    26, 57; groove history, 139; among the
    indie jazz community in Chicago, 121,
    126, 129, 135, 137; racial boundaries,
    23
Hobsbawm, Eric, impact of rock on jazz, 86–87
Hodeir, André, 81
Hommes et problèmes du jazz (1954), 81
honky-tonk, 15; and modernization in country
    music, 65–66, 70; Patsy Cline, 73
Hot Club Sandwich, 42
"Hound Dog" (1956, Elvis Presley), 53
hybridity, 5–6, 17, 161, 168, 185n4; *Bitches
    Brew* (1969, Miles Davis), 96;
    fetishization of, 5, 161; in Tejano culture,
    174–75; Thrill Jockey, 125. *See also*
    genre: mixing and blending

"I Am a Man of Constant Sorrow," 33, 36–37
ideological dimensions genre and
    categorization, 13–14, 151
In a Silent Way (1969). *See* Davis, Miles